LYRICAL LIfE

A Rock 'n' Roll Love Story Told in 200 Song Lyrics

Written by Casey Jones
Illustrated by Mark Malloy

THREE RIVERS PRESS • NEW YORK

20th January 2011

Published by Three Rivers Press, New York, New York
Member of the Crown Publishing Group, a division of Random House, Inc.
www.randomhouse.com

THREE RIVERS PRESS and the Tugboat design are registered trademarks of Random House, Inc.

Printed in Singapore

Design and illustration by Mark Malloy

Library of Congress Cataloging-in-Publication Data

Jones, Casey, 1969–
    Lyrical life : a rock 'n' roll love story told in 200 song lyrics / by Casey Jones and illustrated by Mark Malloy.
    Graphic novel.
    I. Malloy, Mark. II. Title.
PN6727.J64L68 2003
741.5'973—dc21
2003040276

ISBN 1-4000-4886-9

10 9 8 7 6 5 4 3 2 1

First Edition

About the Creators of *Lyrical Life*:

The Author Casey Jones

When not indulging his literary follies and collecting absurd quantities of used records, **Casey Jones** is a marketing strategist for Aloft Group in Newburyport, MA. He lives in Boston and yes, that *is* his real name.

Special thanks to agent extraordinaire Ian Kleinert at the Literary Group, lawyer supreme Chris Fauci, creative guru Jonathan Glatzer, Kendra Boccelli for her love and patience, and his parents for their love of wordplay and goofy humor.

The Illustrator Mark Malloy

Mark Malloy is an artist and designer who is a professor of art at Salem State College in Salem, MA. With the completion of this project, he has lost his primary excuse of the last eighteen months.

He would like to thank Caryn Cove for all her help, along with his parents, Dave, Kathy, & Niki Malloy, Patrick Quirk, Ted Constan, Alison Franklin, Ben and Susanna Gross, Nick MacShane, and the SSC Art Dept.

CHAPTER ONE

AND THEN I SAW HER FACE

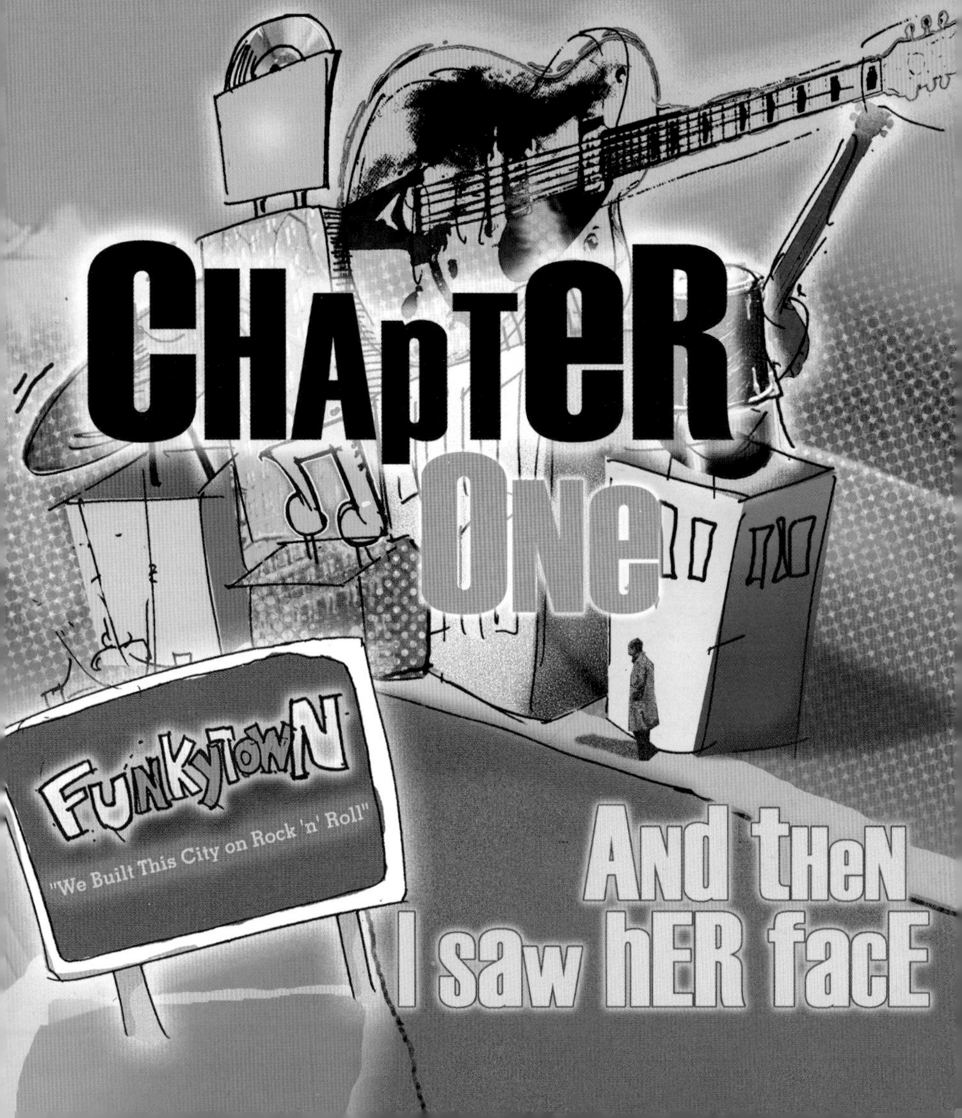
FUNKYTOWN
"We Built This City on Rock 'n' Roll"

It's nine o'clock on a Saturday. The regular crowd shuffles in.

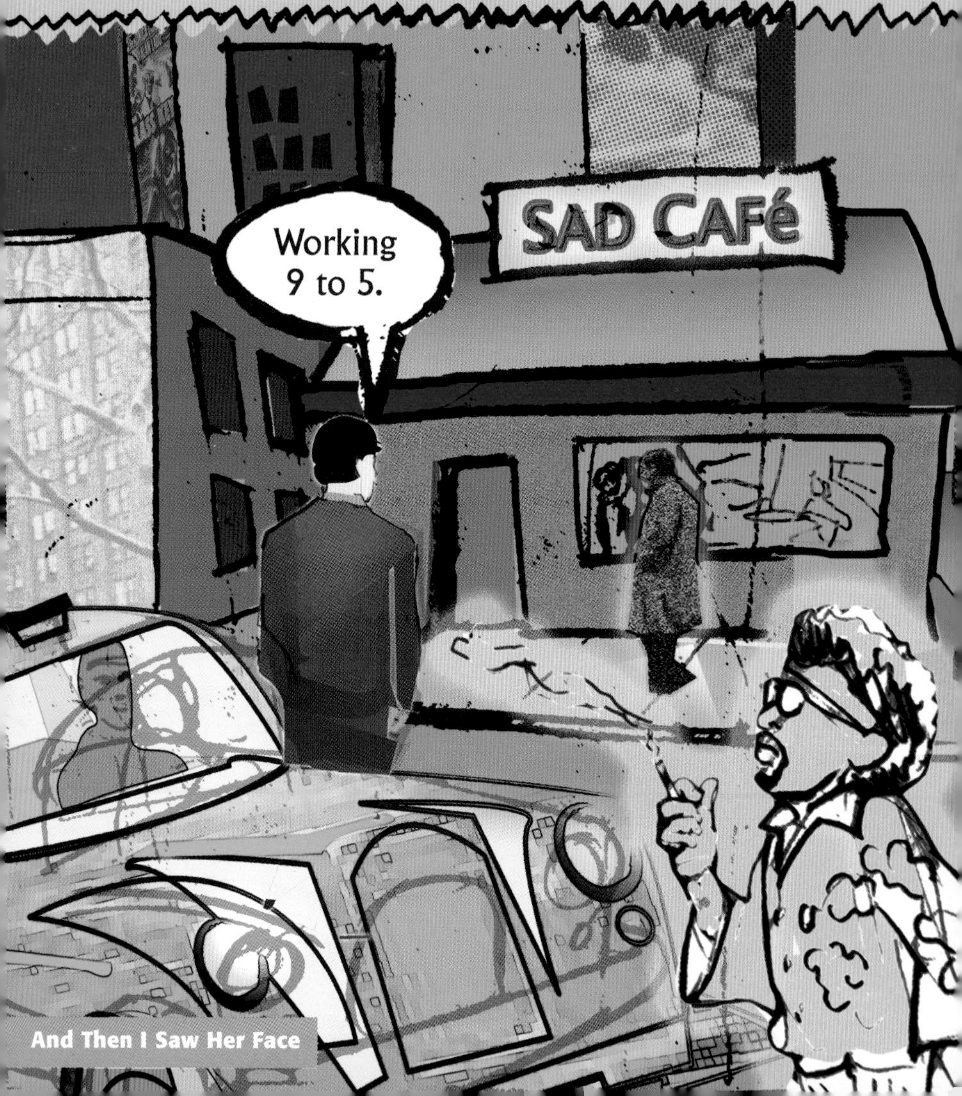
SAD CAFé
Working 9 to 5.

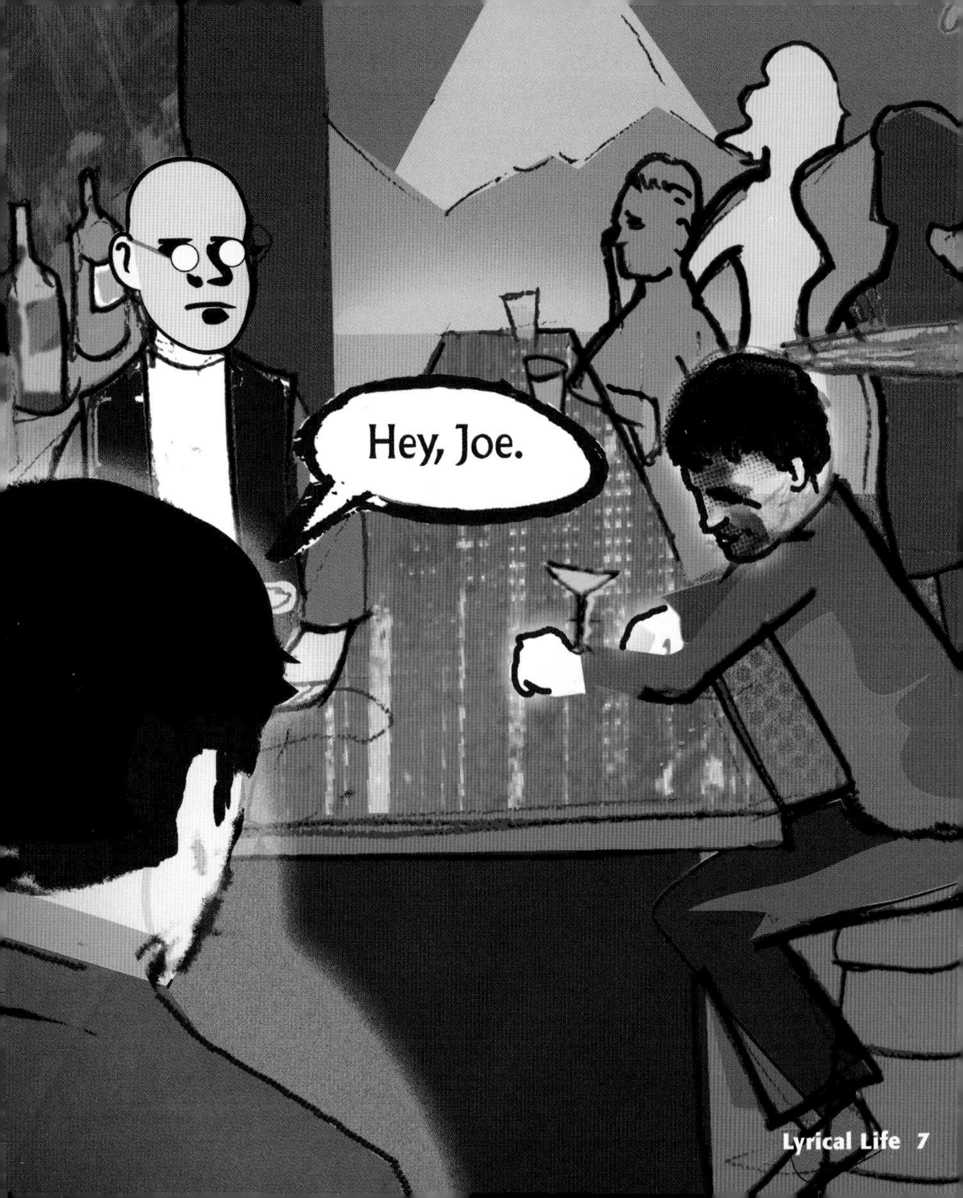
Hey, Joe.

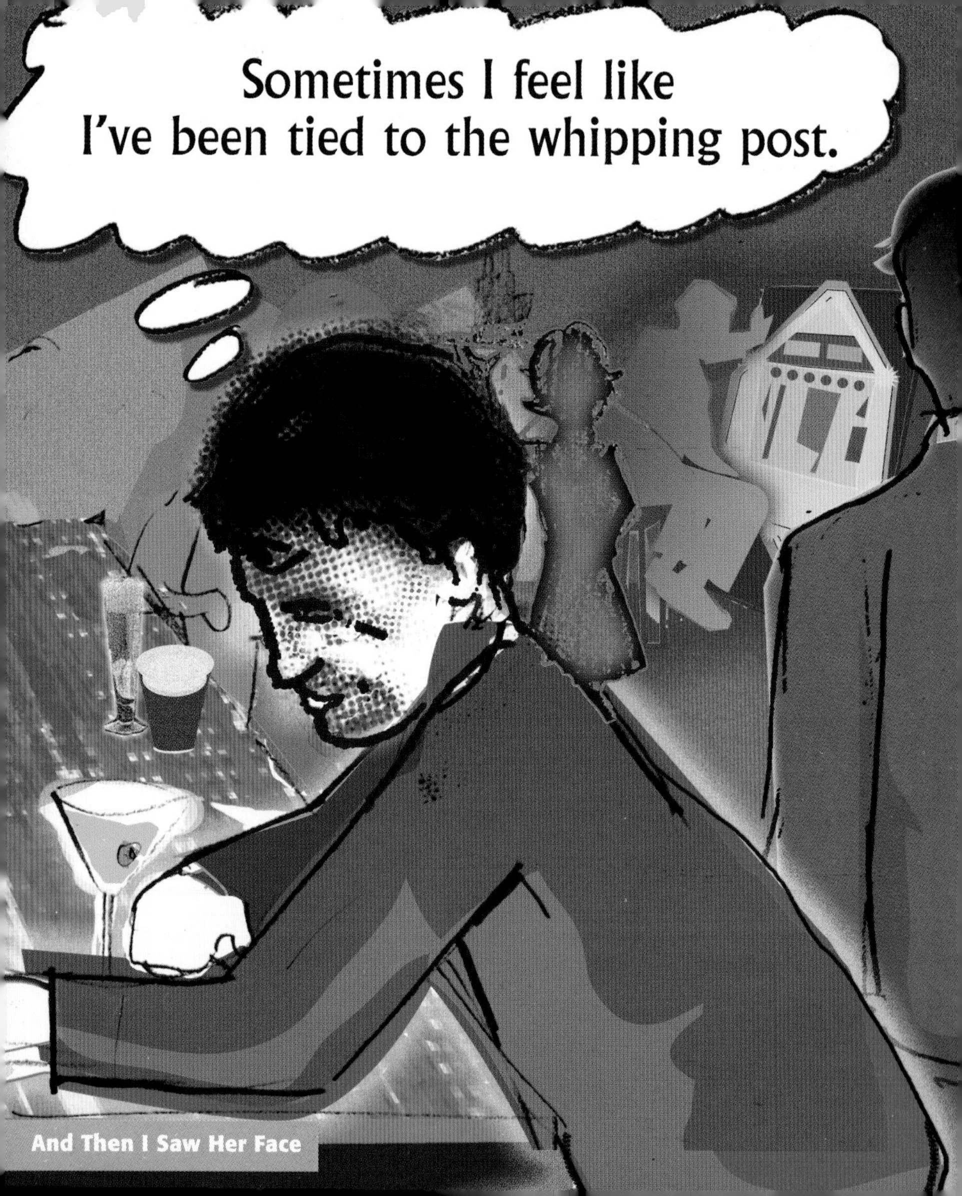
Sometimes I feel like
I've been tied to the whipping post.

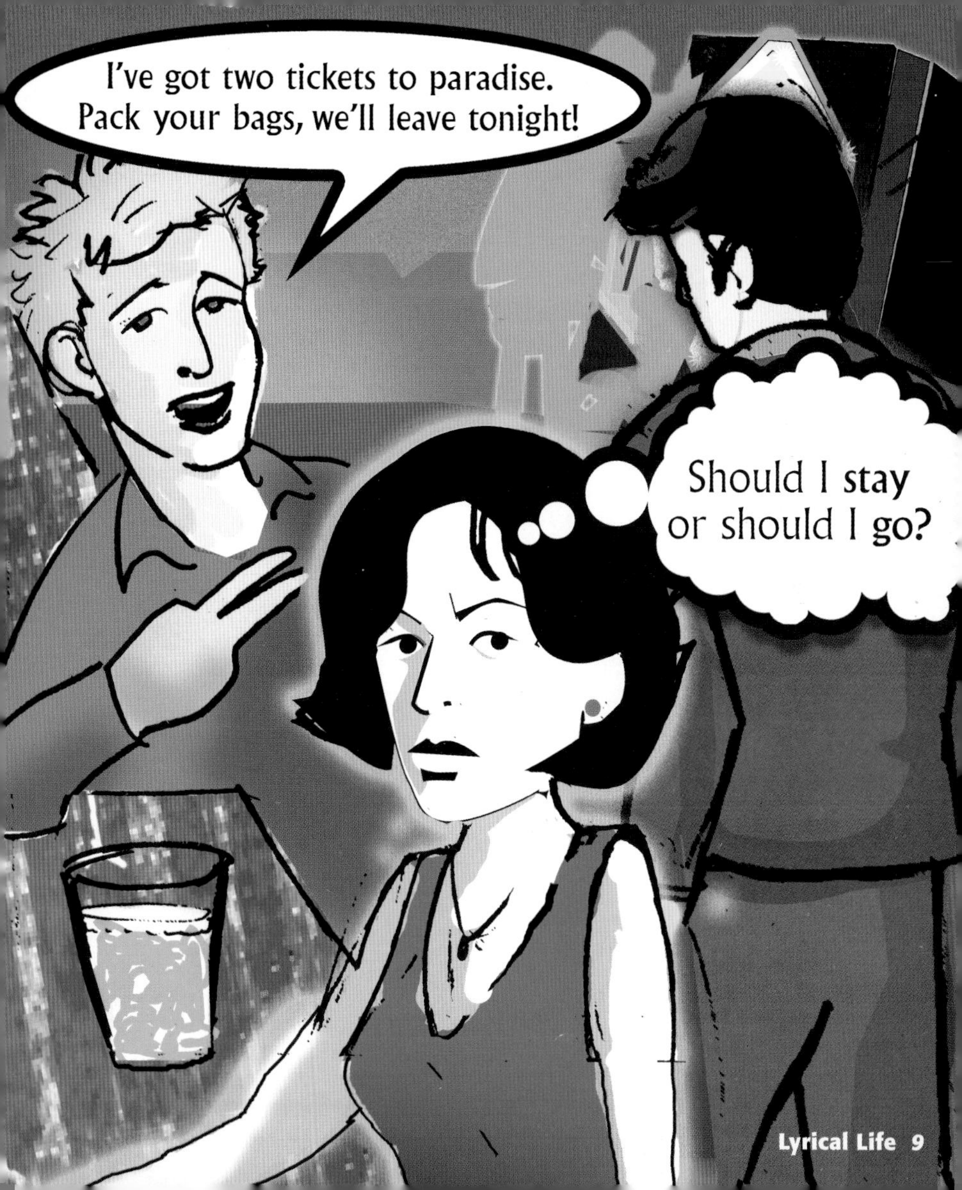
I've got two tickets to paradise.
Pack your bags, we'll leave tonight!
Should I stay
or should I go?

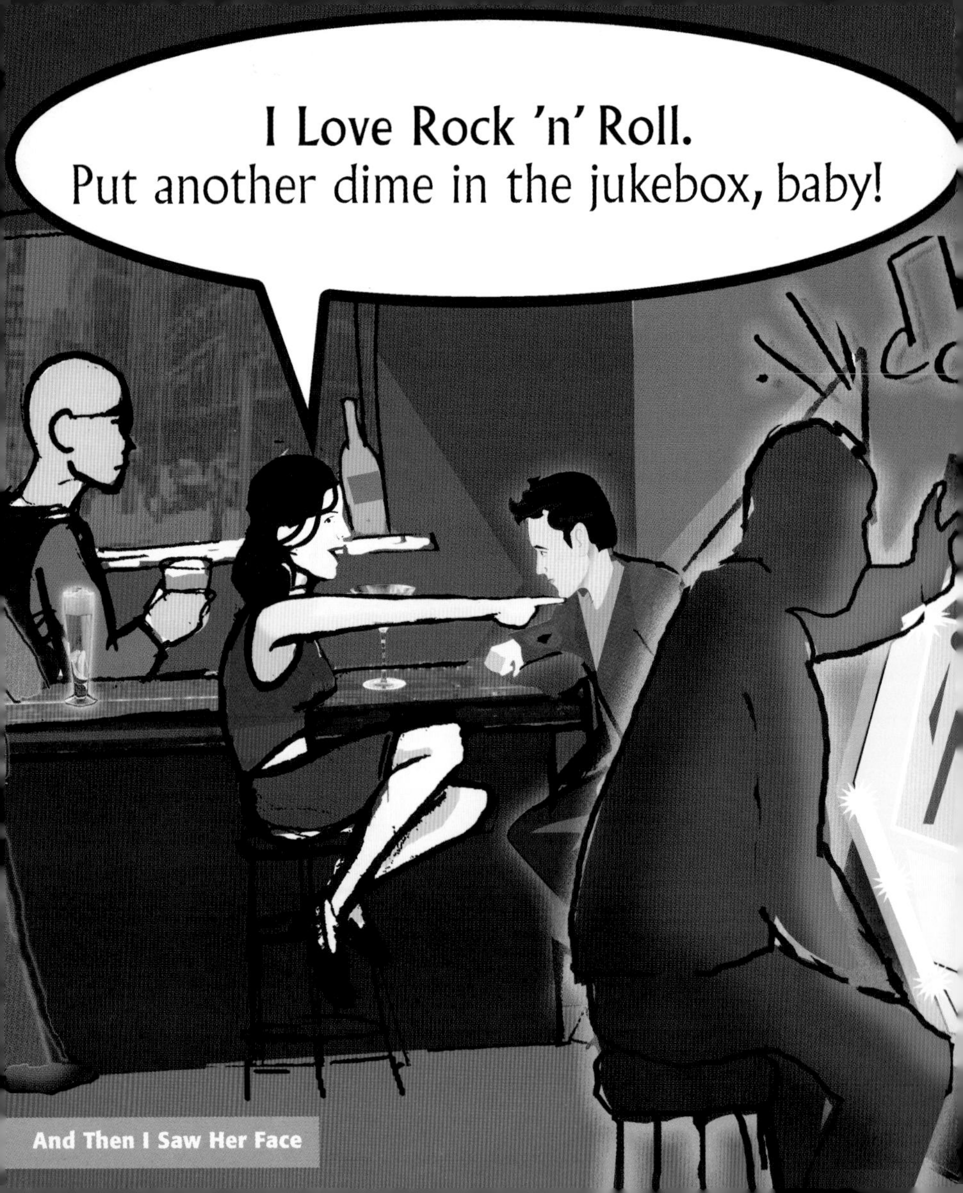
I Love Rock 'n' Roll.
Put another dime in the jukebox, baby!
And Then I Saw Her Face

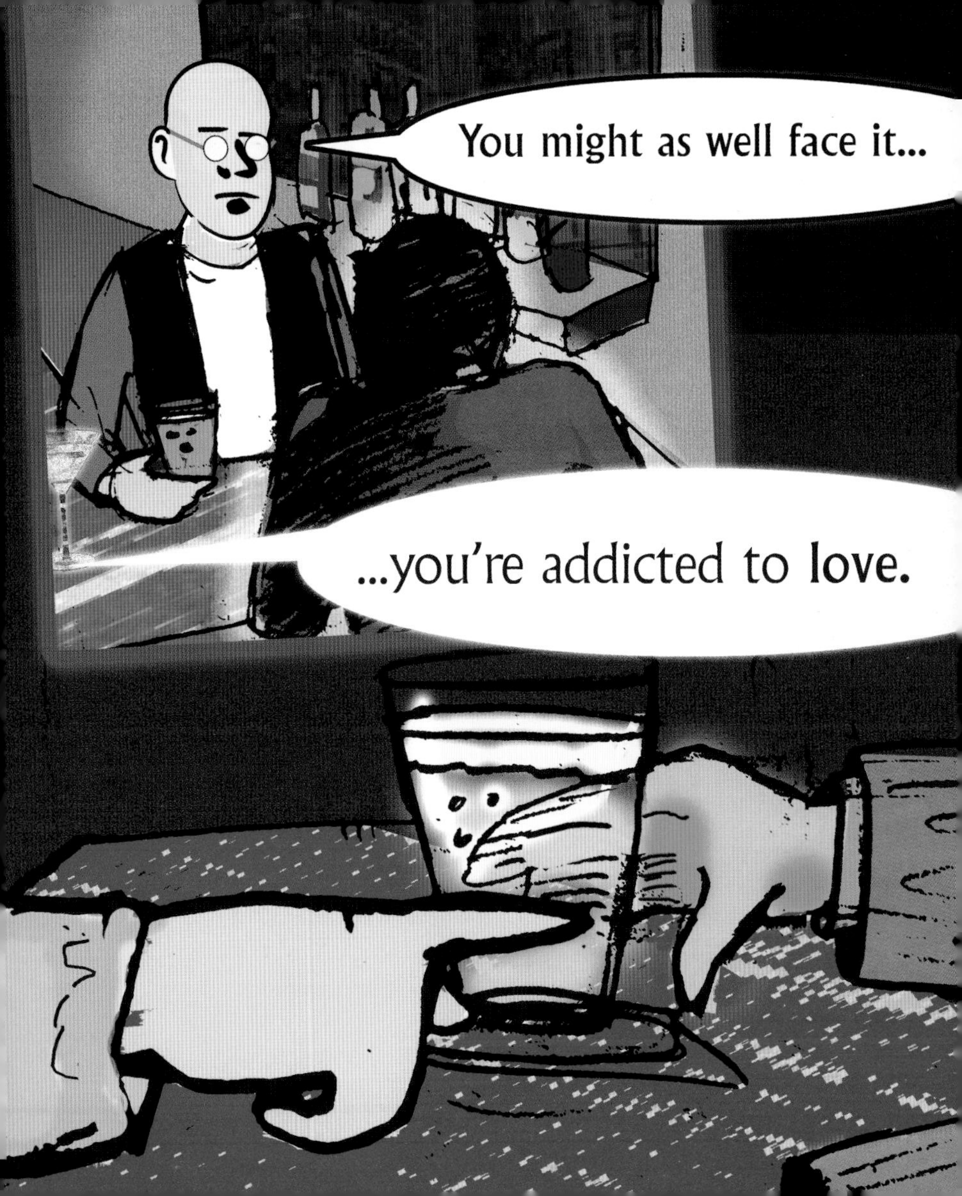
You might as well face it...
...you're addicted to **love**.

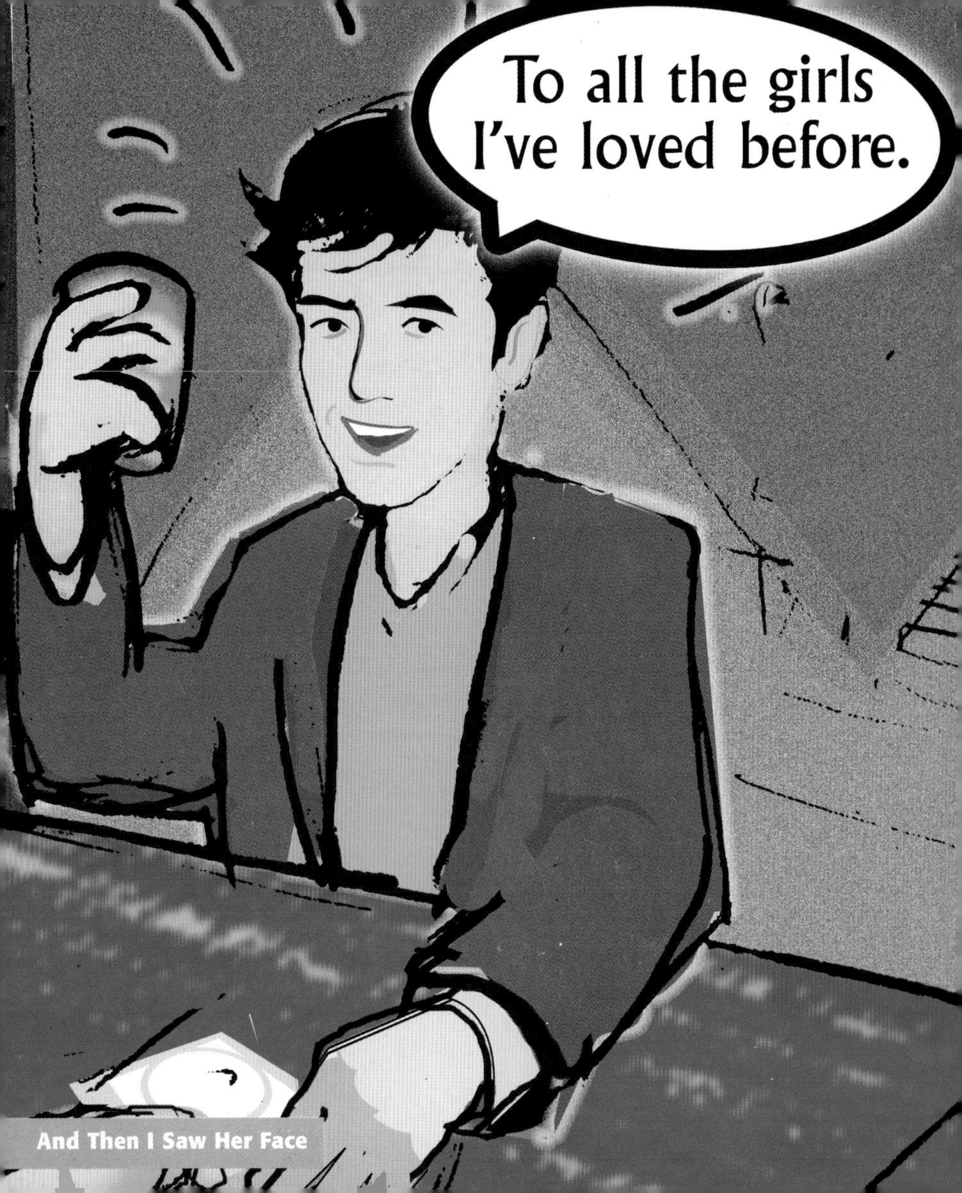
To all the girls I've loved before.
And Then I Saw Her Face

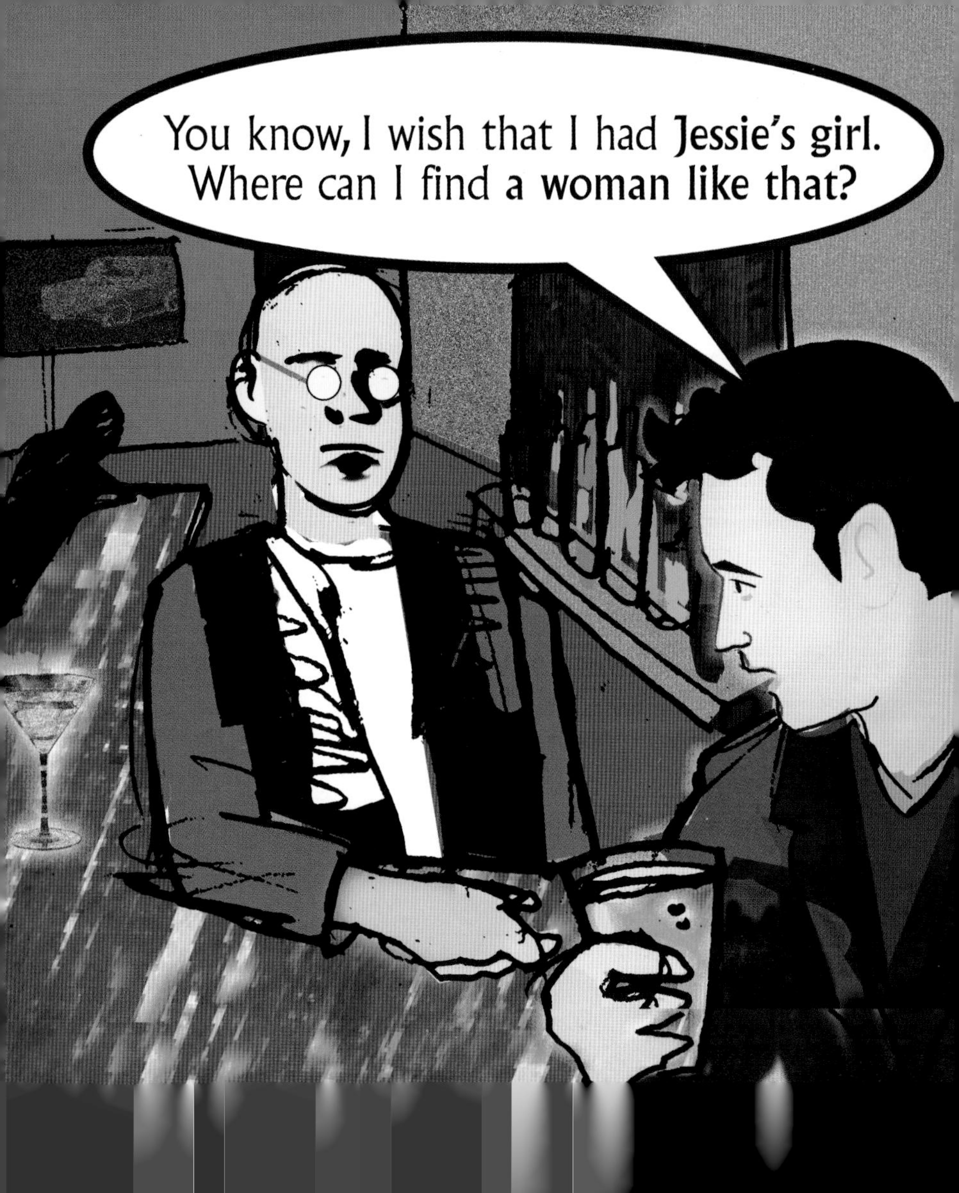
You know, I wish that I had Jessie's girl.
Where can I find a woman like that?

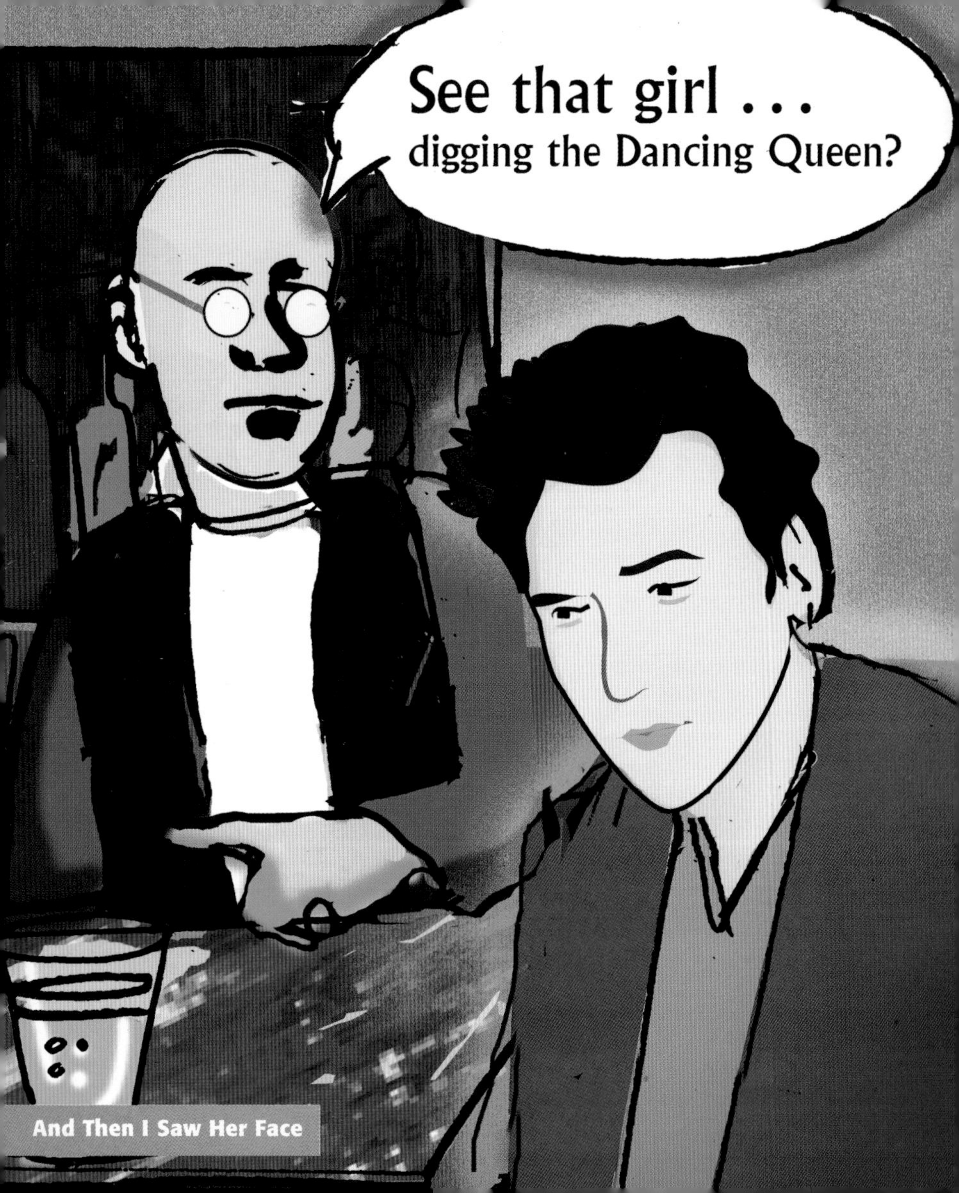
See that girl . . .
digging the Dancing Queen?

And then I saw her face!

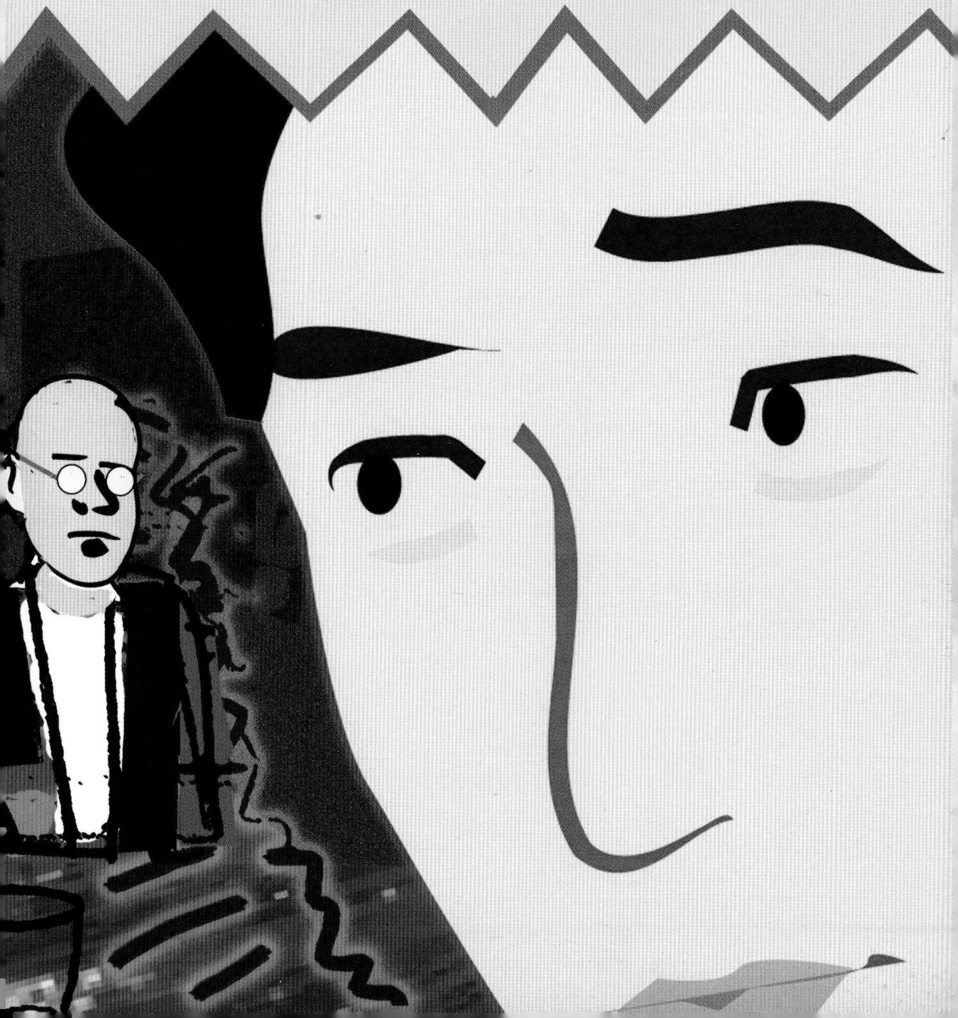

Her name was **Lola** . . .

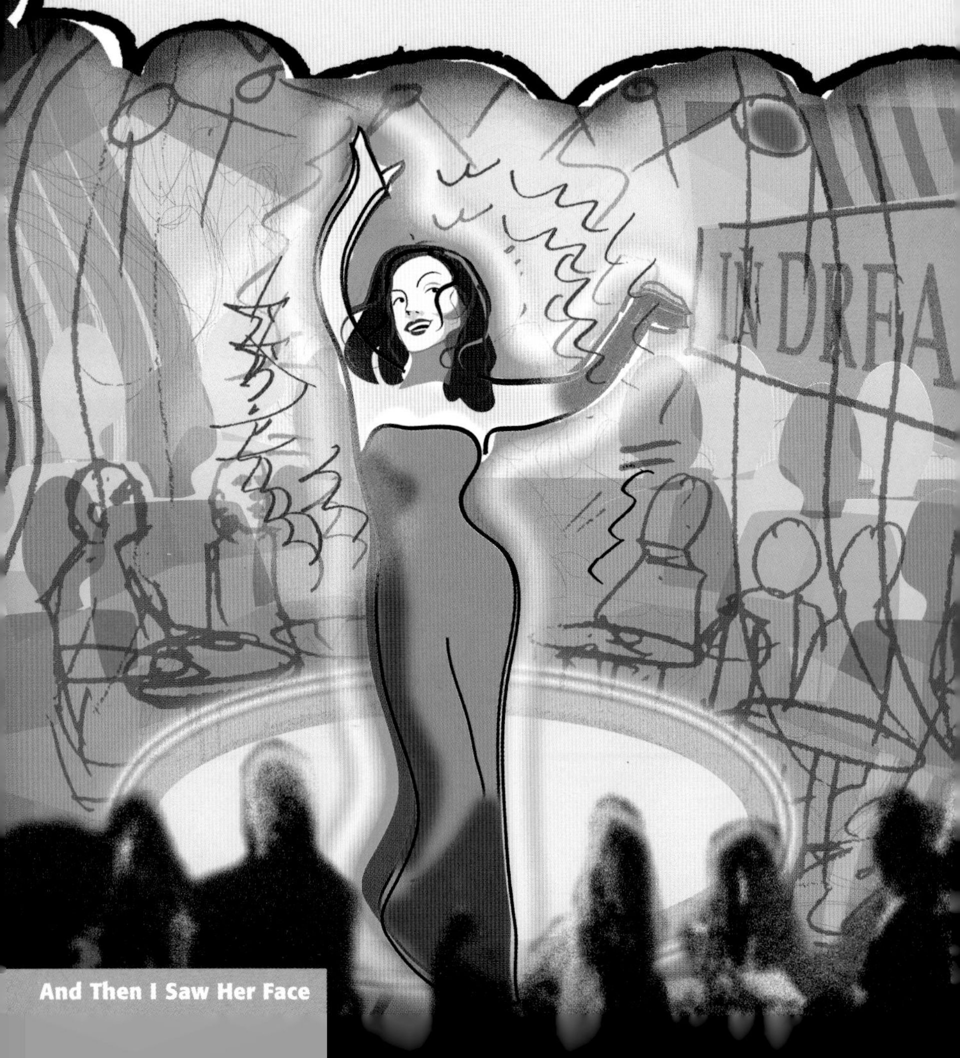

And Then I Saw Her Face

. . . she was a **showgirl.**

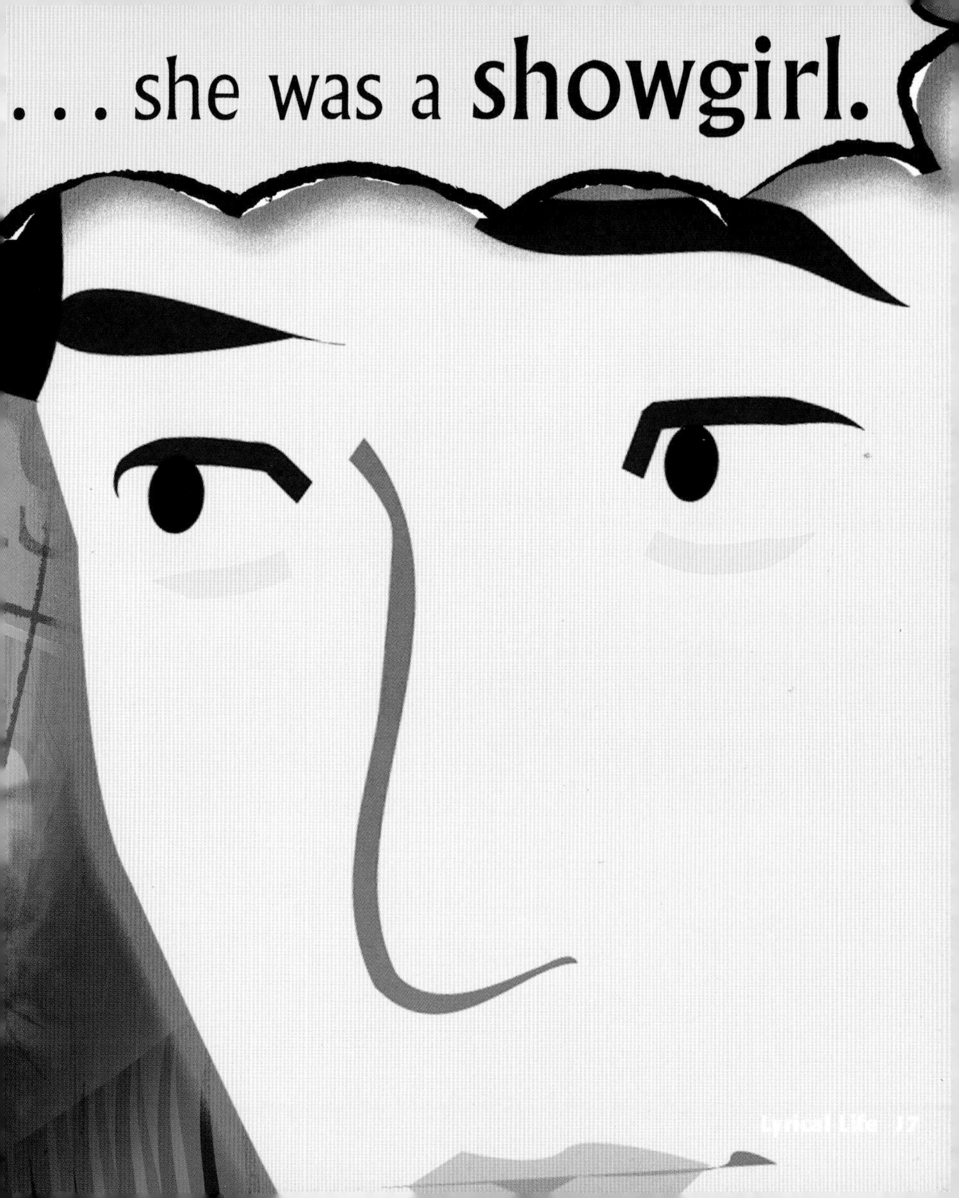

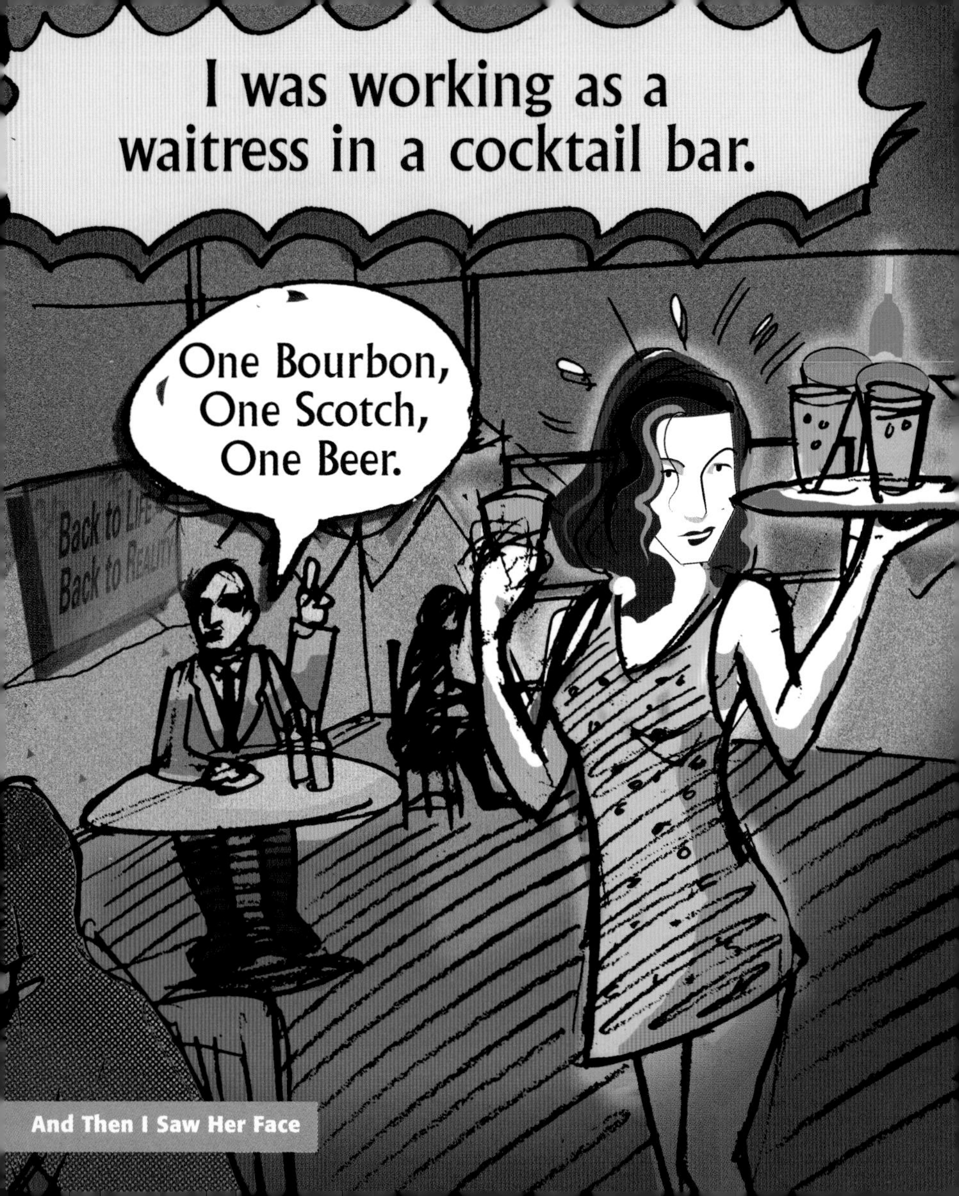
I was working as a waitress in a cocktail bar.
One Bourbon, One Scotch, One Beer.

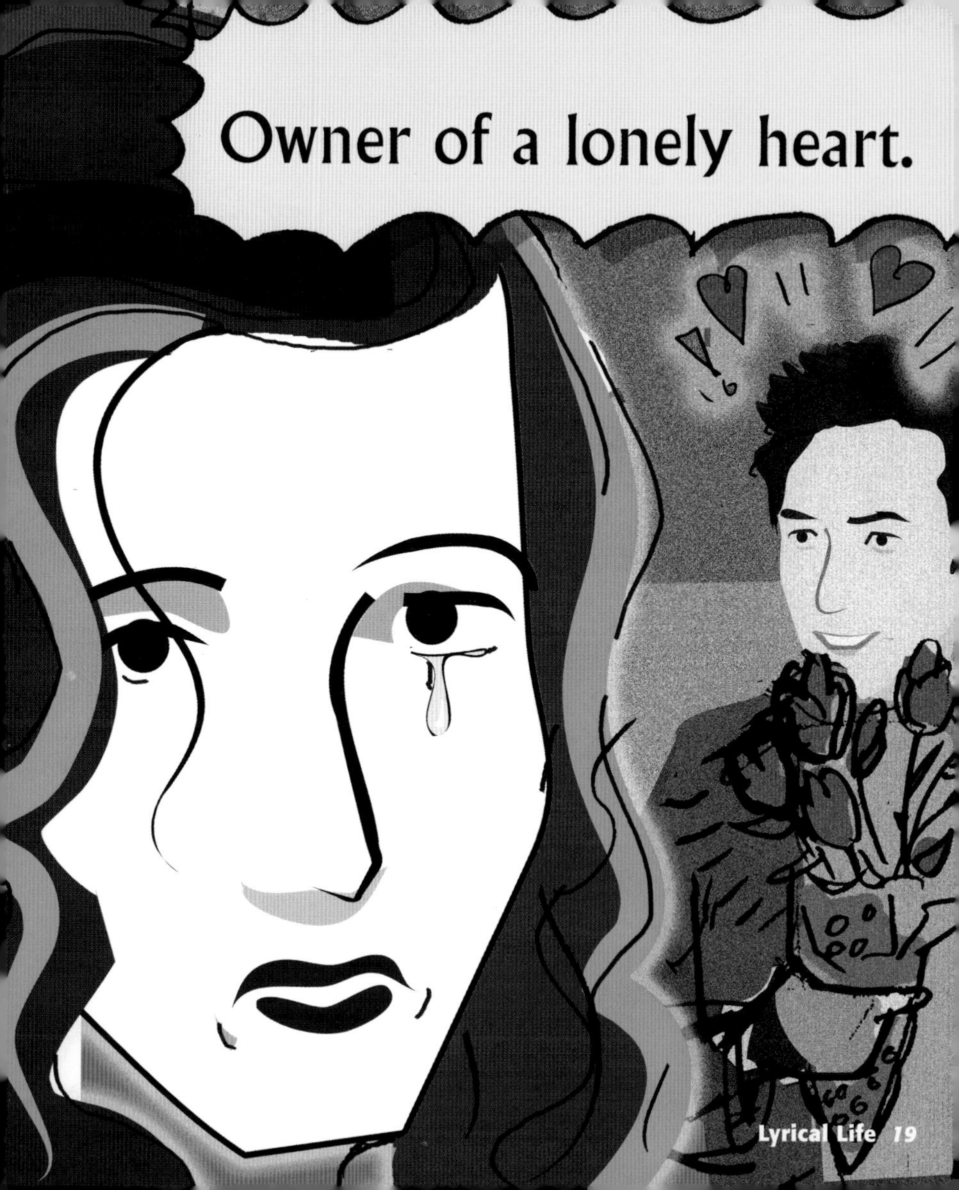
Owner of a lonely heart.

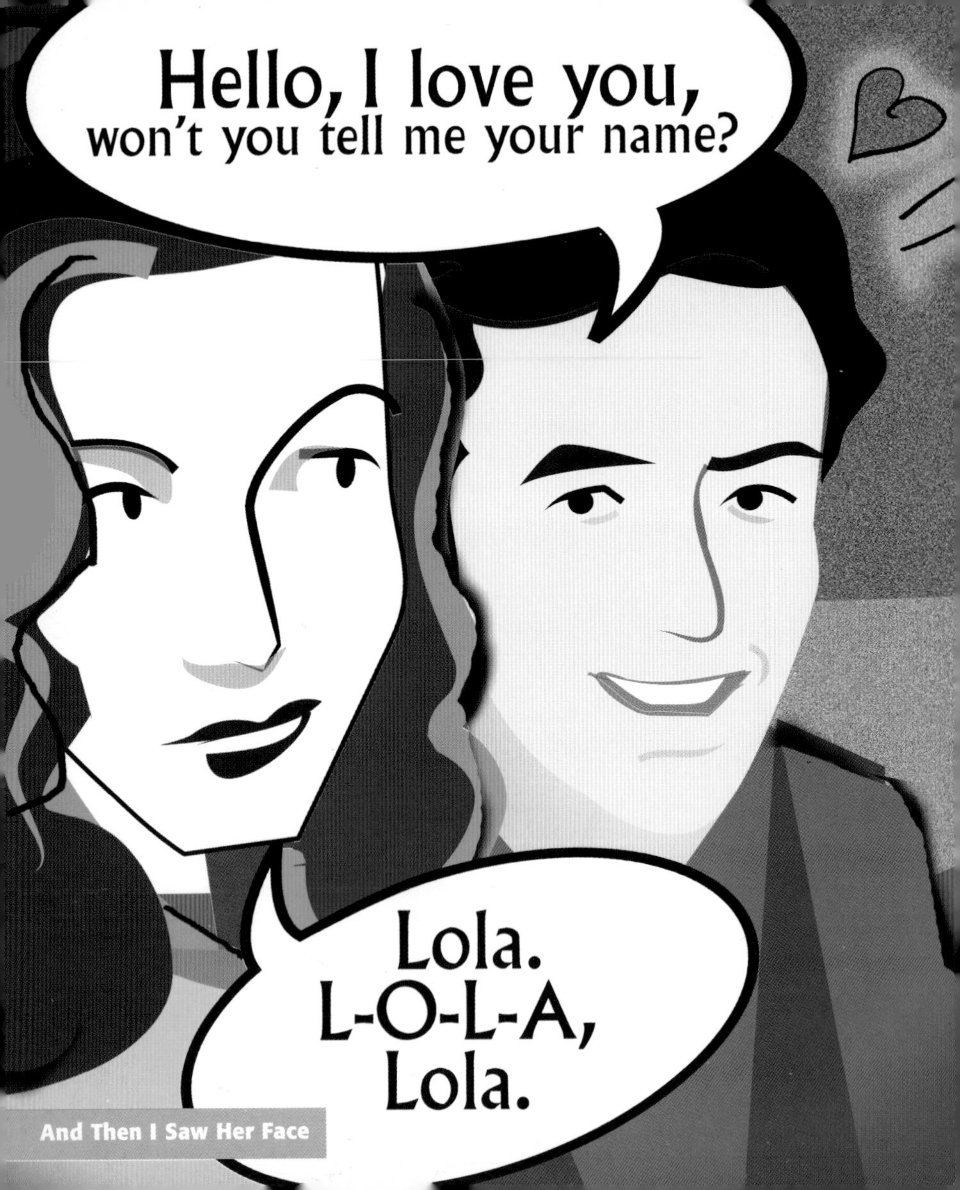
Hello, I love you, won't you tell me your name?
Lola. L-O-L-A, Lola.
And Then I Saw Her Face

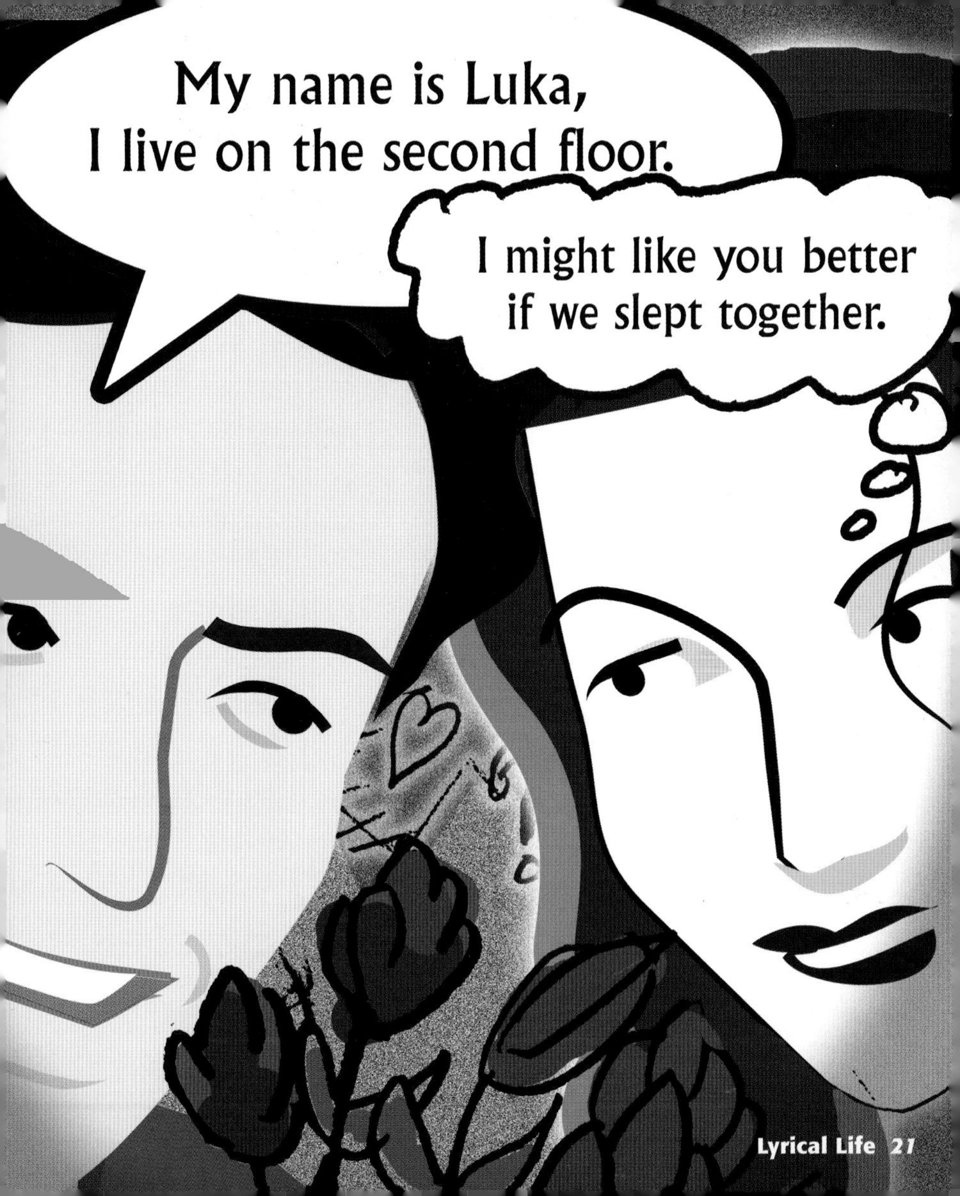
My name is Luka,
I live on the second floor.
I might like you better
if we slept together.

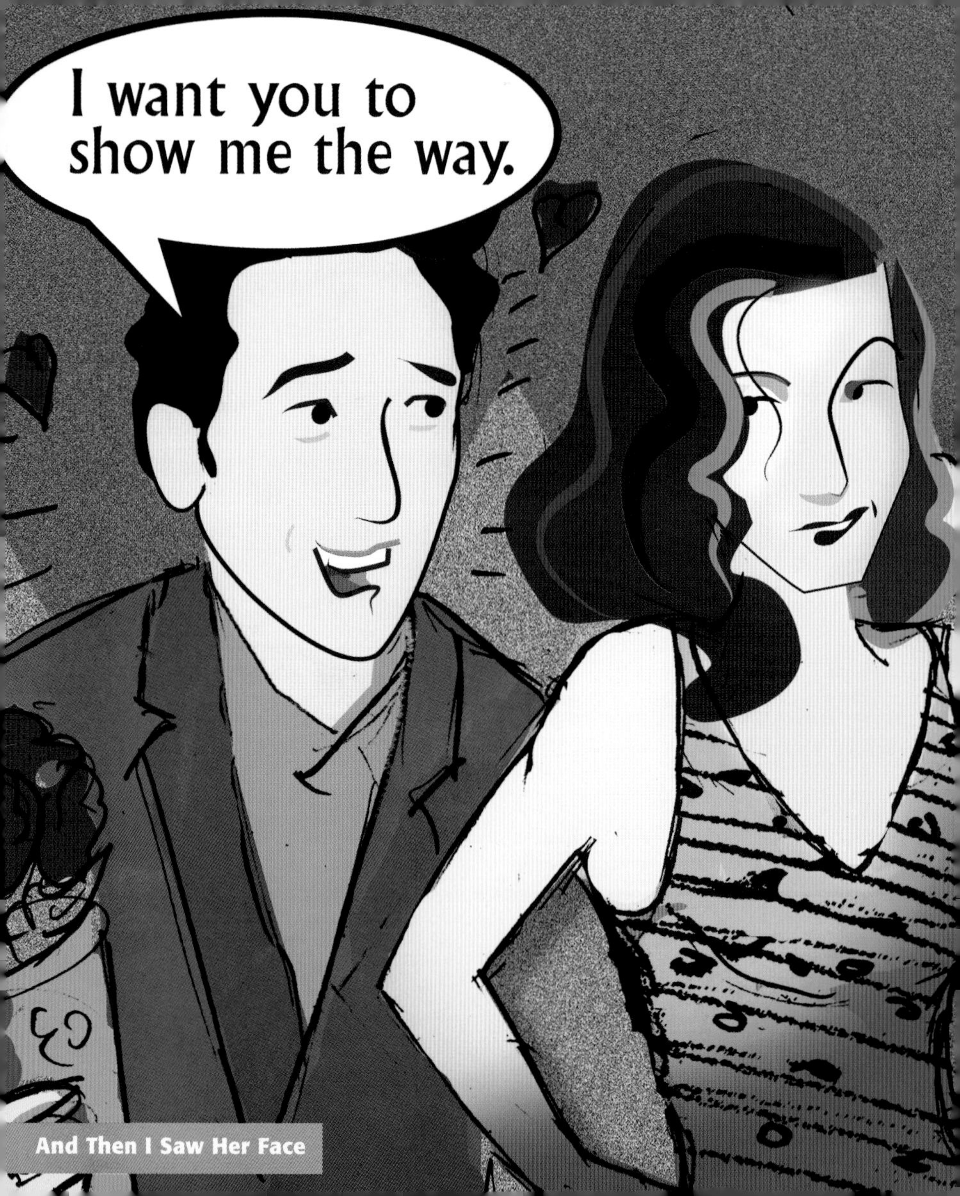
I want you to show me the way.

And Then I Saw Her Face

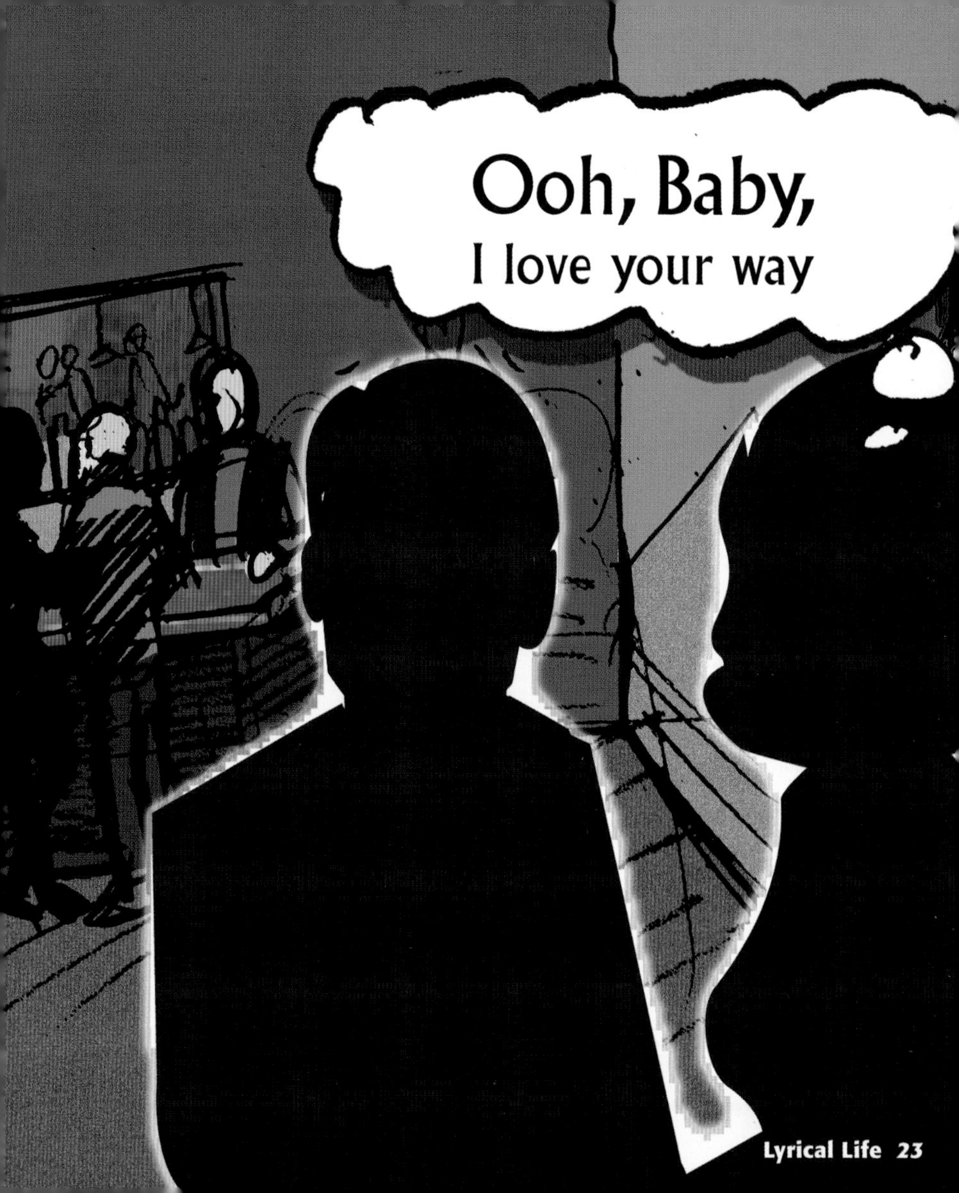
Ooh, Baby,
I love your way

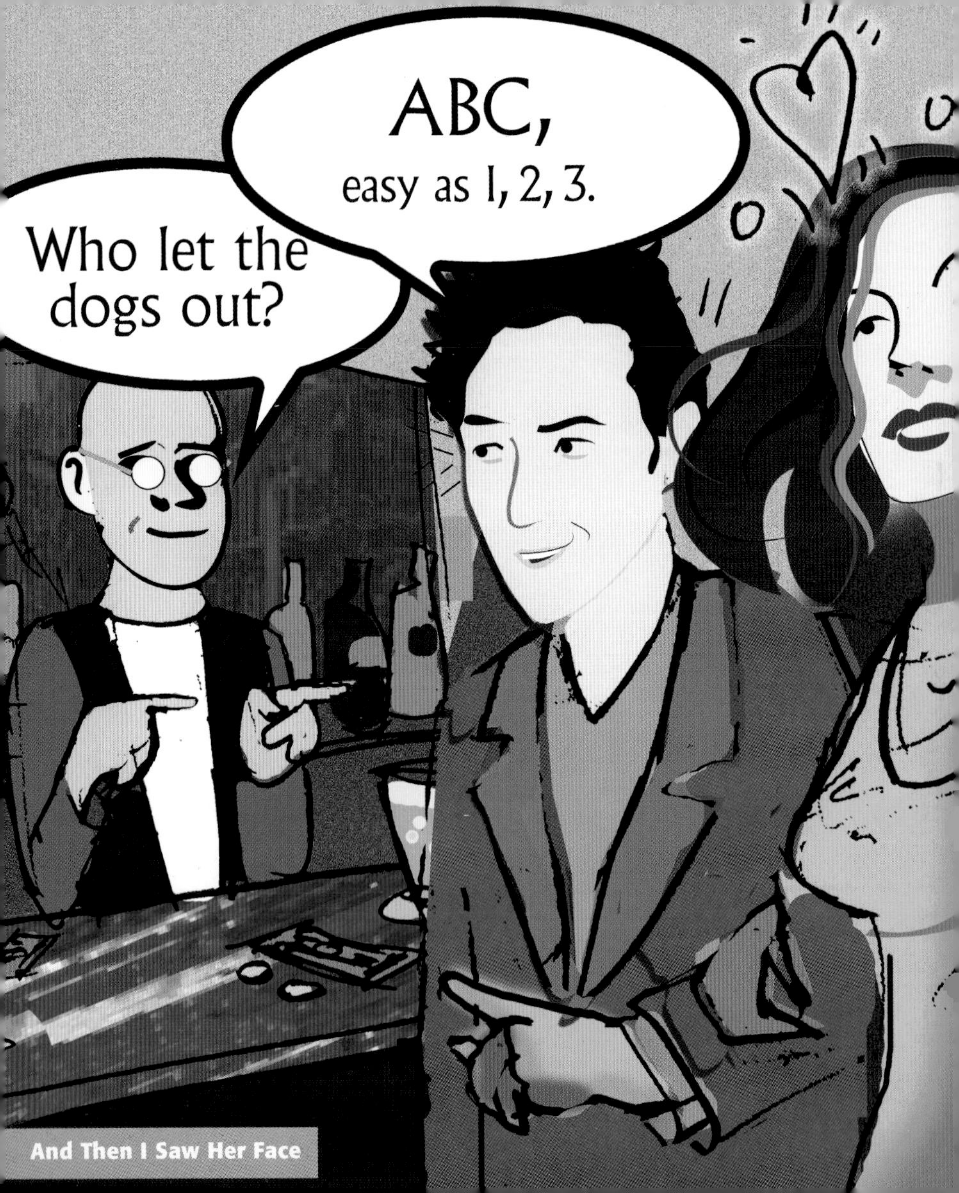
Who let the dogs out?
ABC, easy as 1, 2, 3.

And Then I Saw Her Face

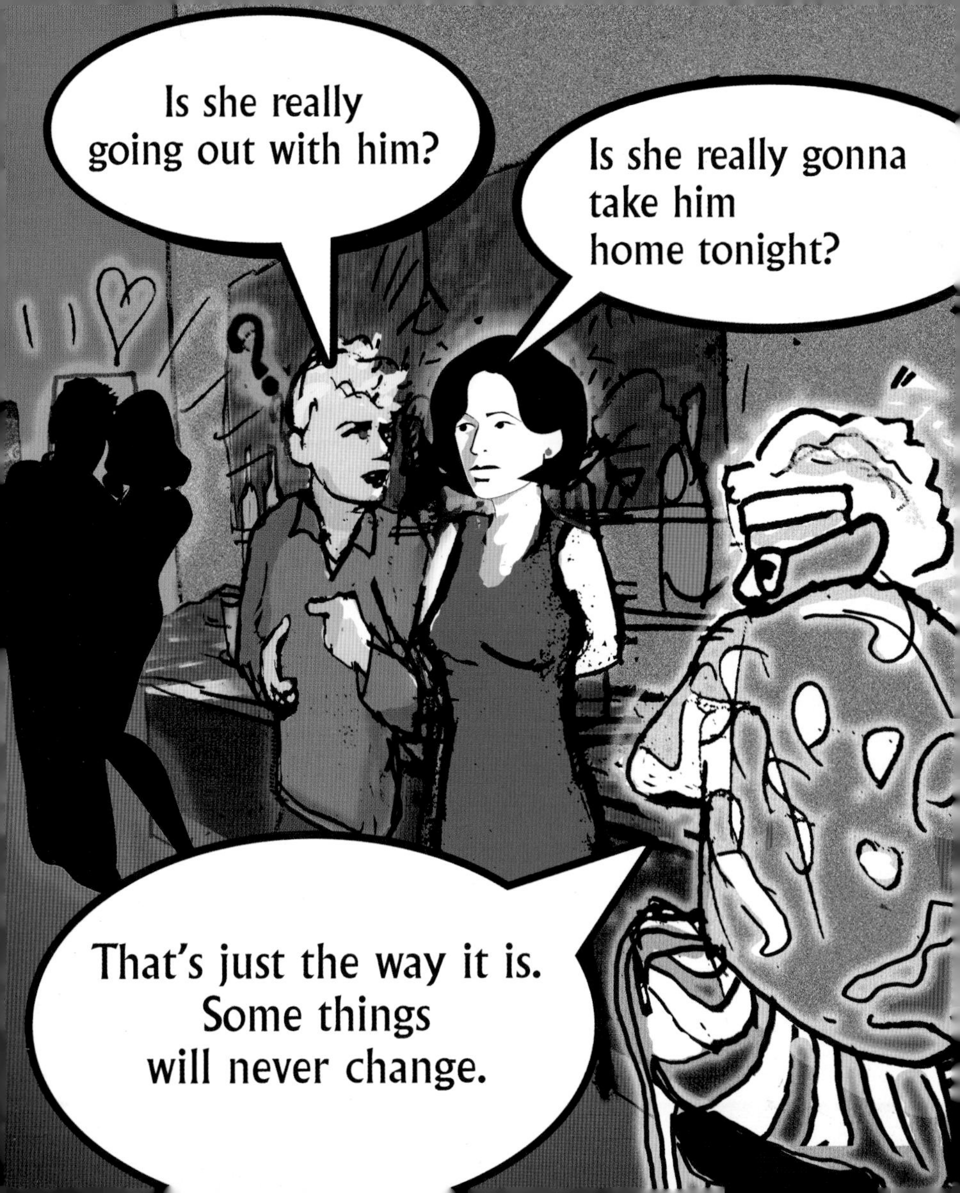
Is she really going out with him?
Is she really gonna take him home tonight?
That's just the way it is. Some things will never change.

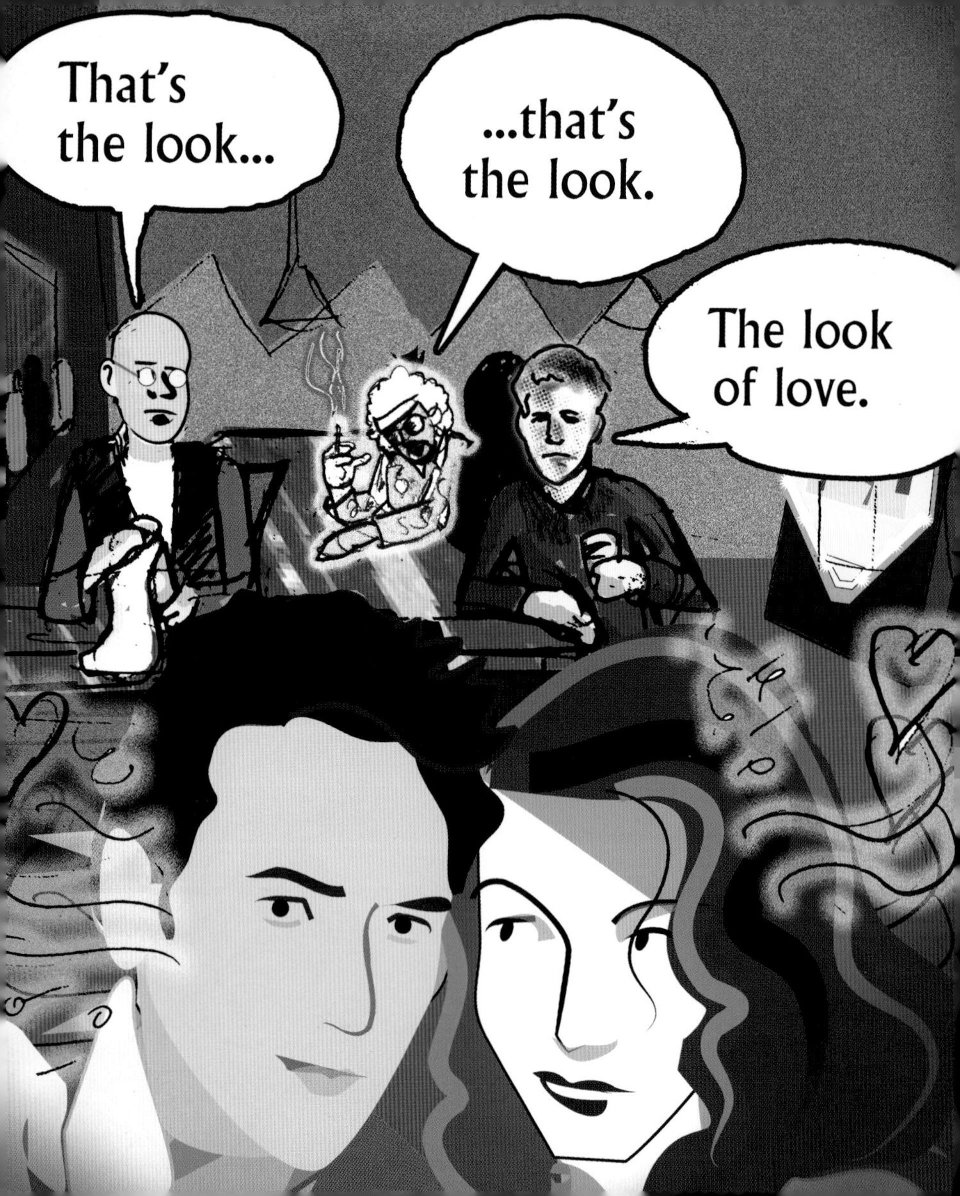
That's the look...
...that's the look.
The look of love.

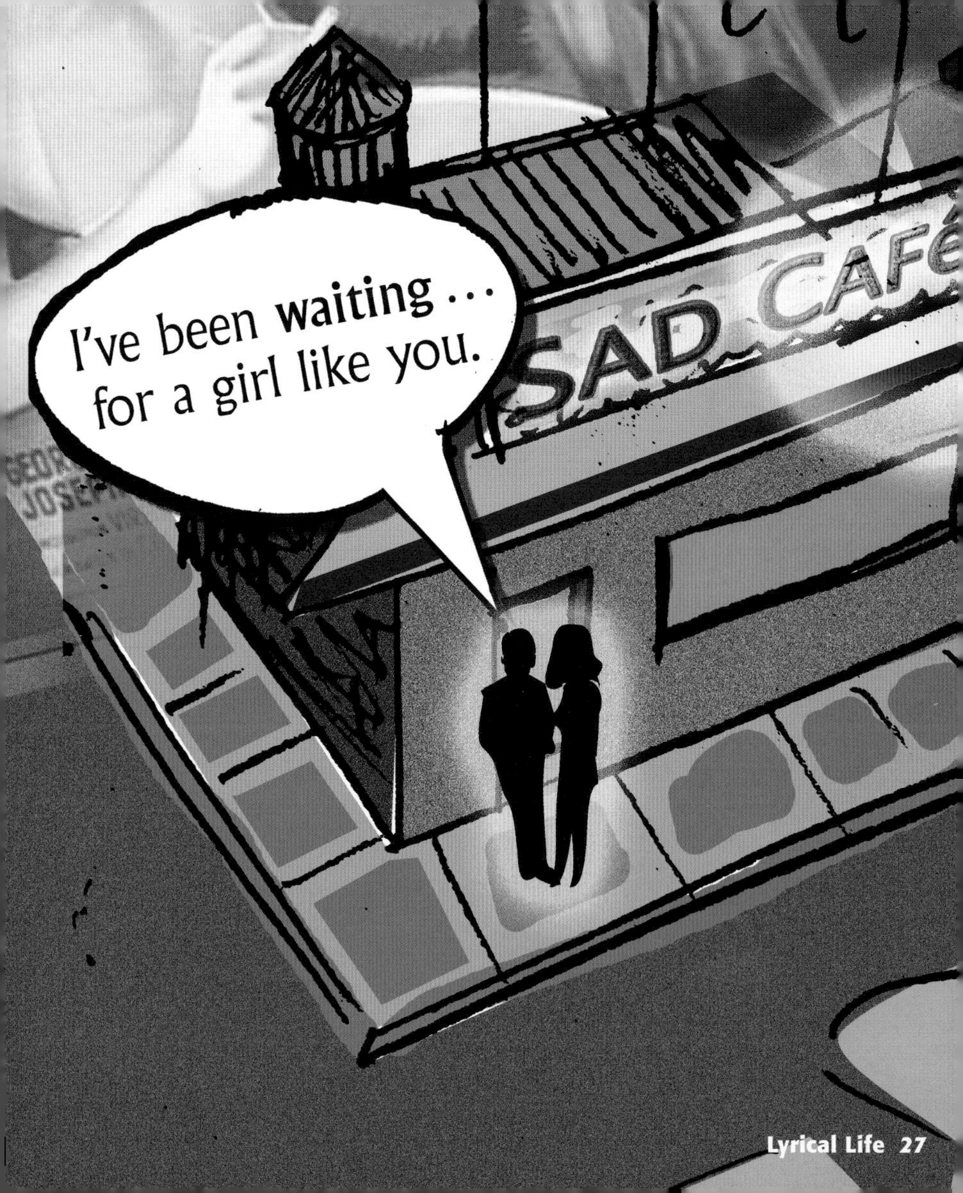
I've been waiting . . .
for a girl like you.
SAD CAFÉ

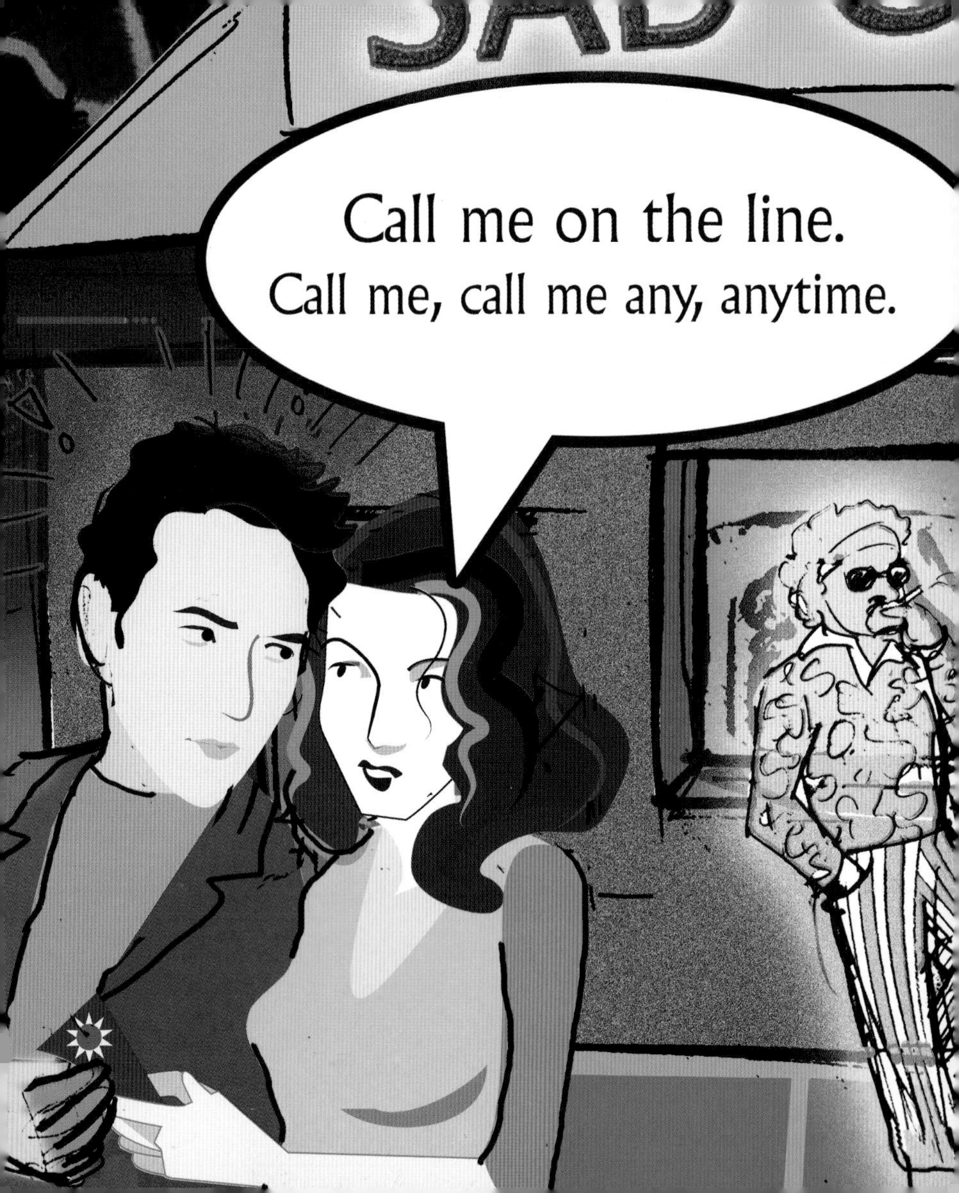
Call me on the line.
Call me, call me any, anytime.

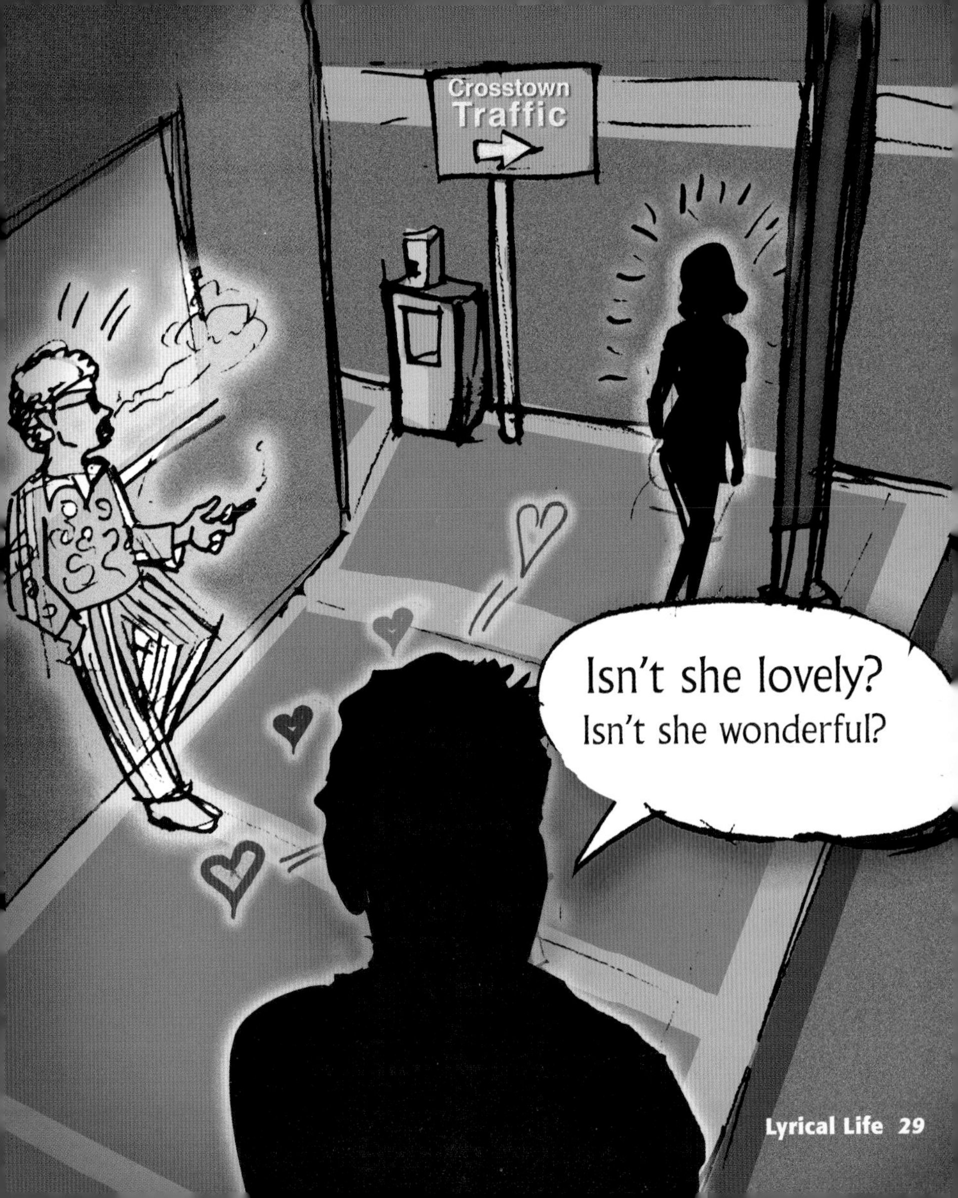
Crosstown
Traffic
Isn't she lovely?
Isn't she wonderful?

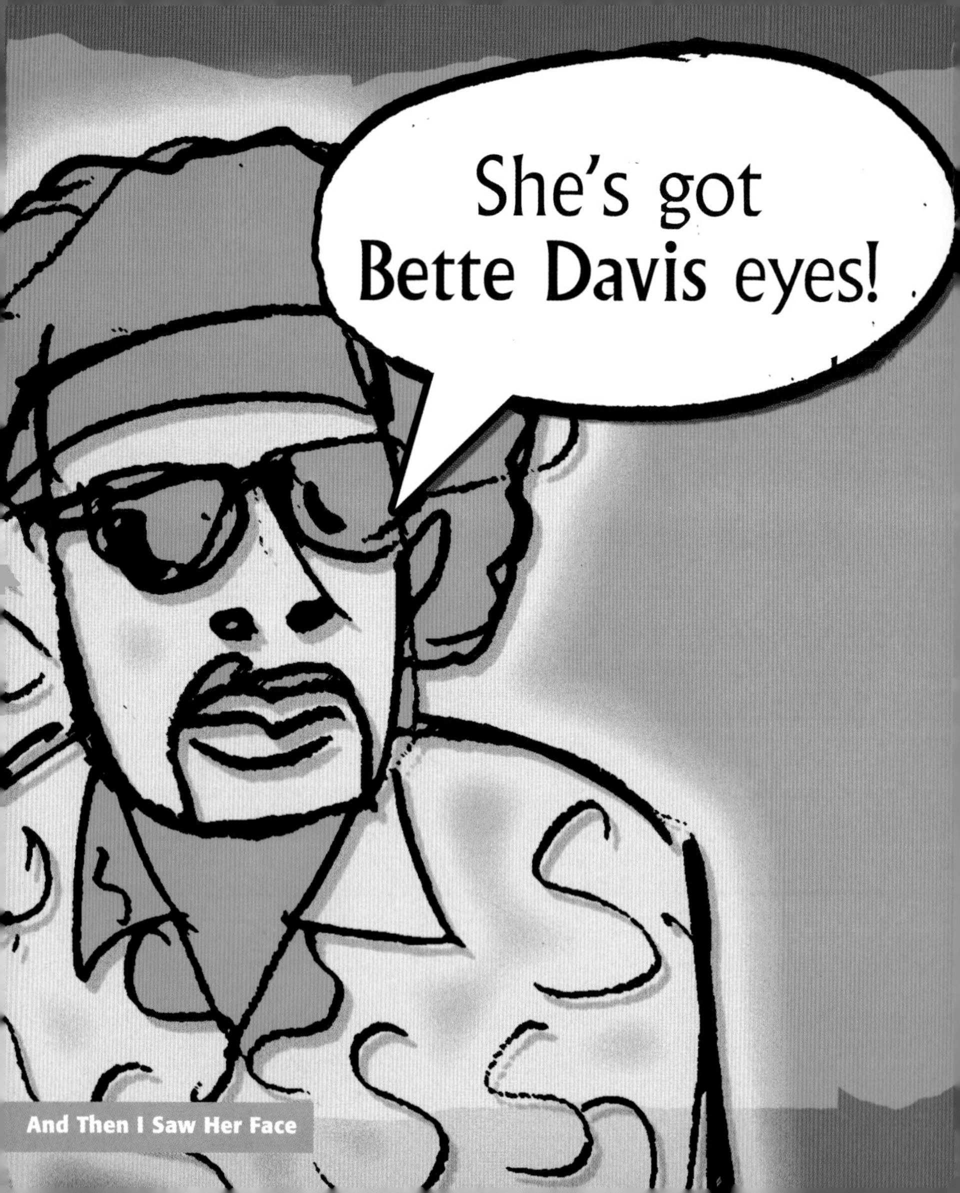
She's got
Bette Davis eyes!

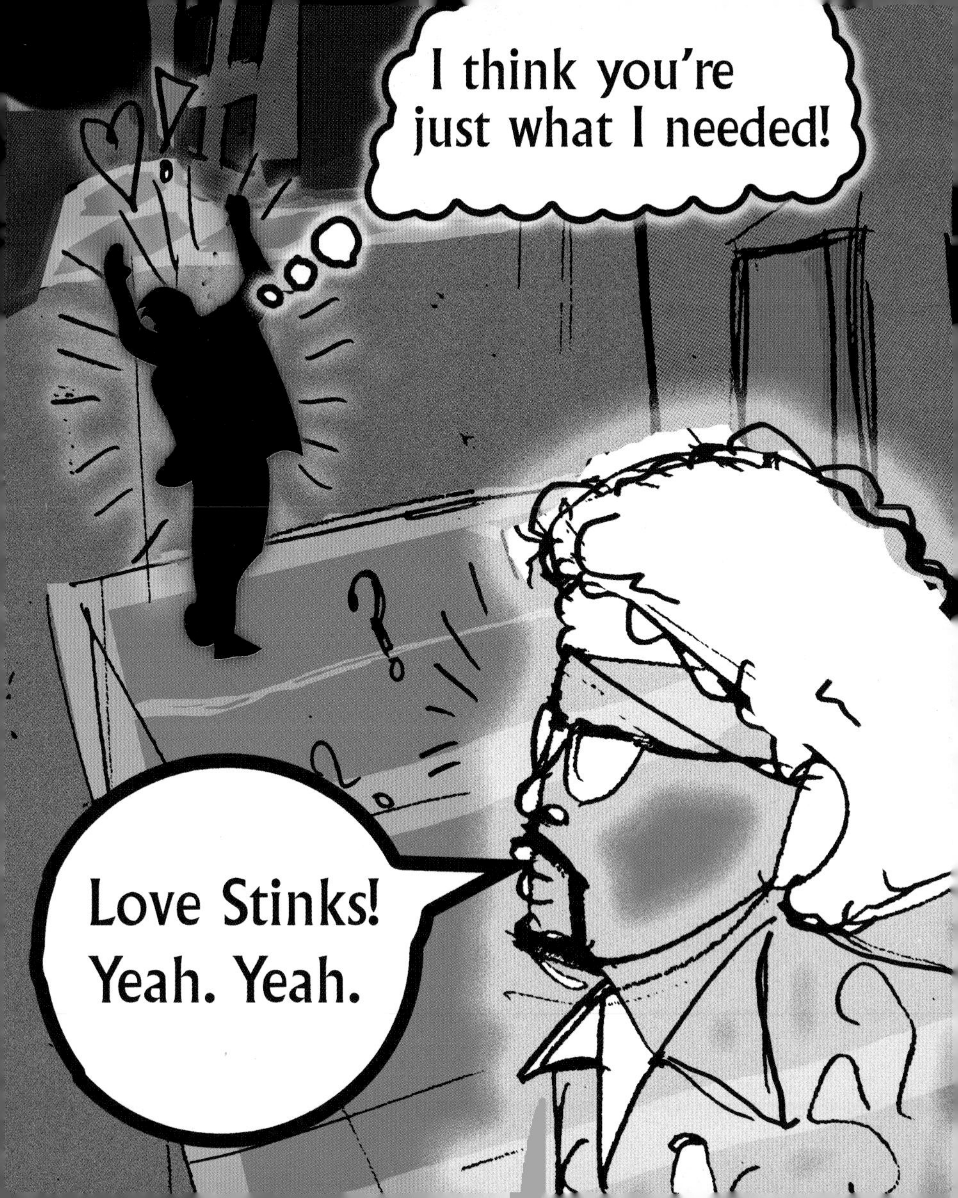
I think you're just what I needed!
Love Stinks! Yeah. Yeah.

Chapter Two

I'll Melt With You

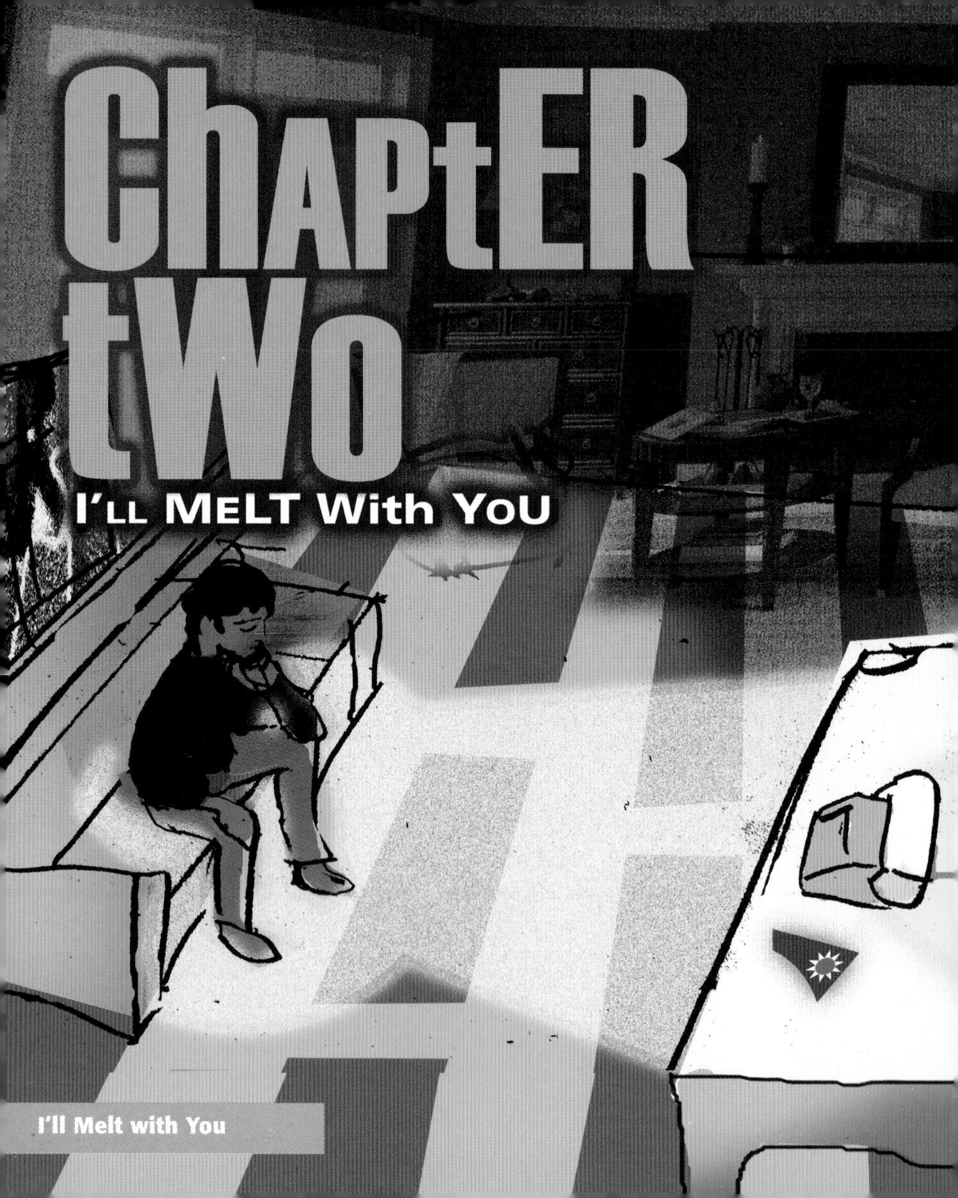

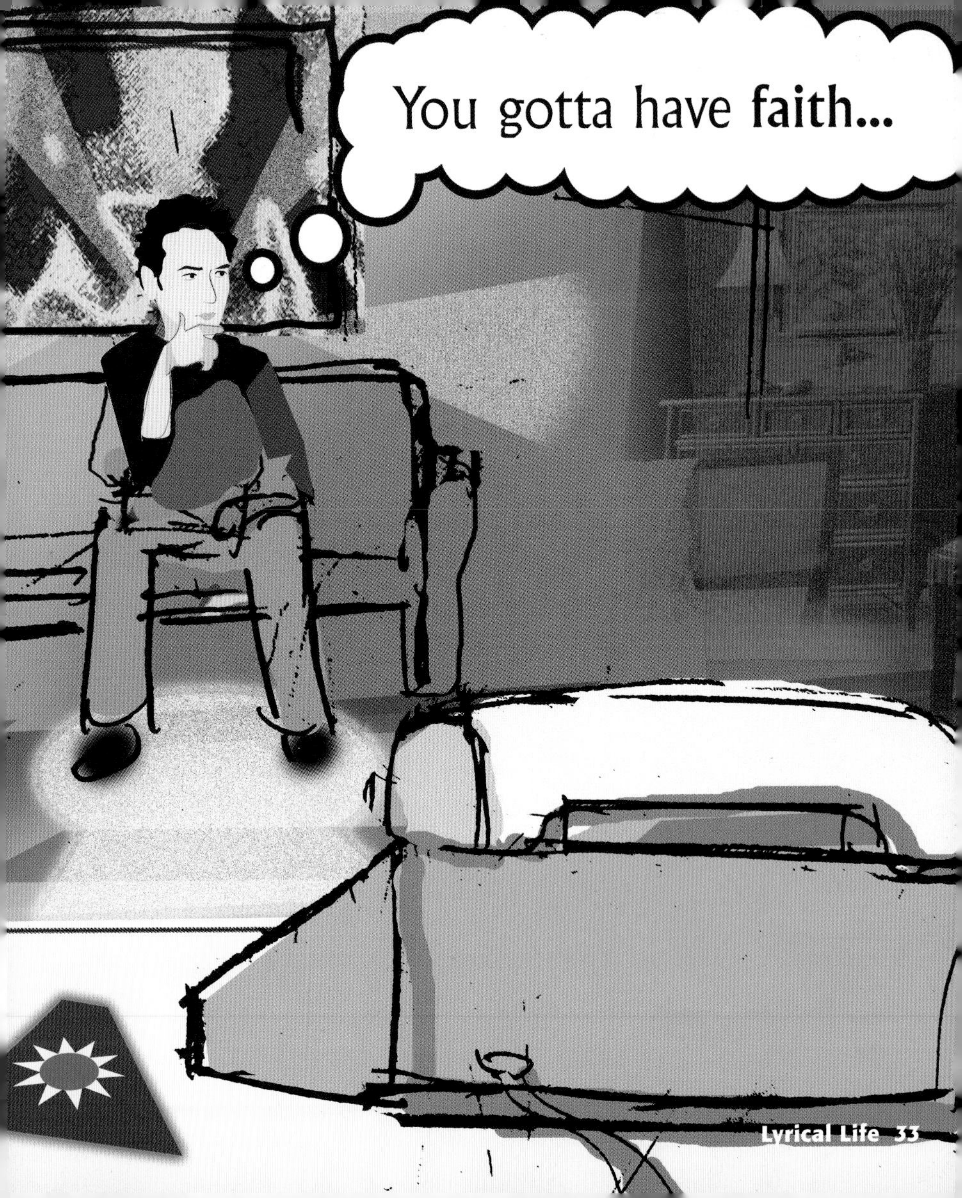
You gotta have faith...

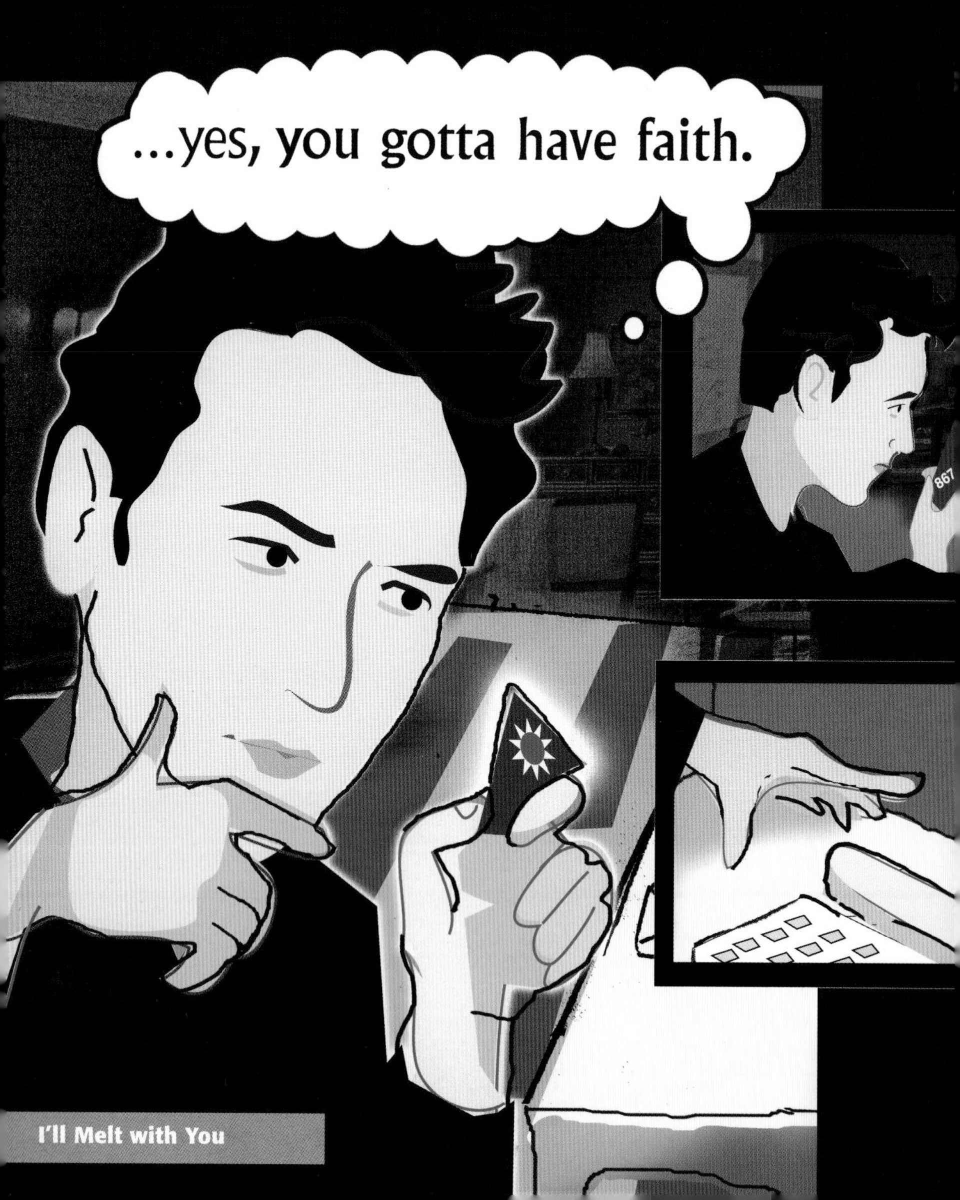
...yes, you gotta have faith.
867

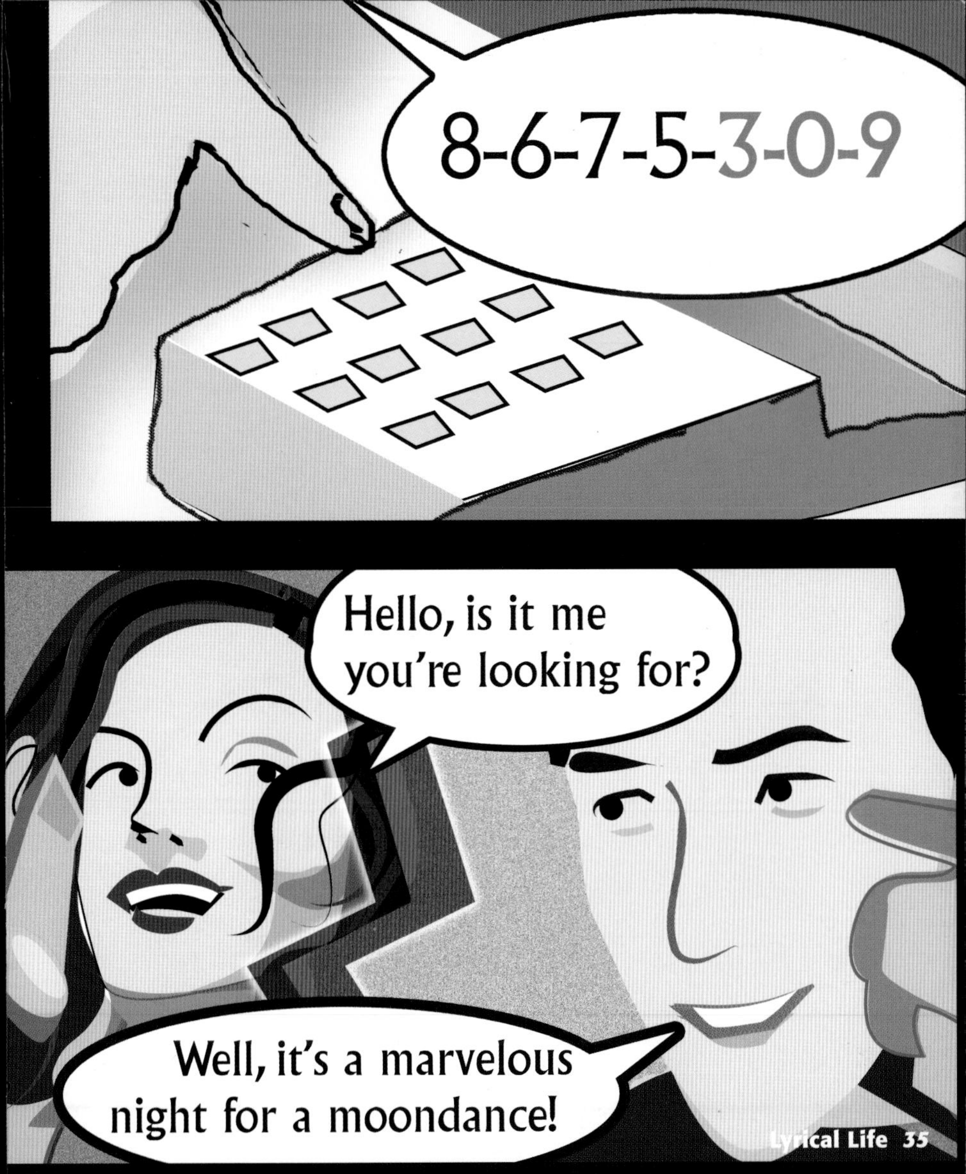
8-6-7-5-3-0-9
Hello, is it me
you're looking for?
Well, it's a marvelous
night for a moondance!

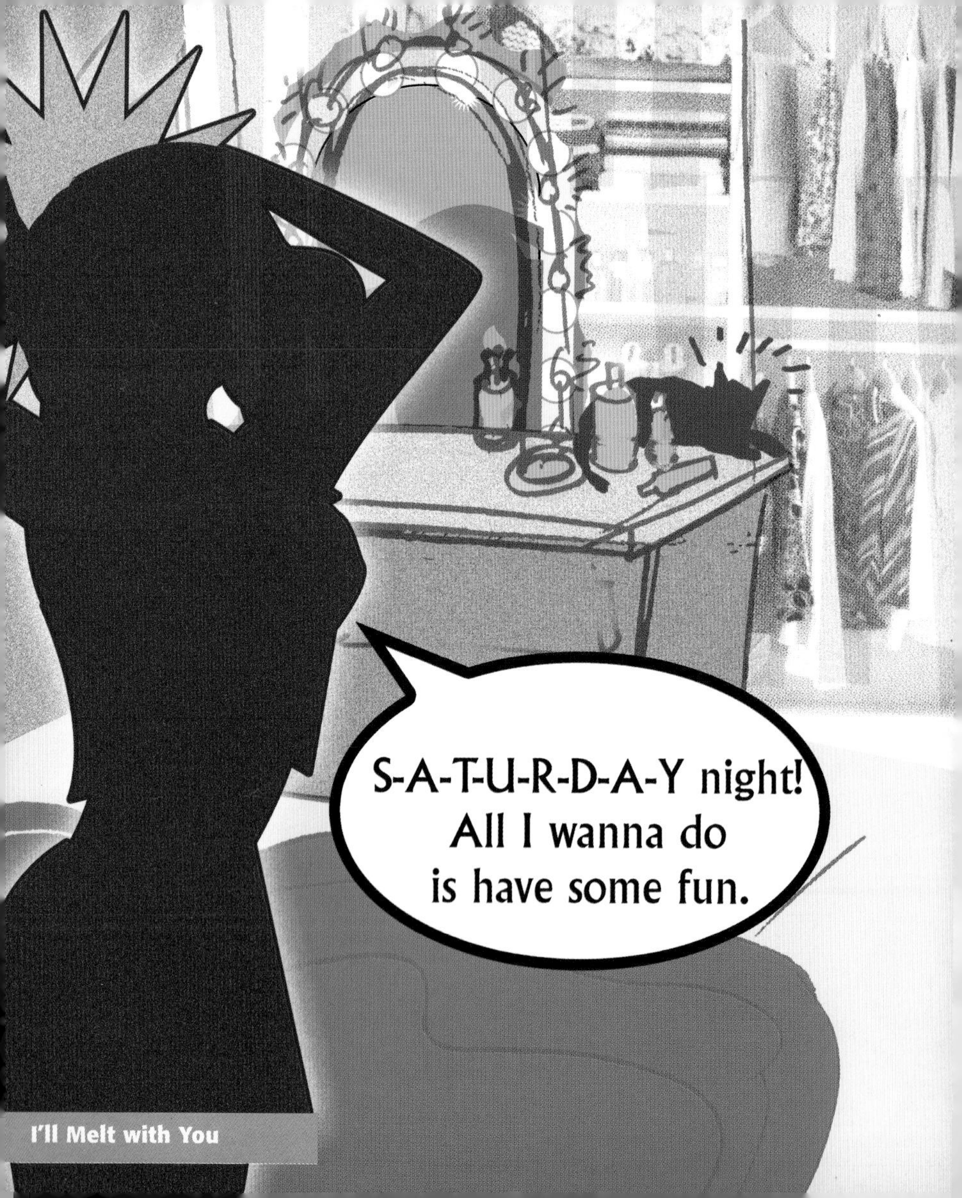
S-A-T-U-R-D-A-Y night!
All I wanna do
is have some fun.

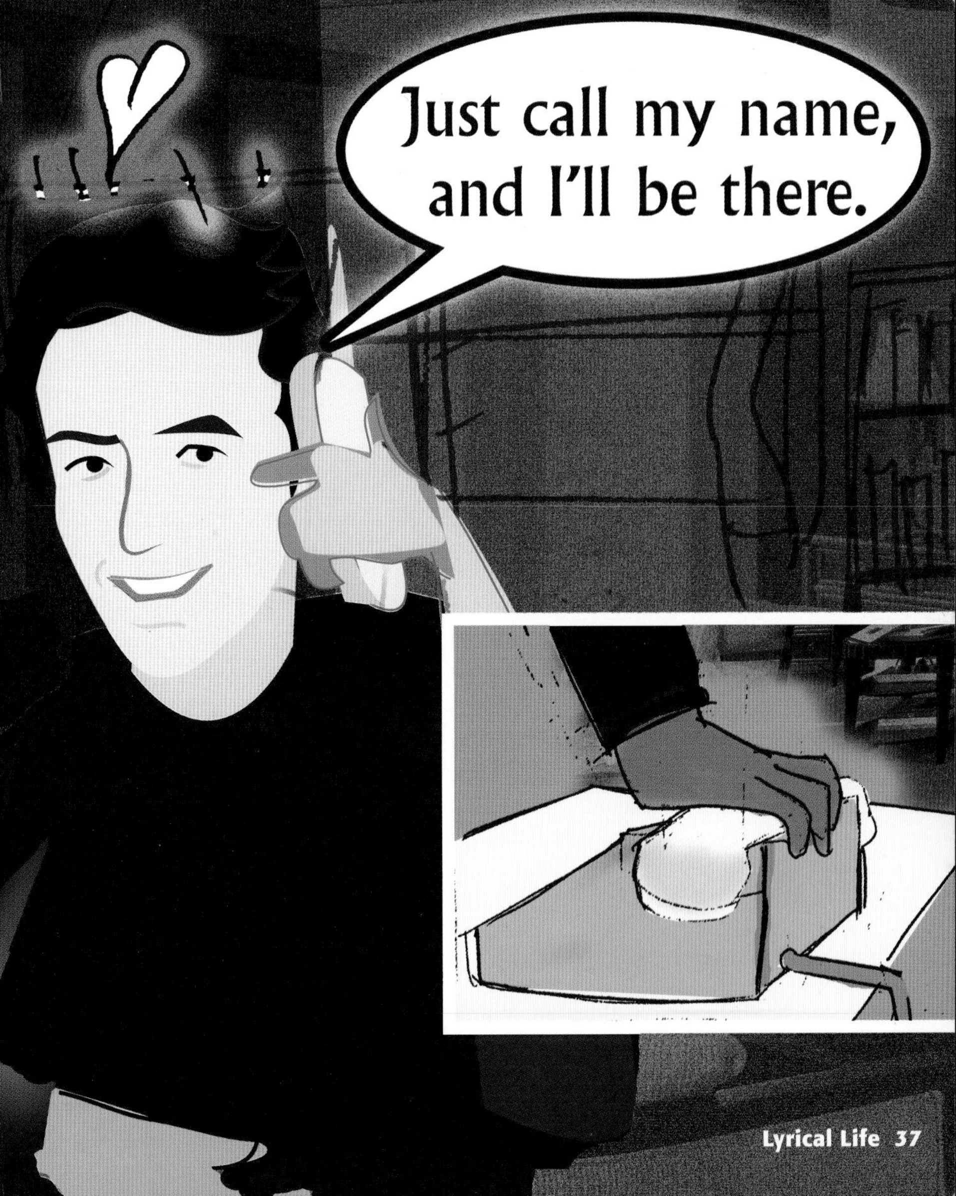
Just call my name, and I'll be there.

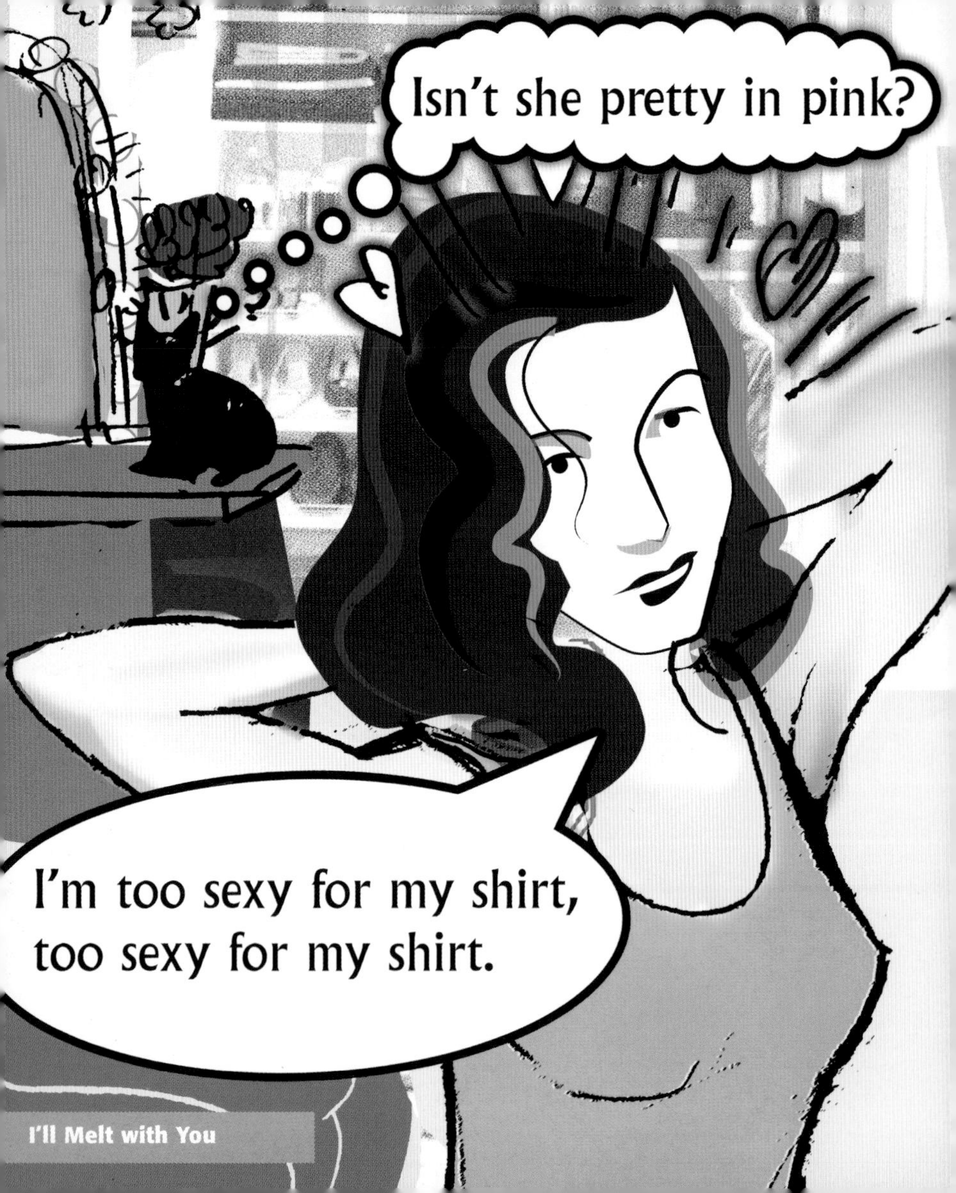
Isn't she pretty in pink?
I'm too sexy for my shirt, too sexy for my shirt.

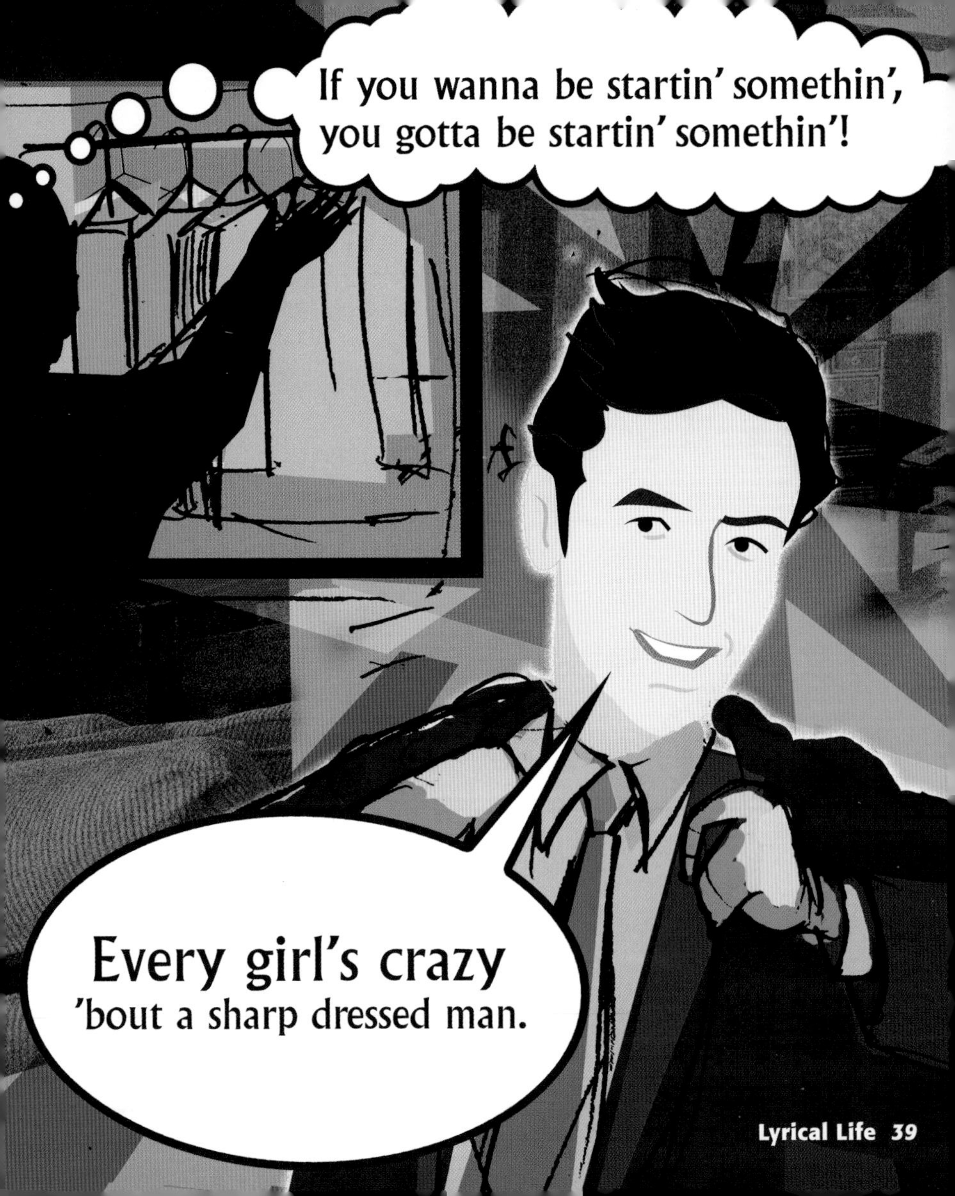
If you wanna be startin' somethin', you gotta be startin' somethin'!
Every girl's crazy 'bout a sharp dressed man.

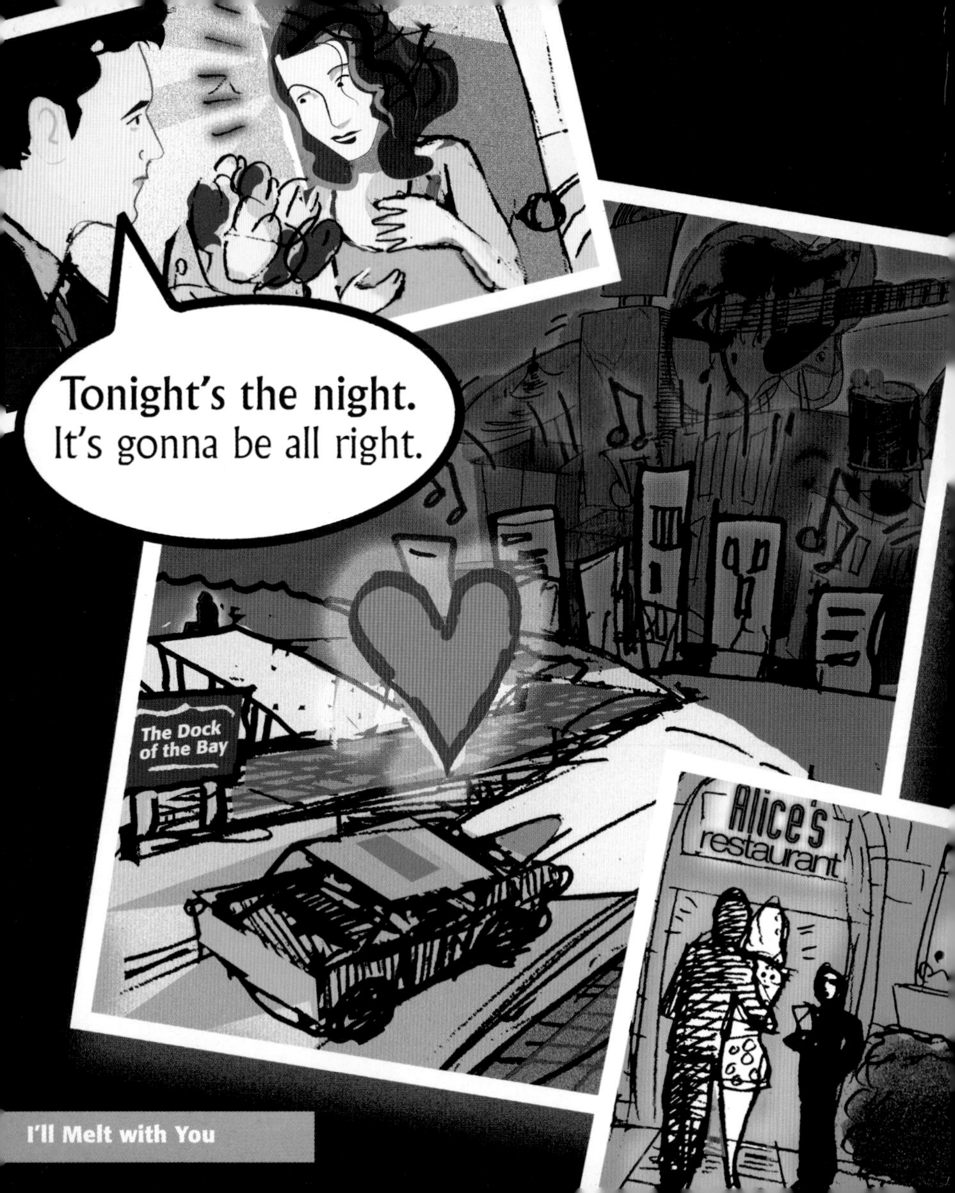
Tonight's the night.
It's gonna be all right.
The Dock of the Bay
Alice's restaurant

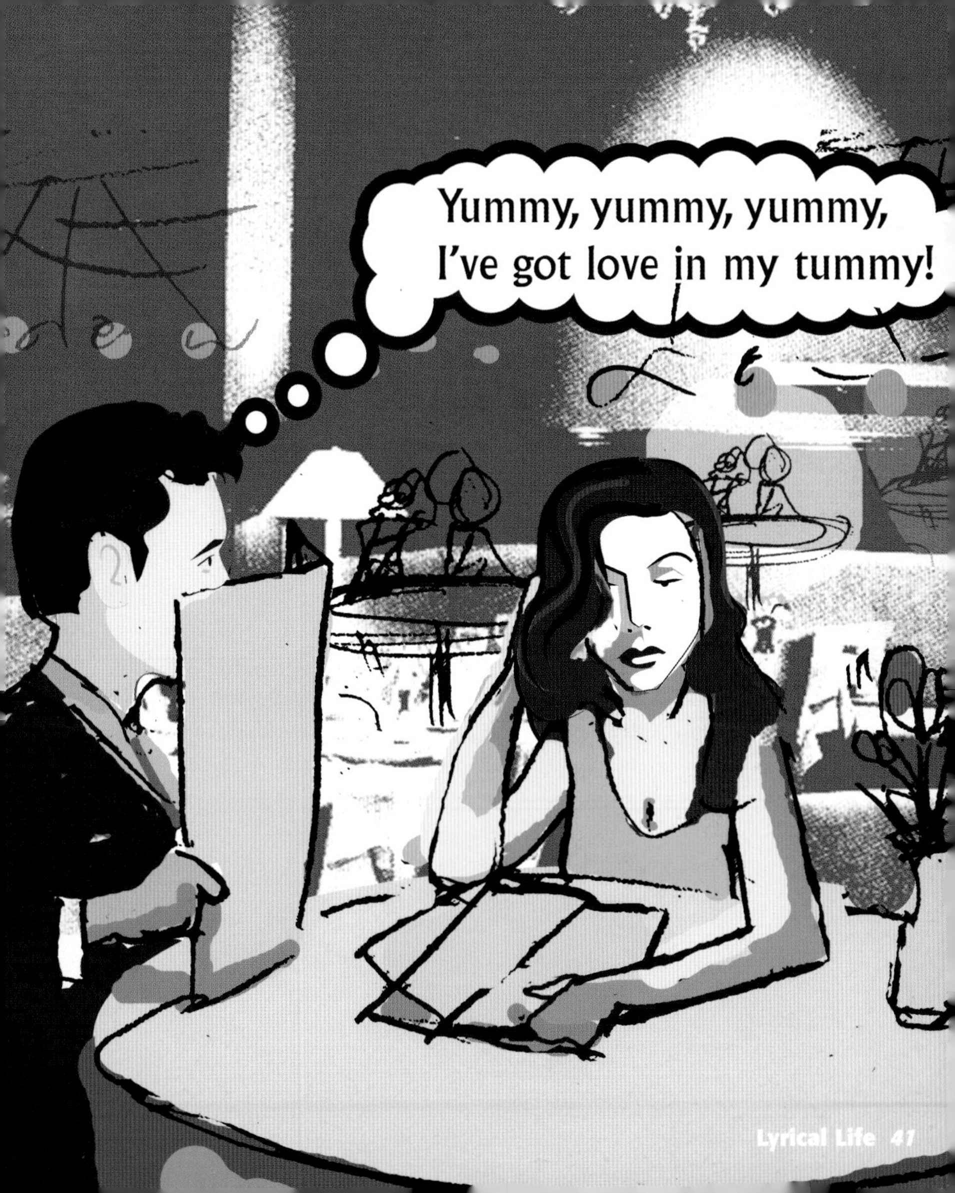
Yummy, yummy, yummy,
I've got love in my tummy!

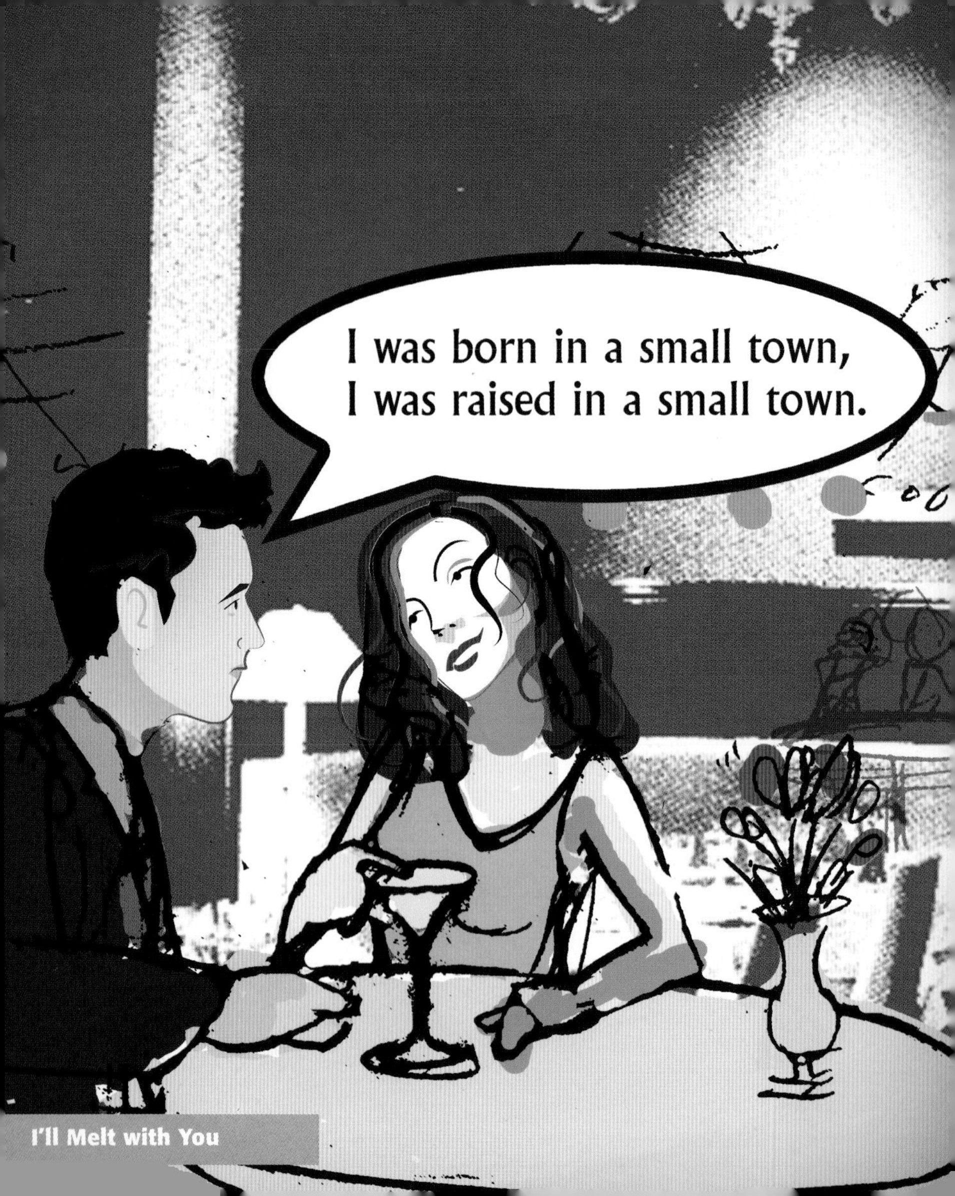
I was born in a small town,
I was raised in a small town.

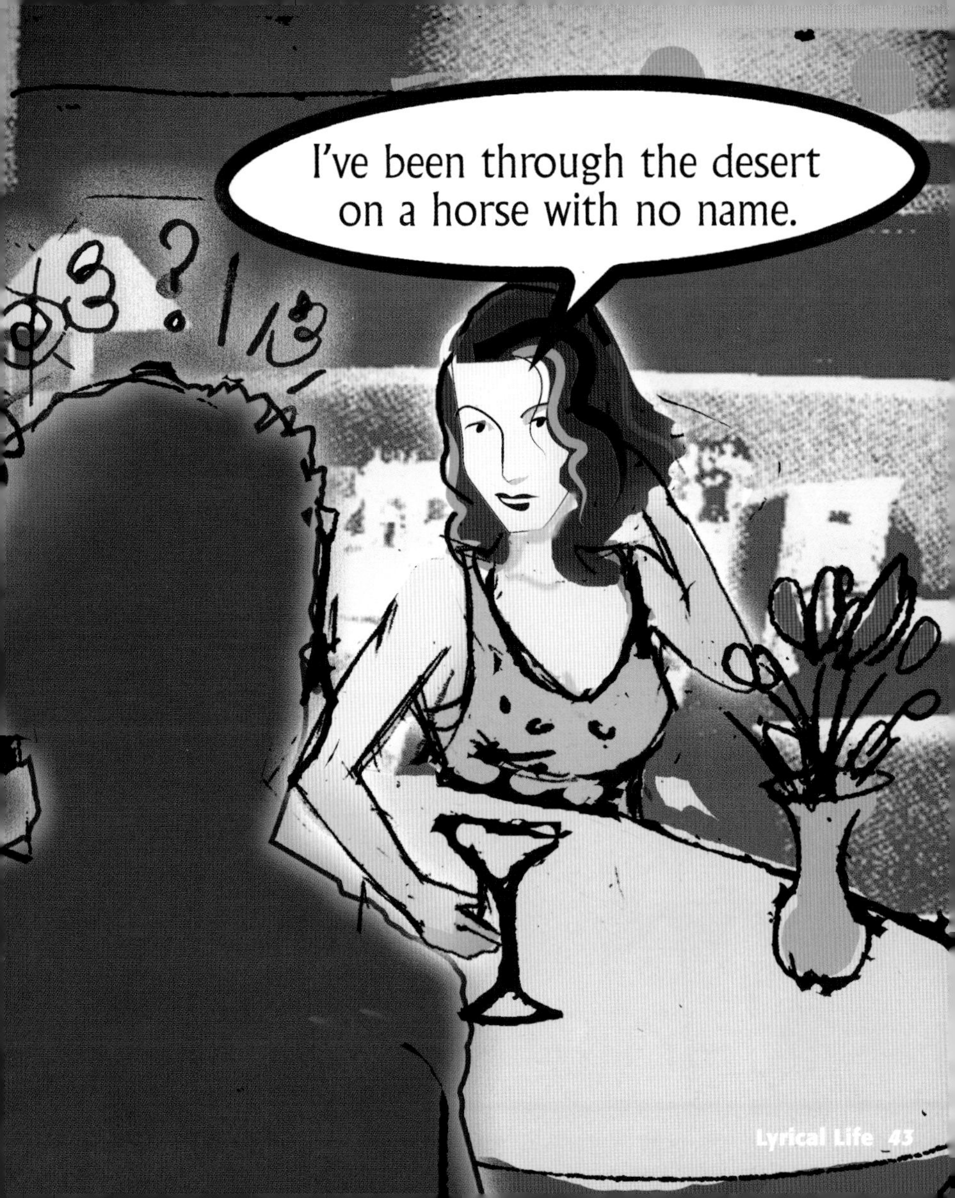
I've been through the desert on a horse with no name.

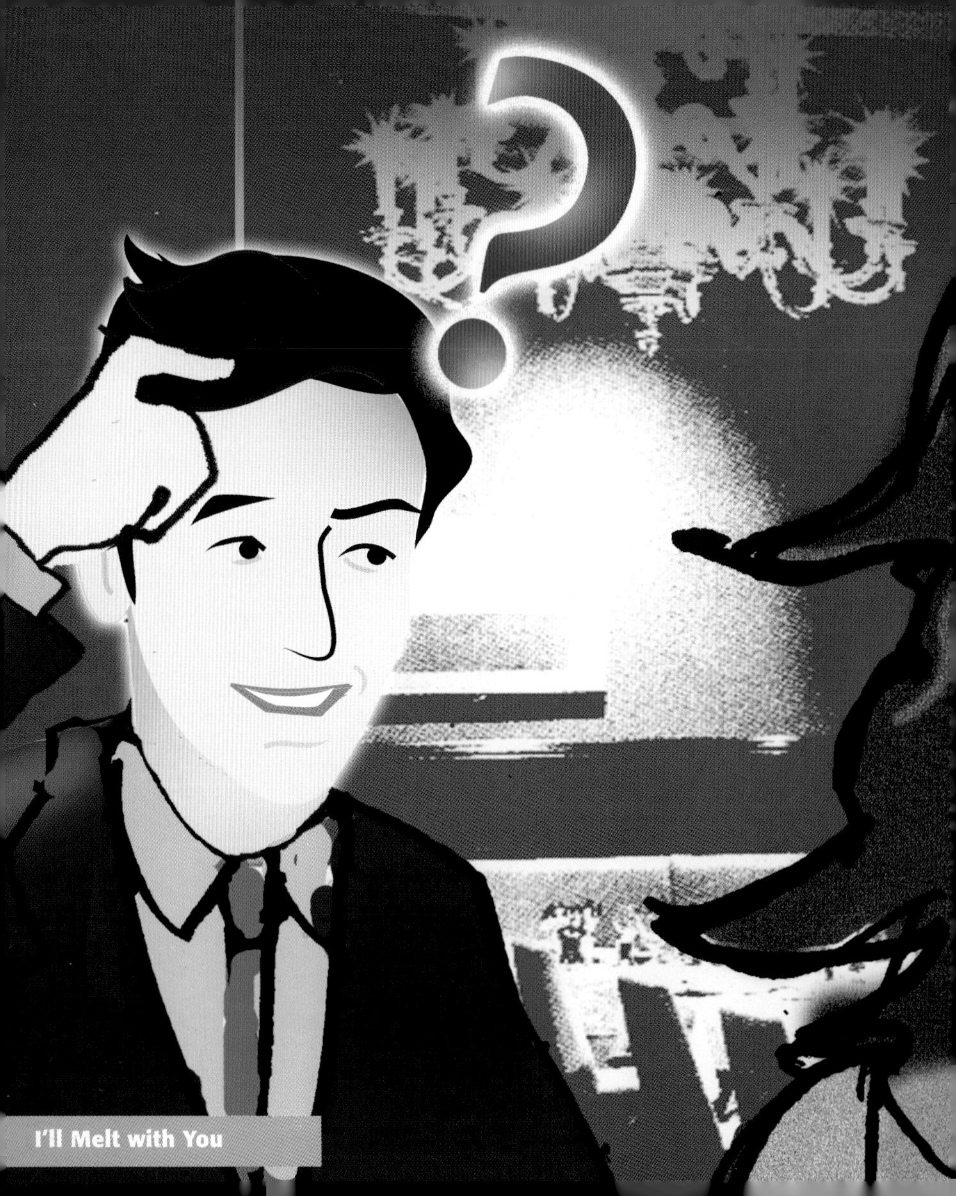

I'll Melt with You

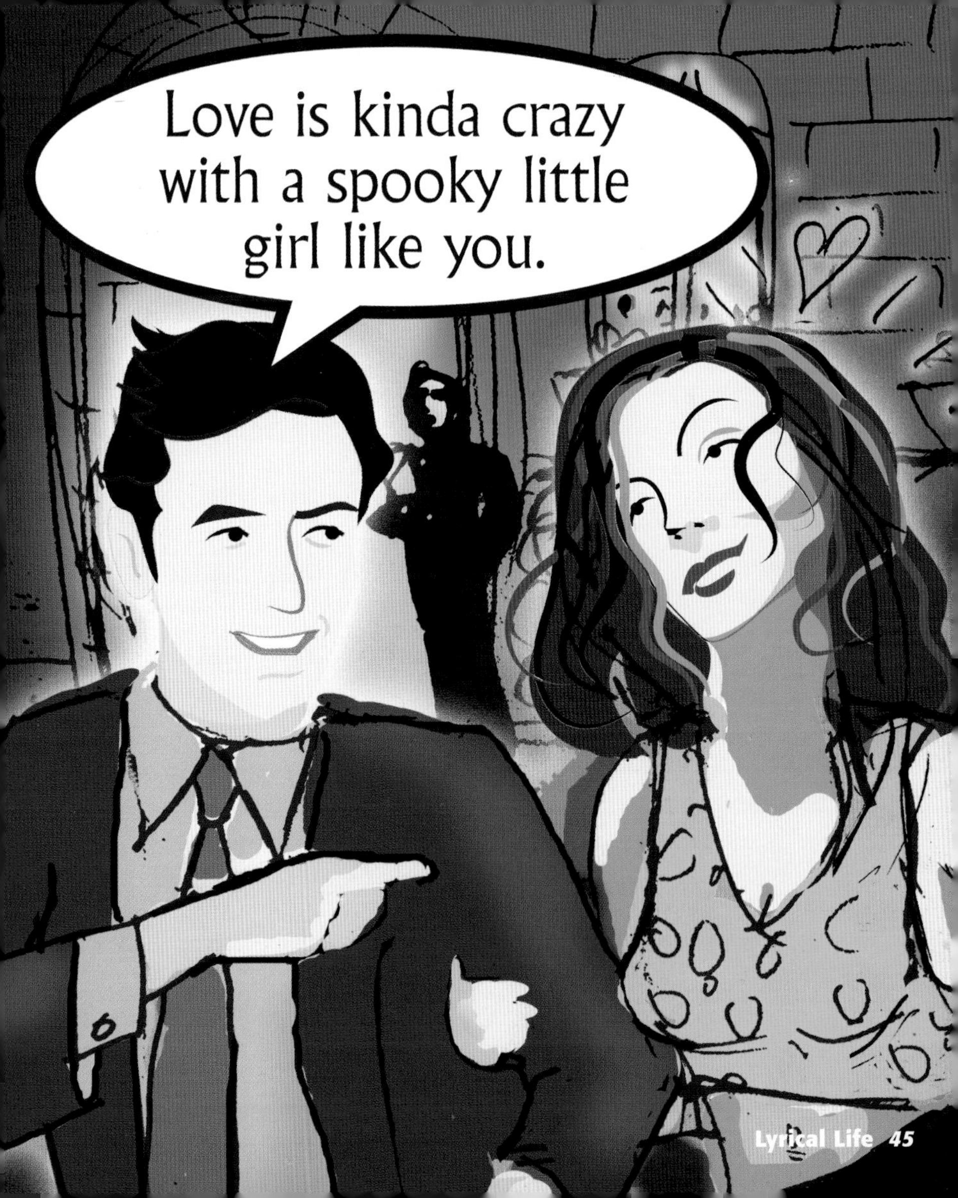
Love is kinda crazy with a spooky little girl like you.

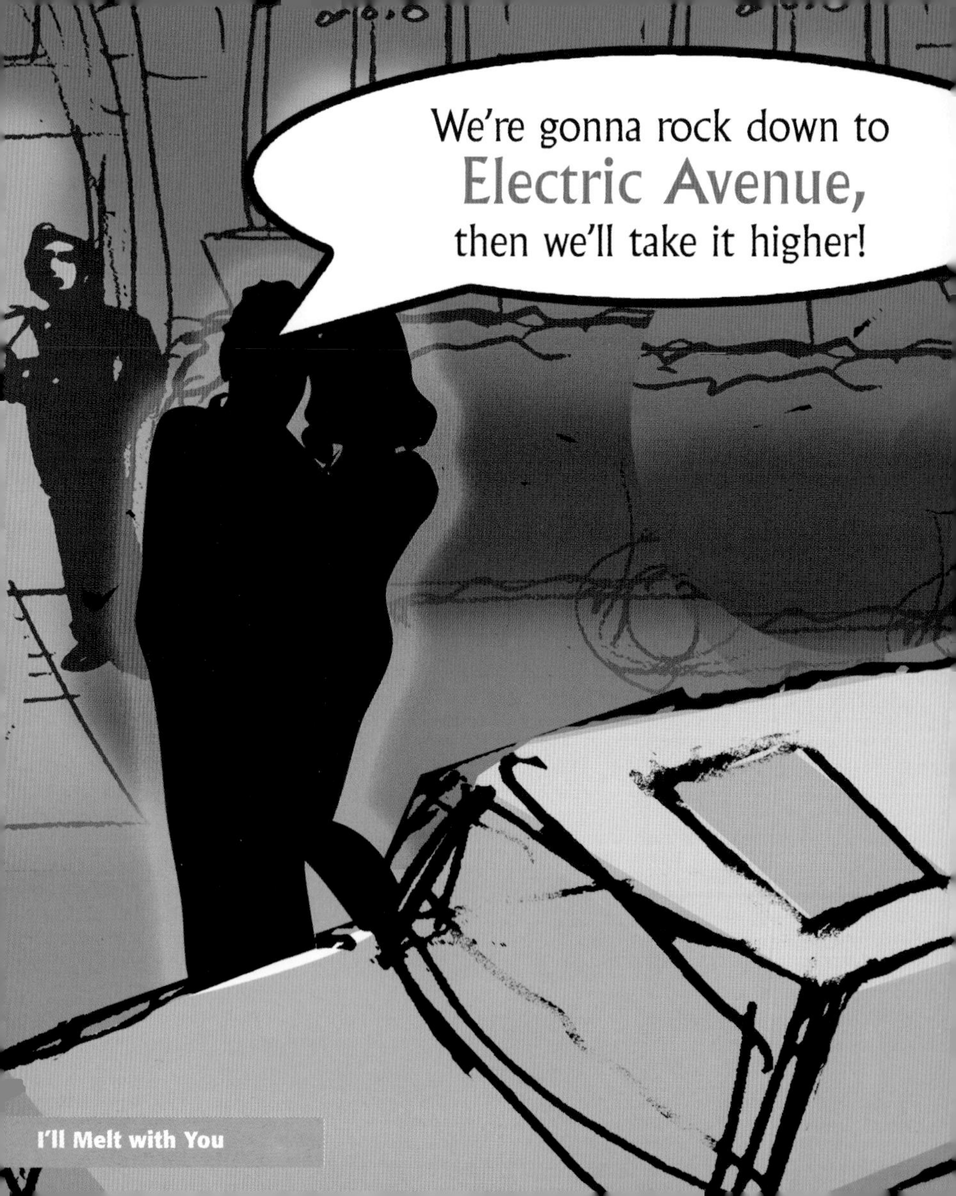
We're gonna rock down to
Electric Avenue,
then we'll take it higher!

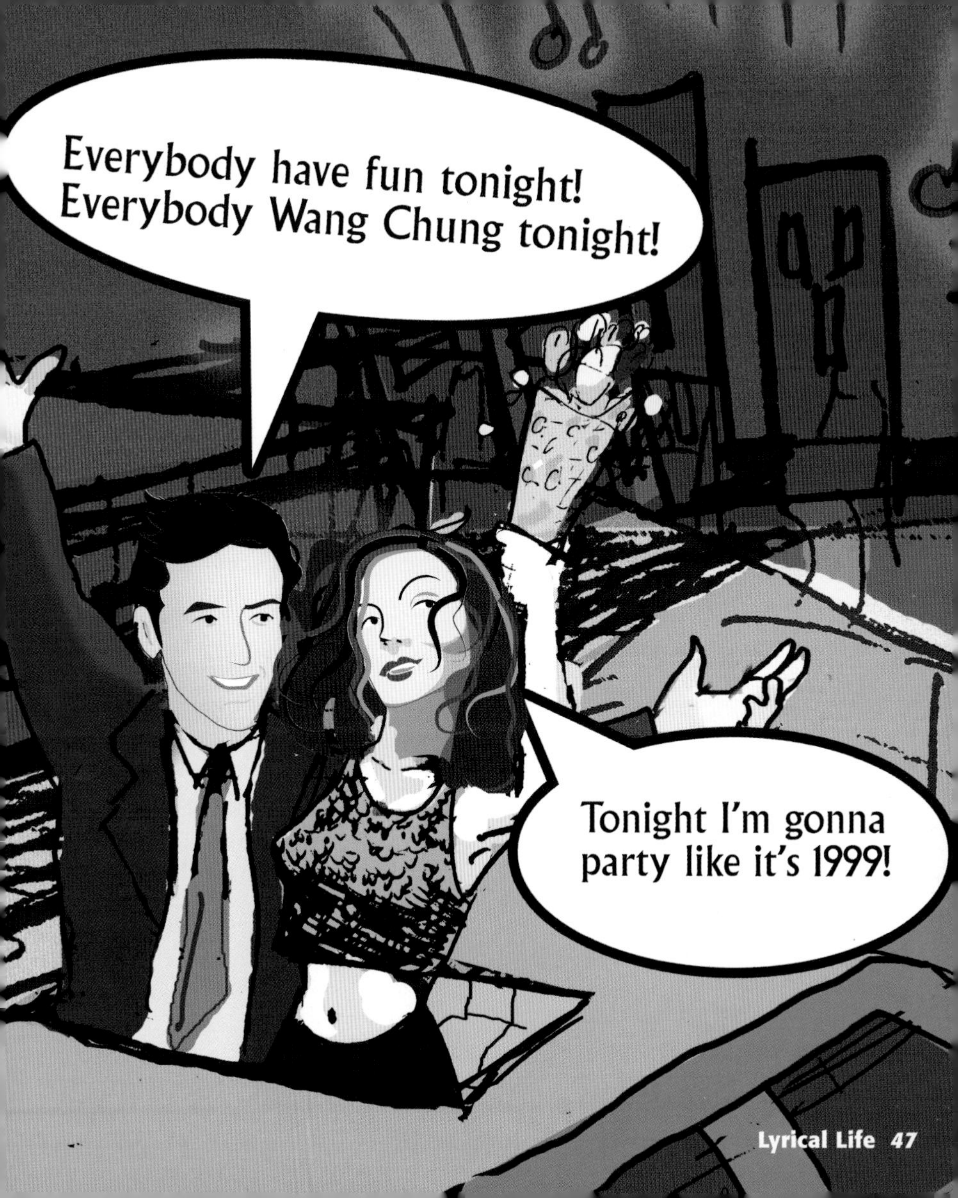
Everybody have fun tonight!
Everybody Wang Chung tonight!
Tonight I'm gonna party like it's 1999!

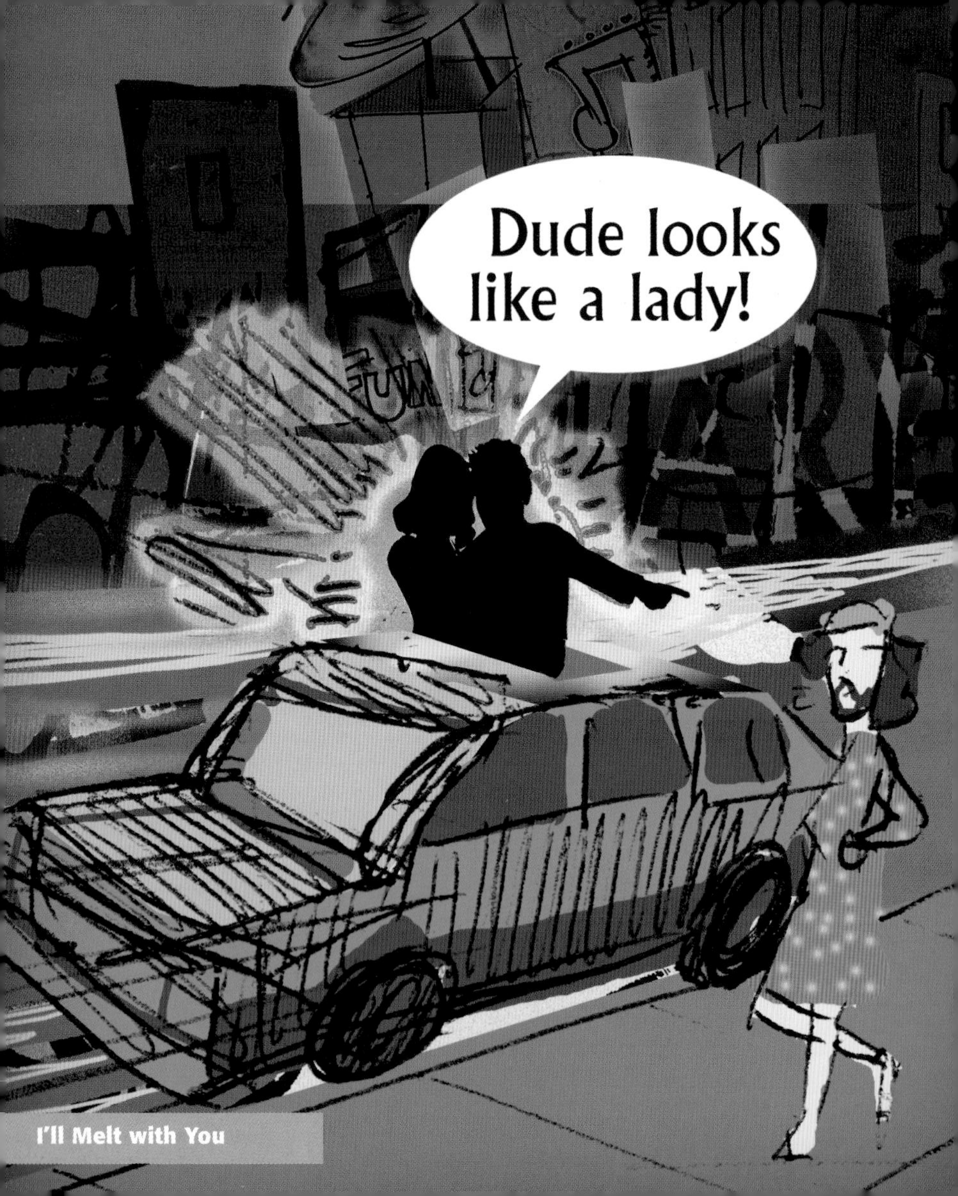
Dude looks like a lady!

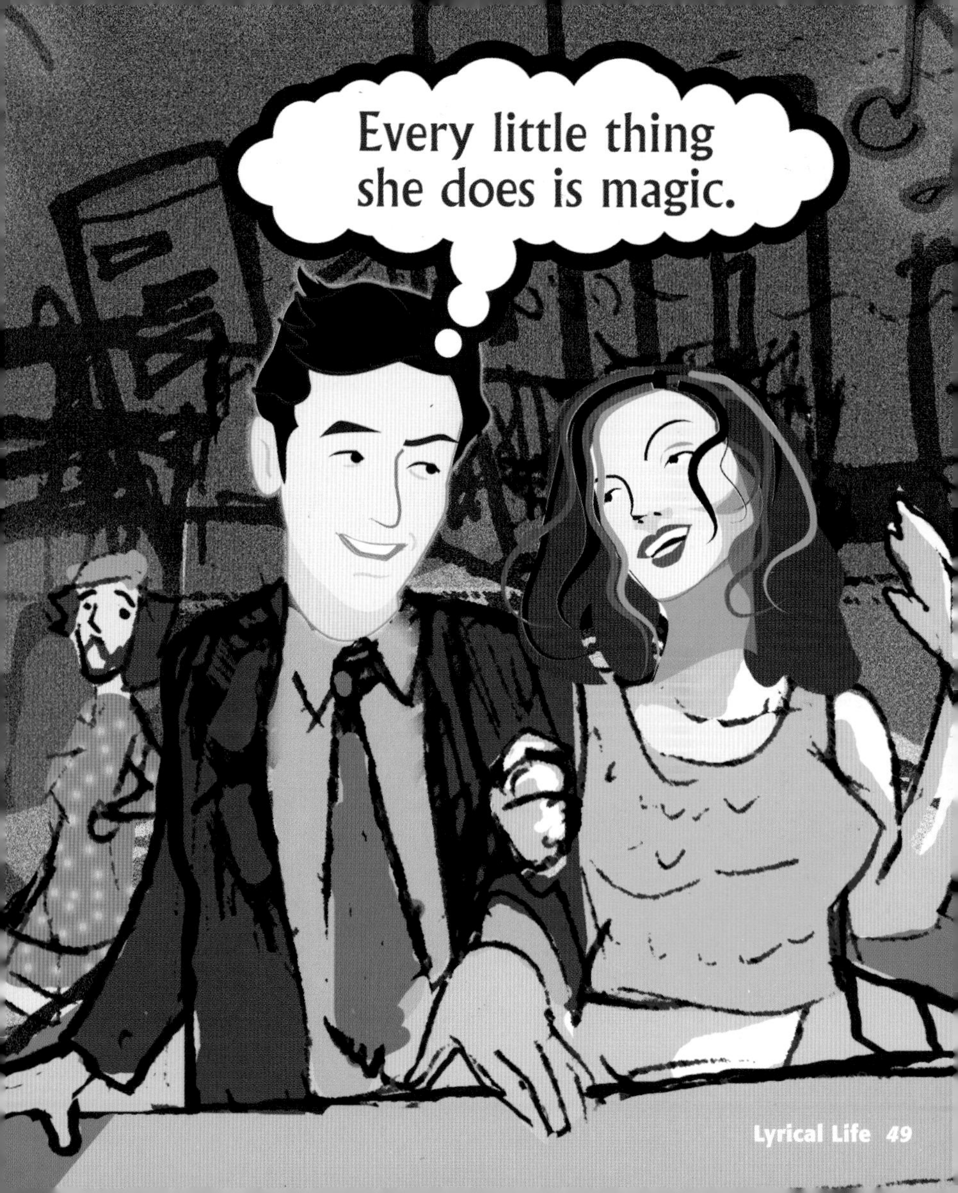
Every little thing
she does is magic.

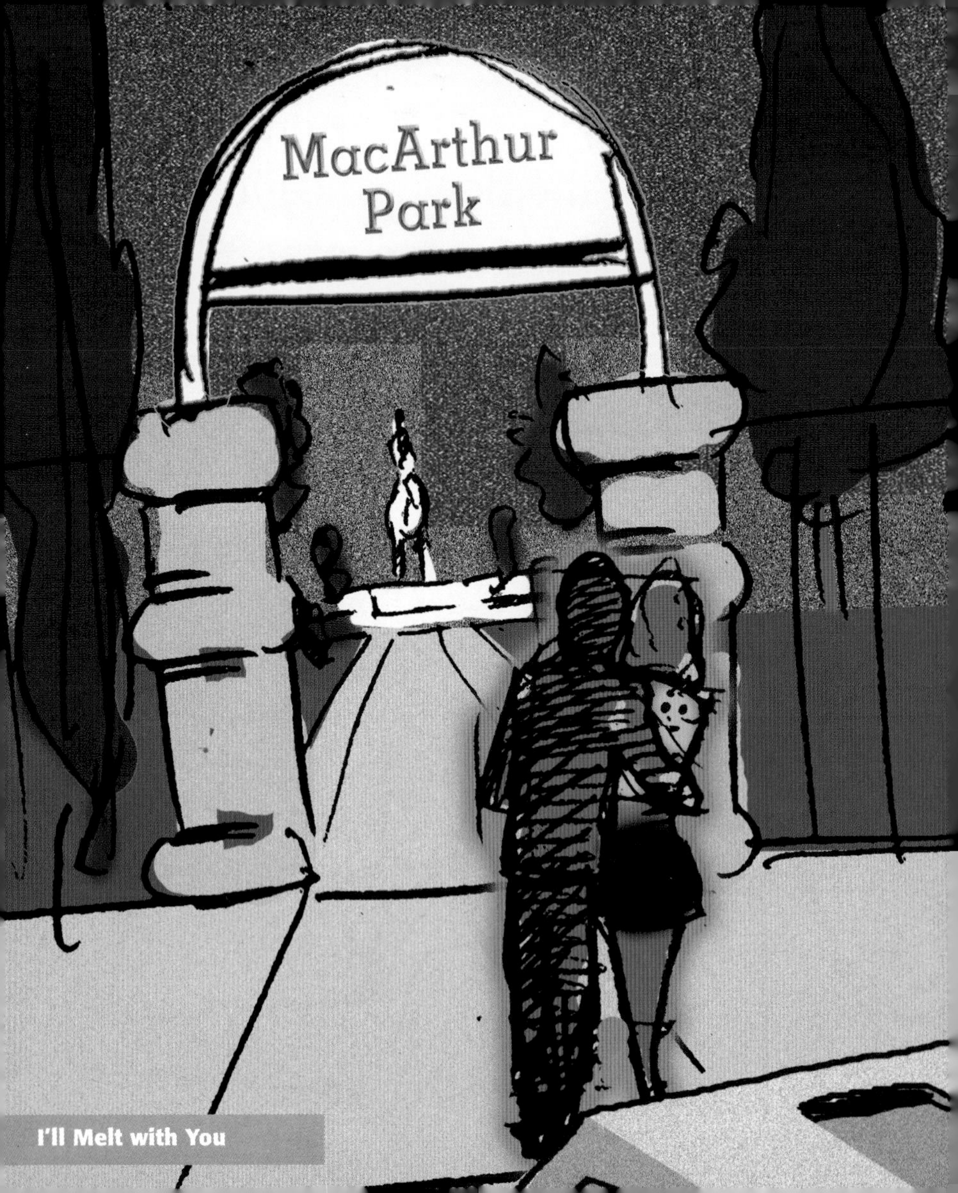
MacArthur
Park

I'll Melt with You

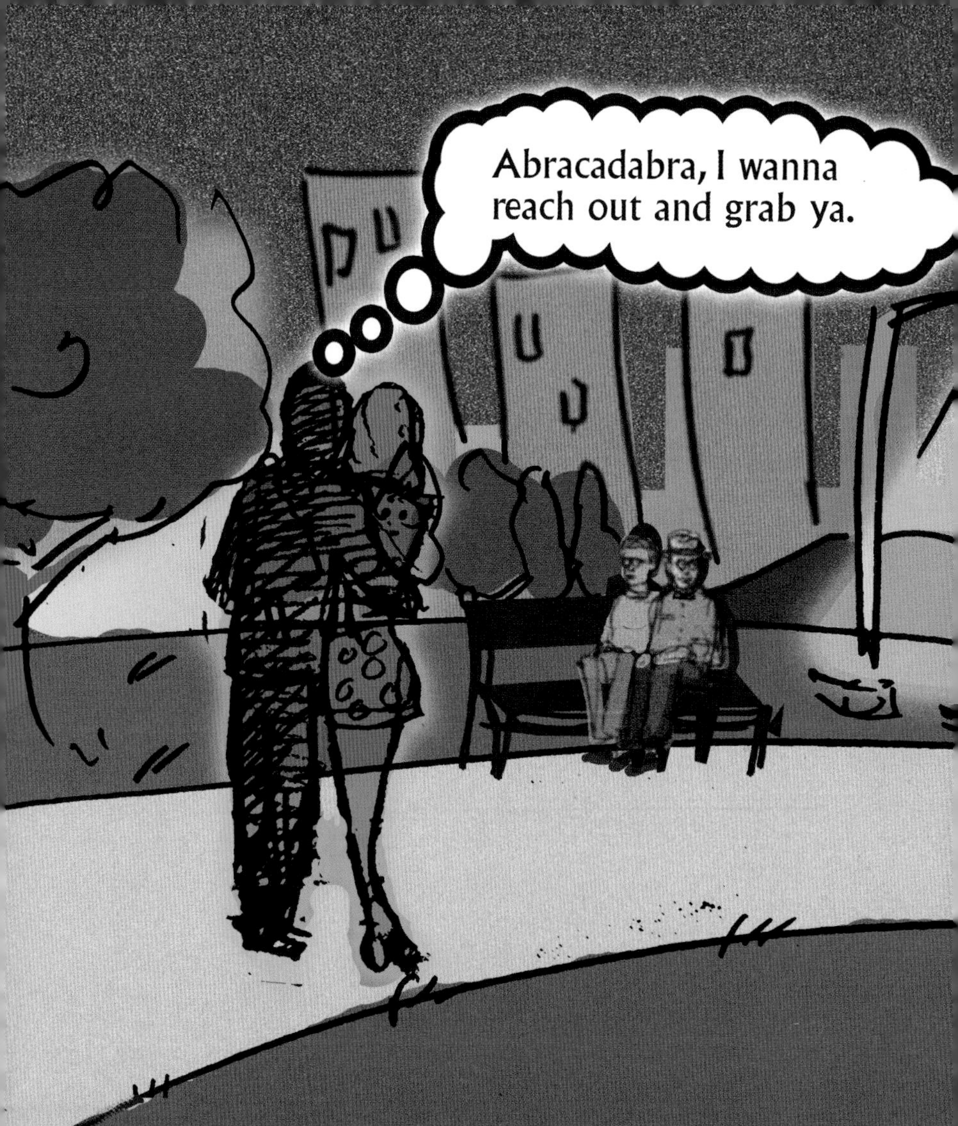
Abracadabra, I wanna reach out and grab ya.

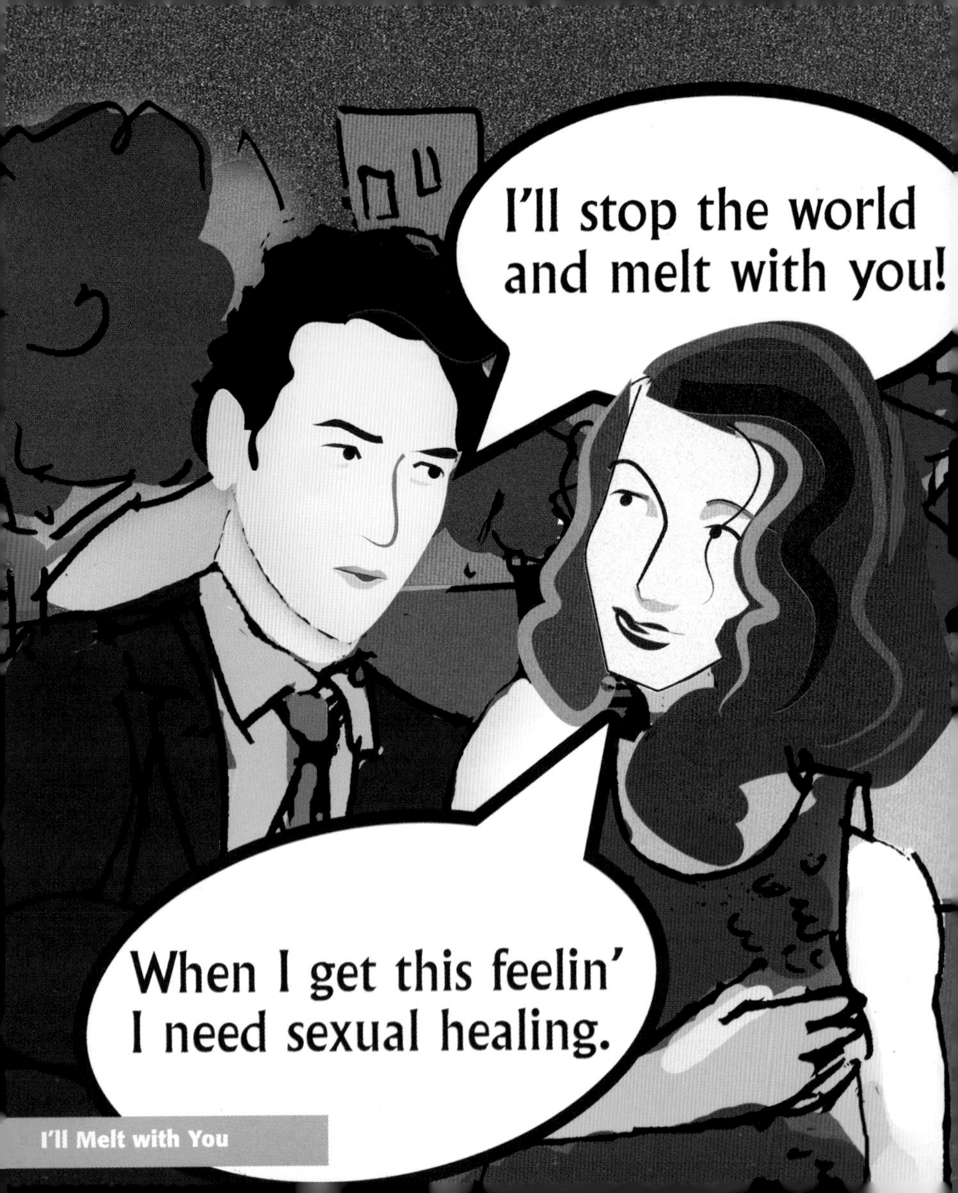
I'll stop the world and melt with you!
When I get this feelin' I need sexual healing.

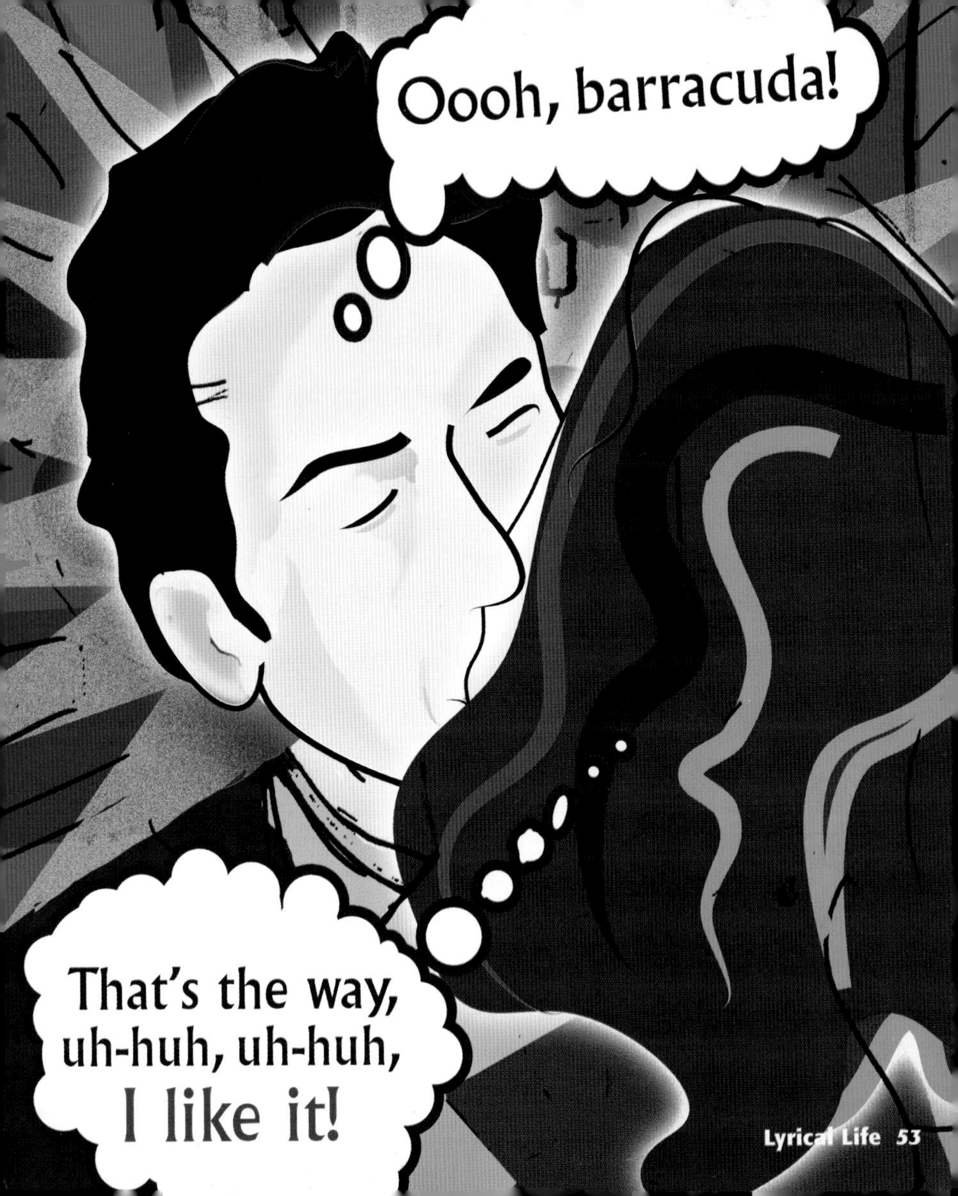
Oooh, barracuda!
That's the way, uh-huh, uh-huh, I like it!

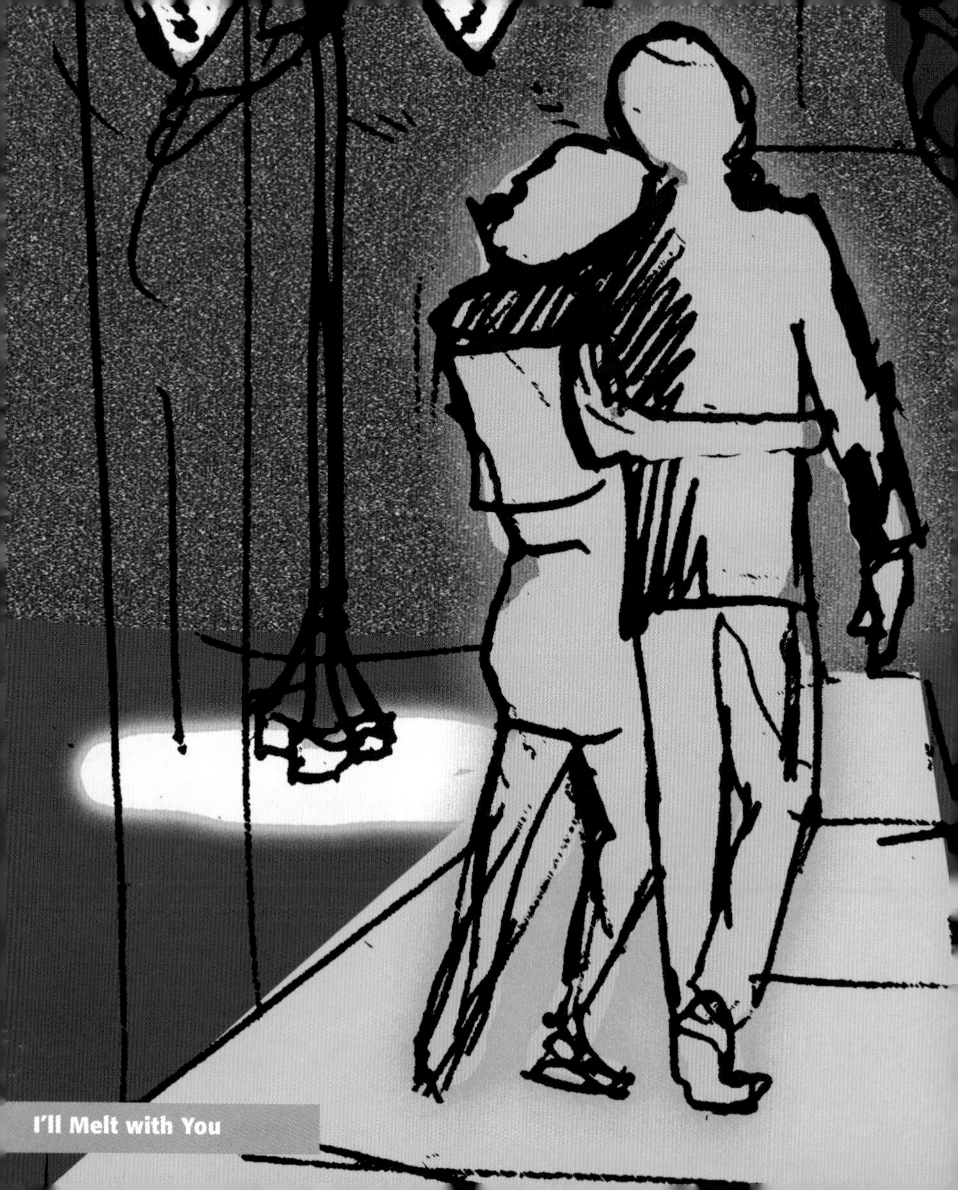

I'll Melt with You

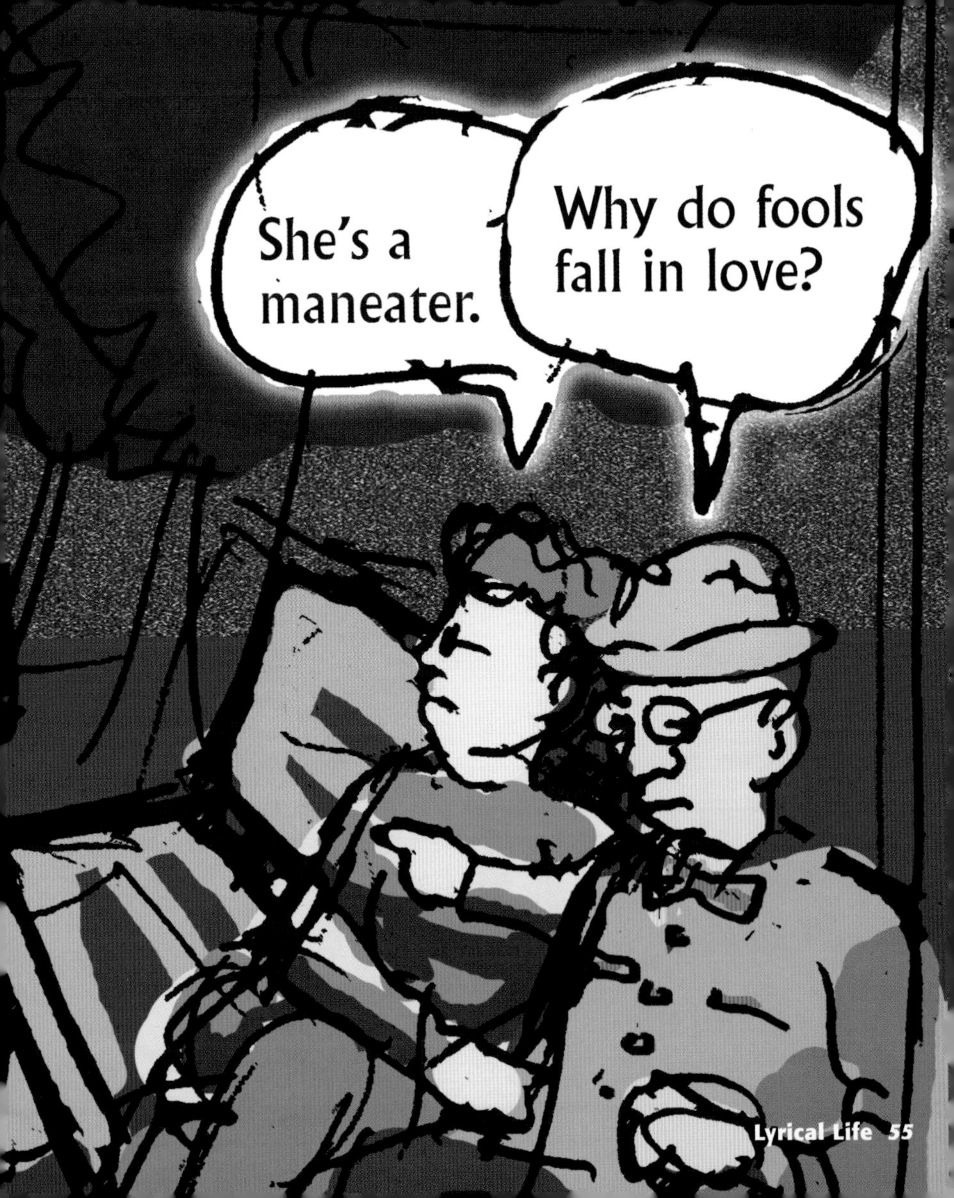
She's a maneater.
Why do fools fall in love?

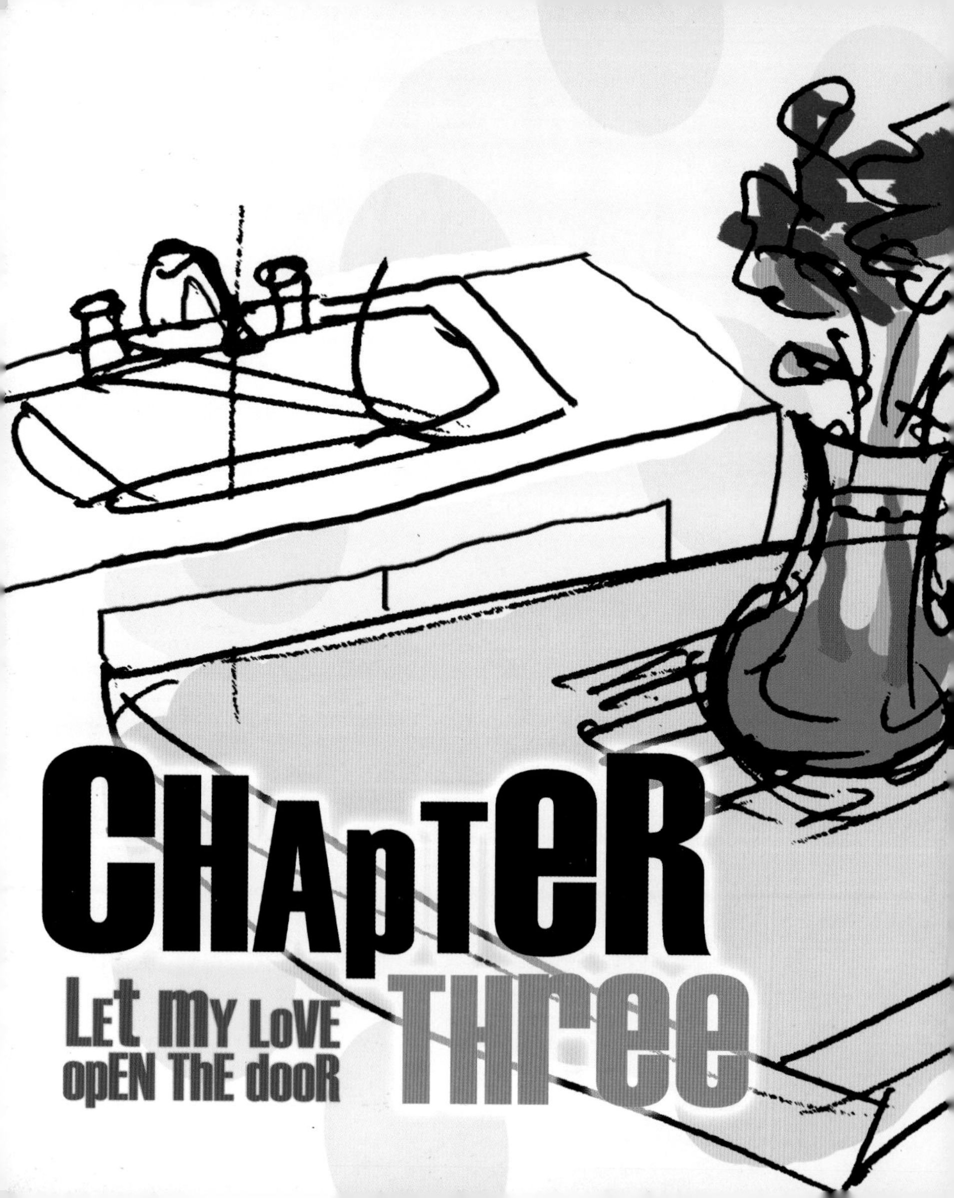

Chapter Three

Let My Love Open the Door

At first I was afraid, I was petrified.

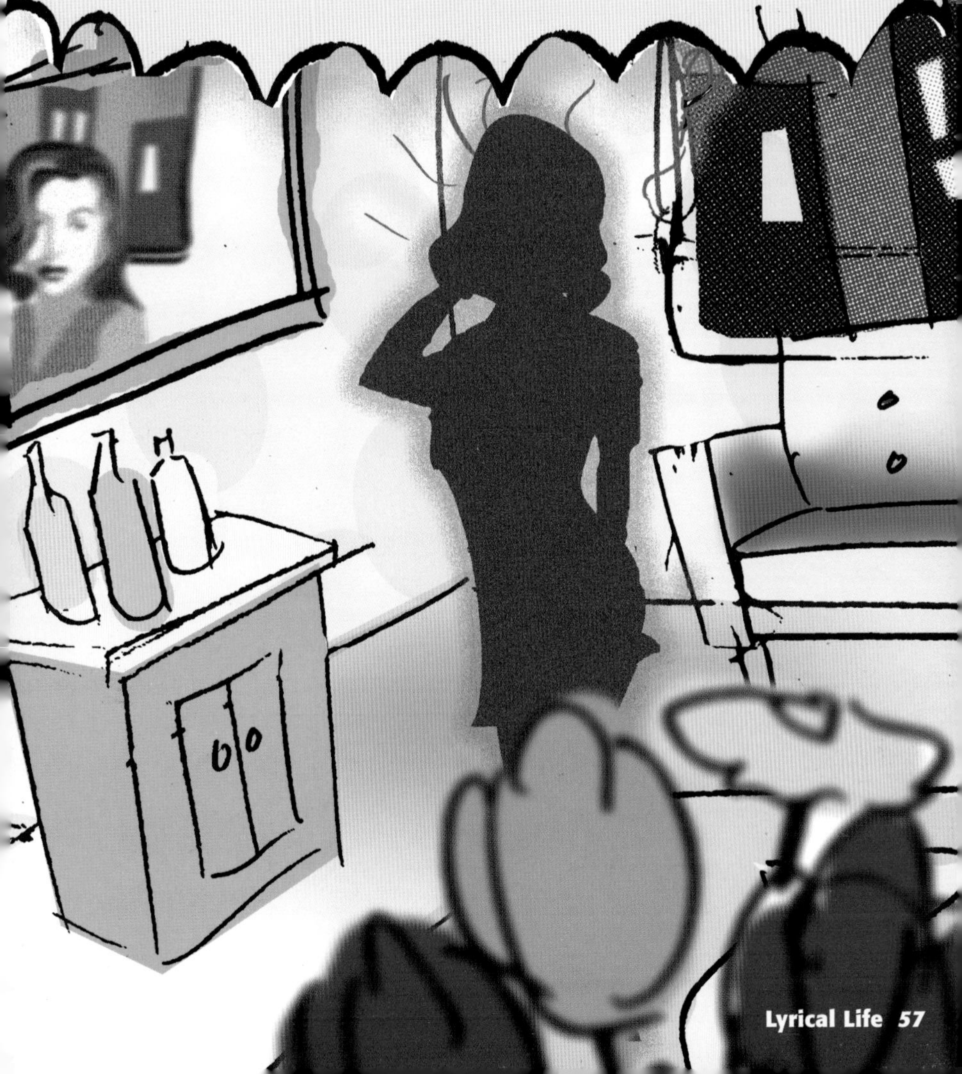

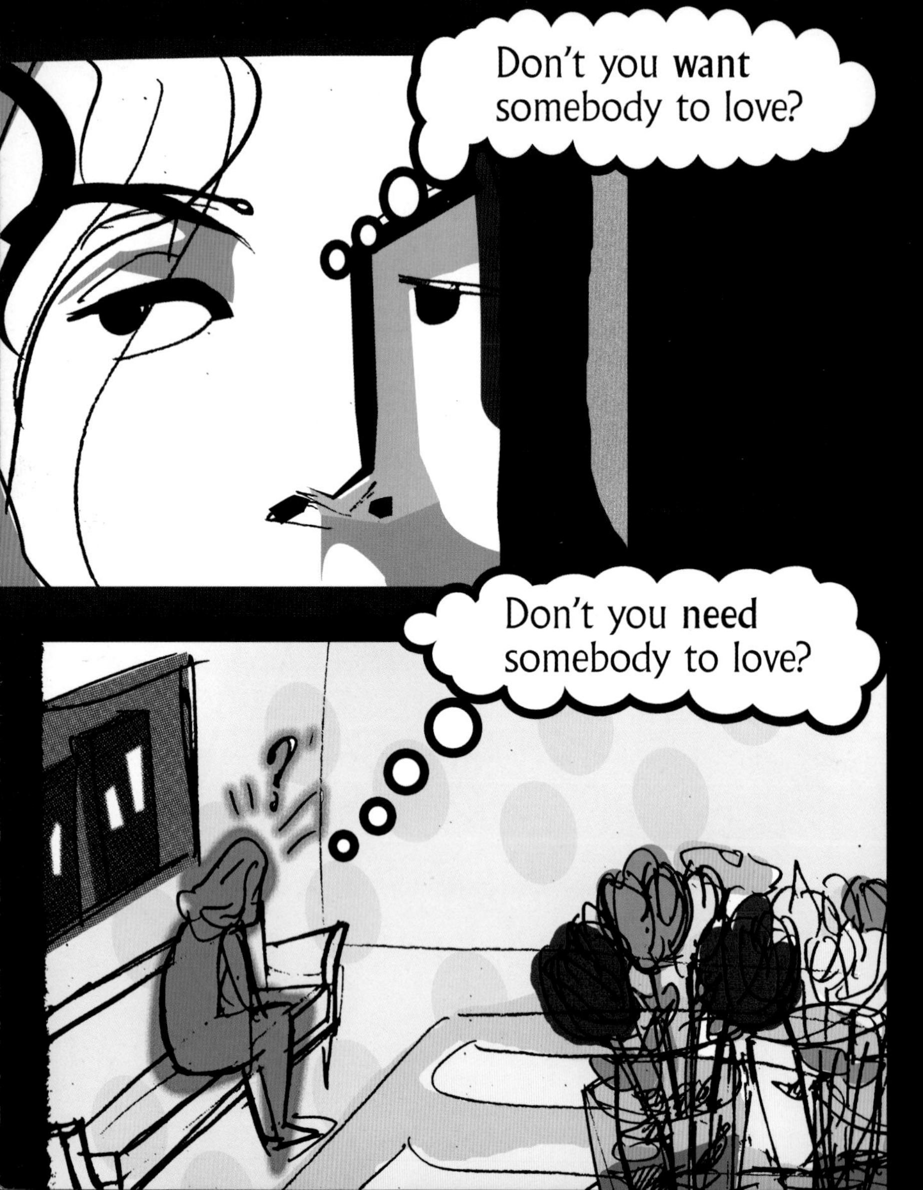
Don't you **want** somebody to love?
Don't you **need** somebody to love?

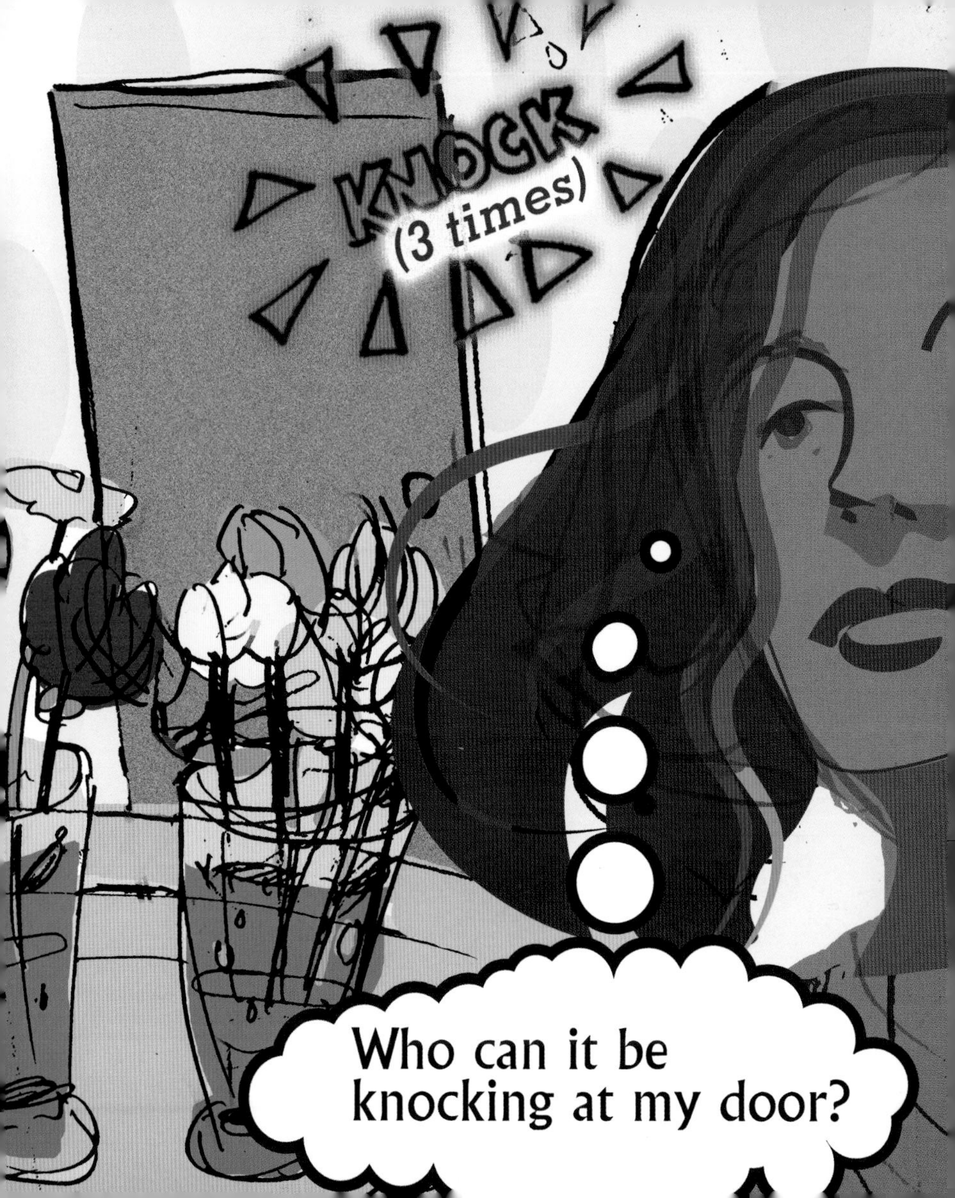
KNOCK
(3 times)
Who can it be knocking at my door?

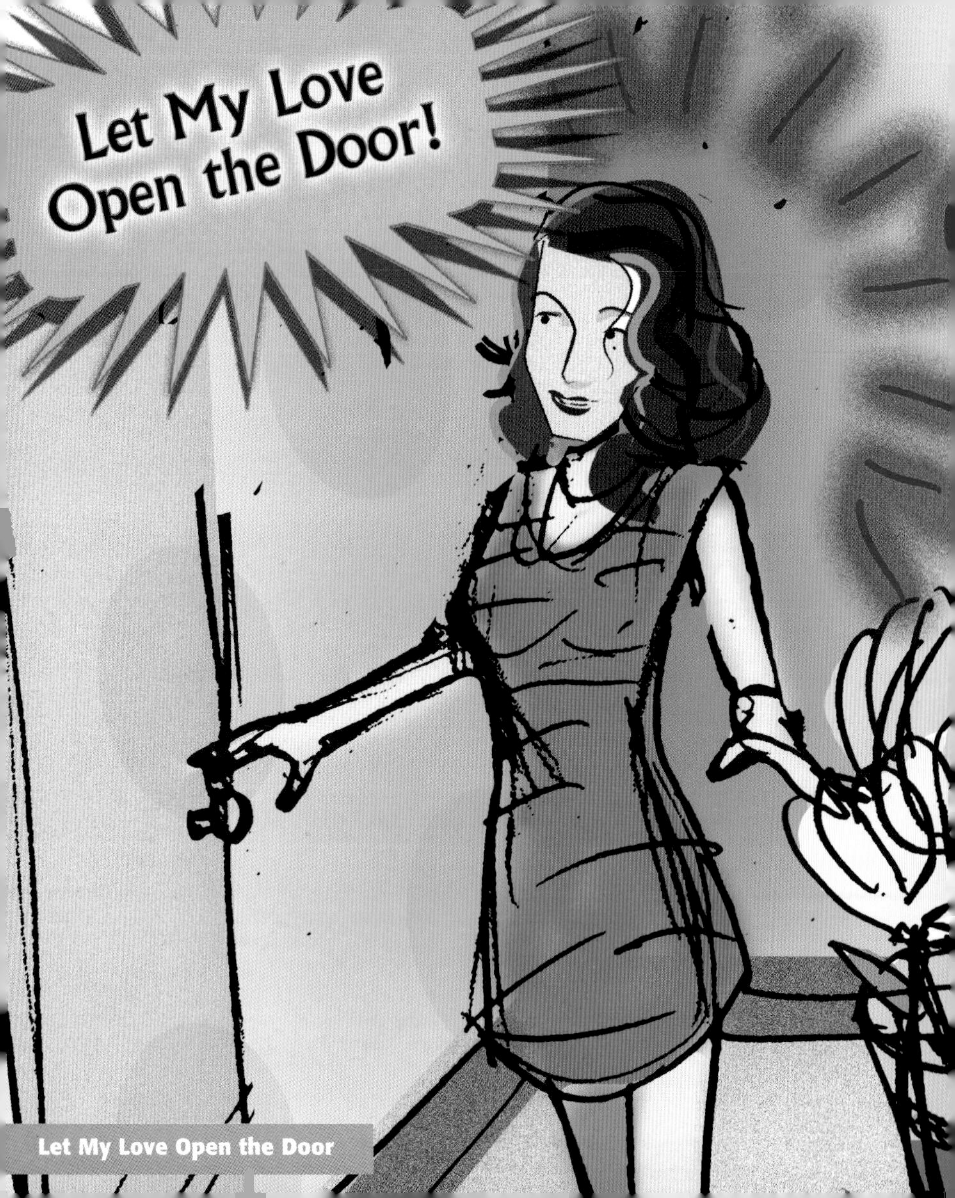
Let My Love
Open the Door!

Let My Love Open the Door

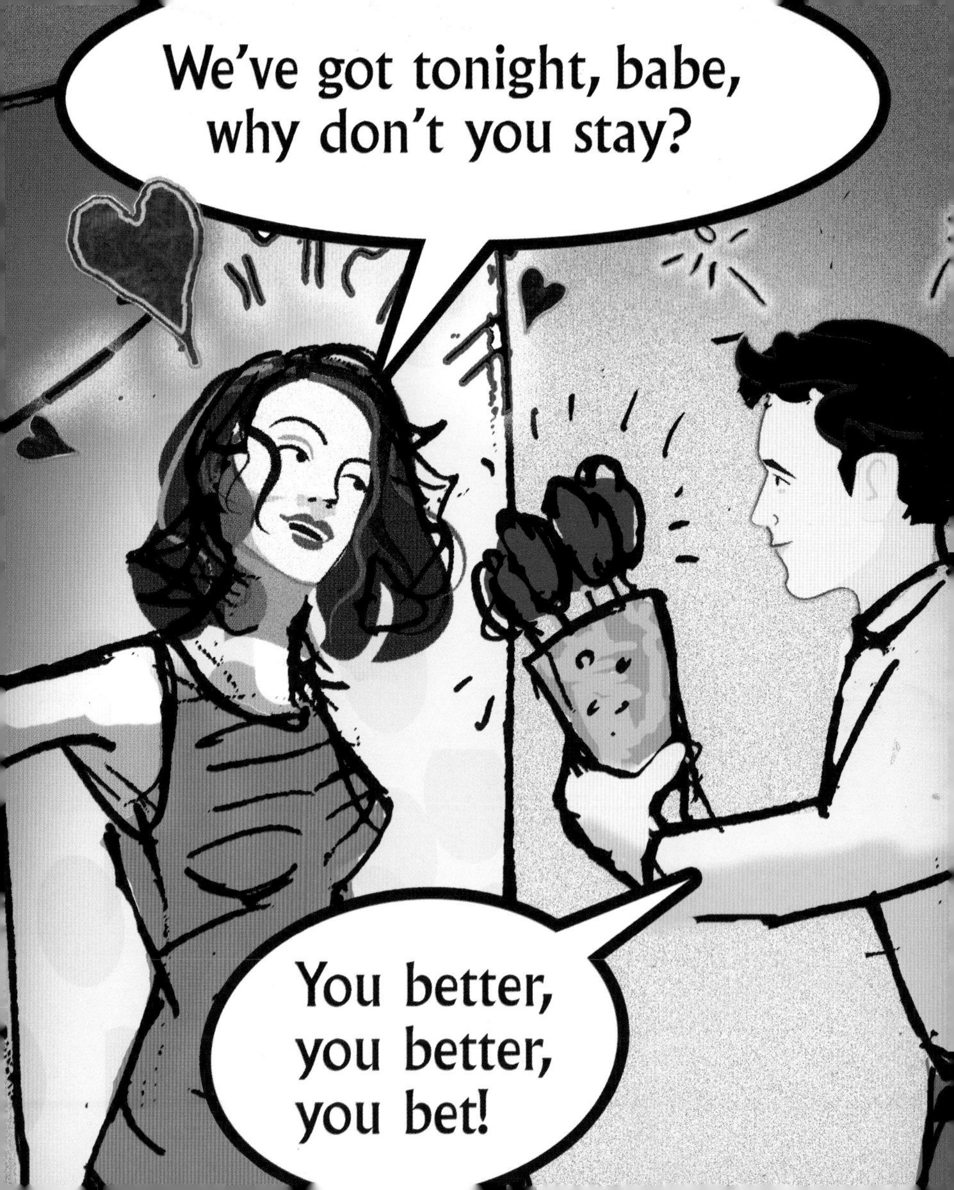
We've got tonight, babe, why don't you stay?
You better, you better, you bet!

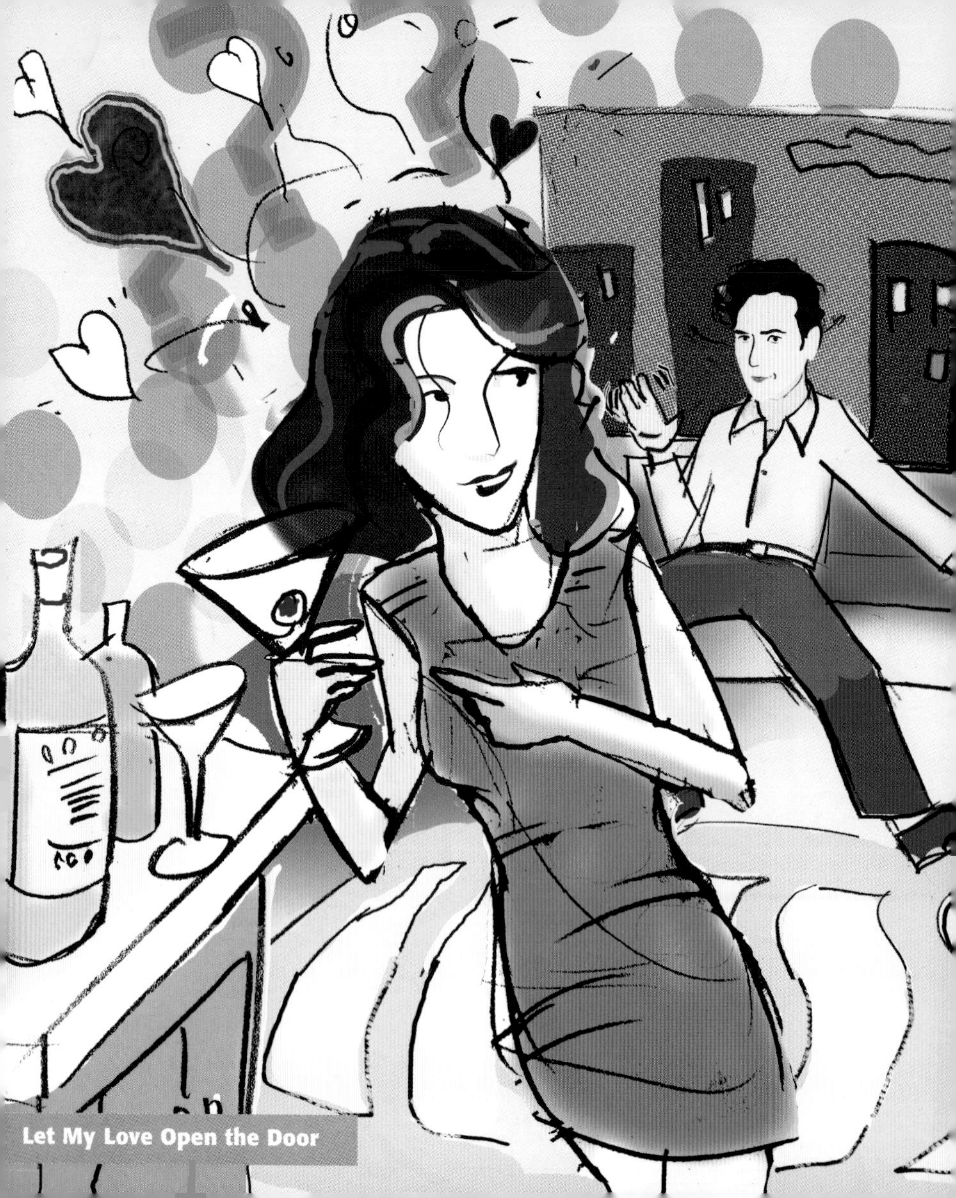

Let My Love Open the Door

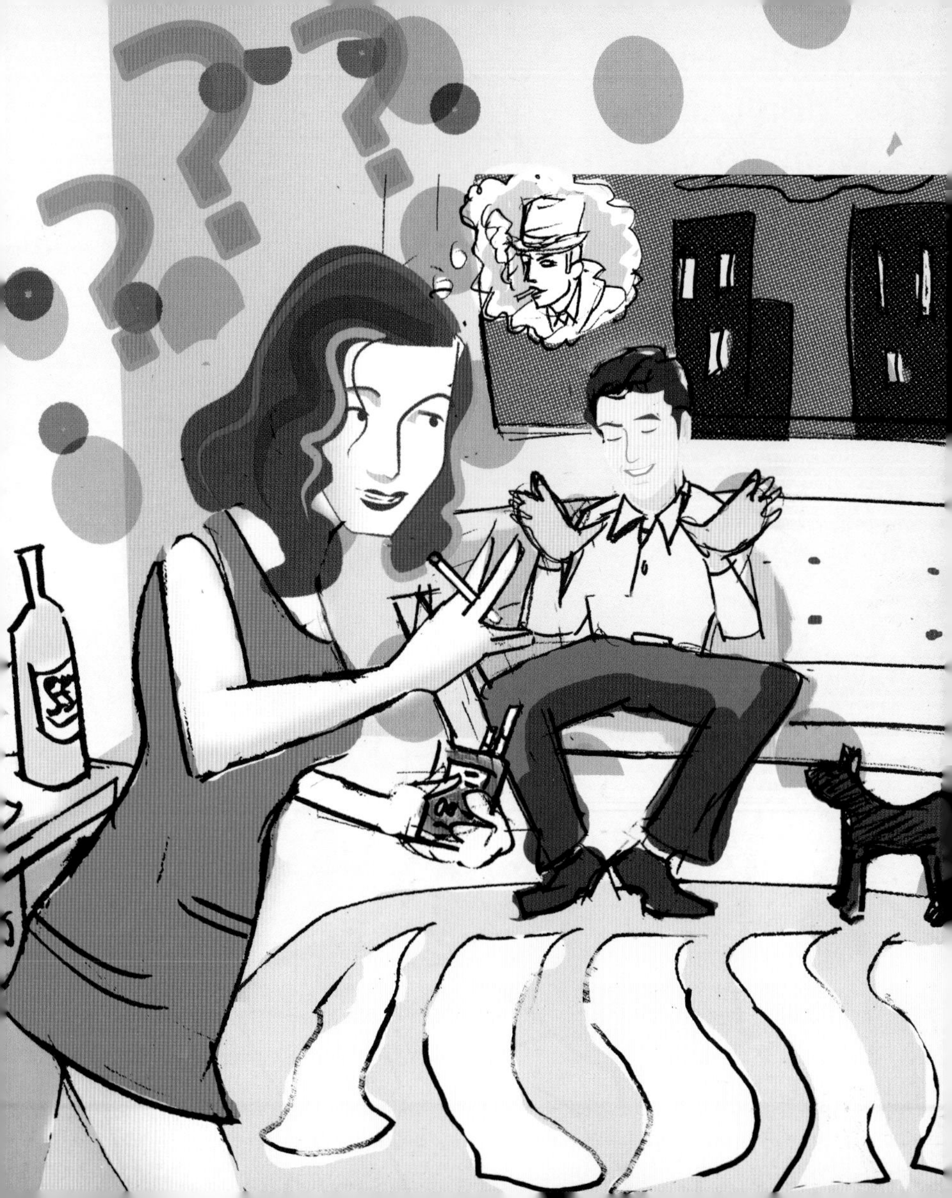

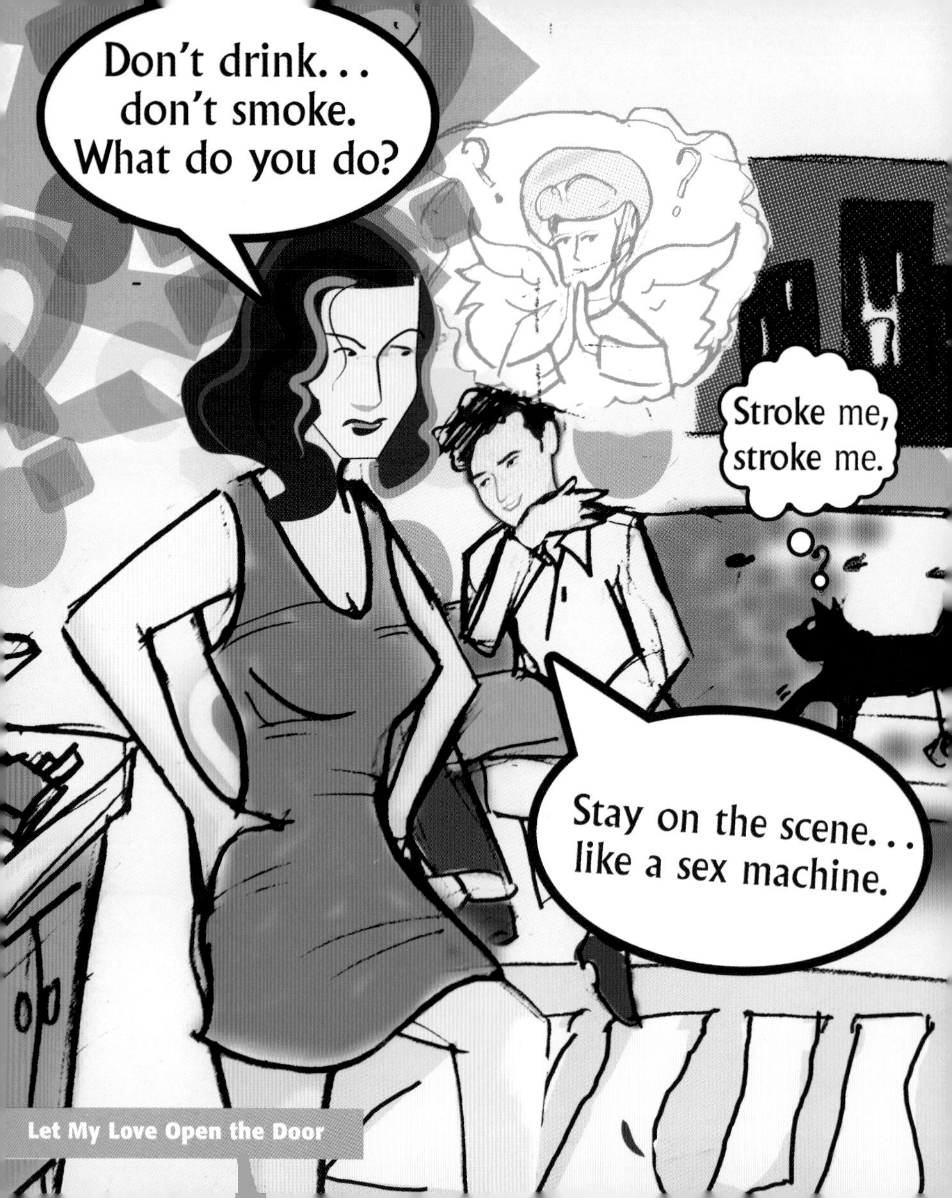
Don't drink. . .
don't smoke.
What do you do?
Stroke me,
stroke me.
Stay on the scene. . .
like a sex machine.

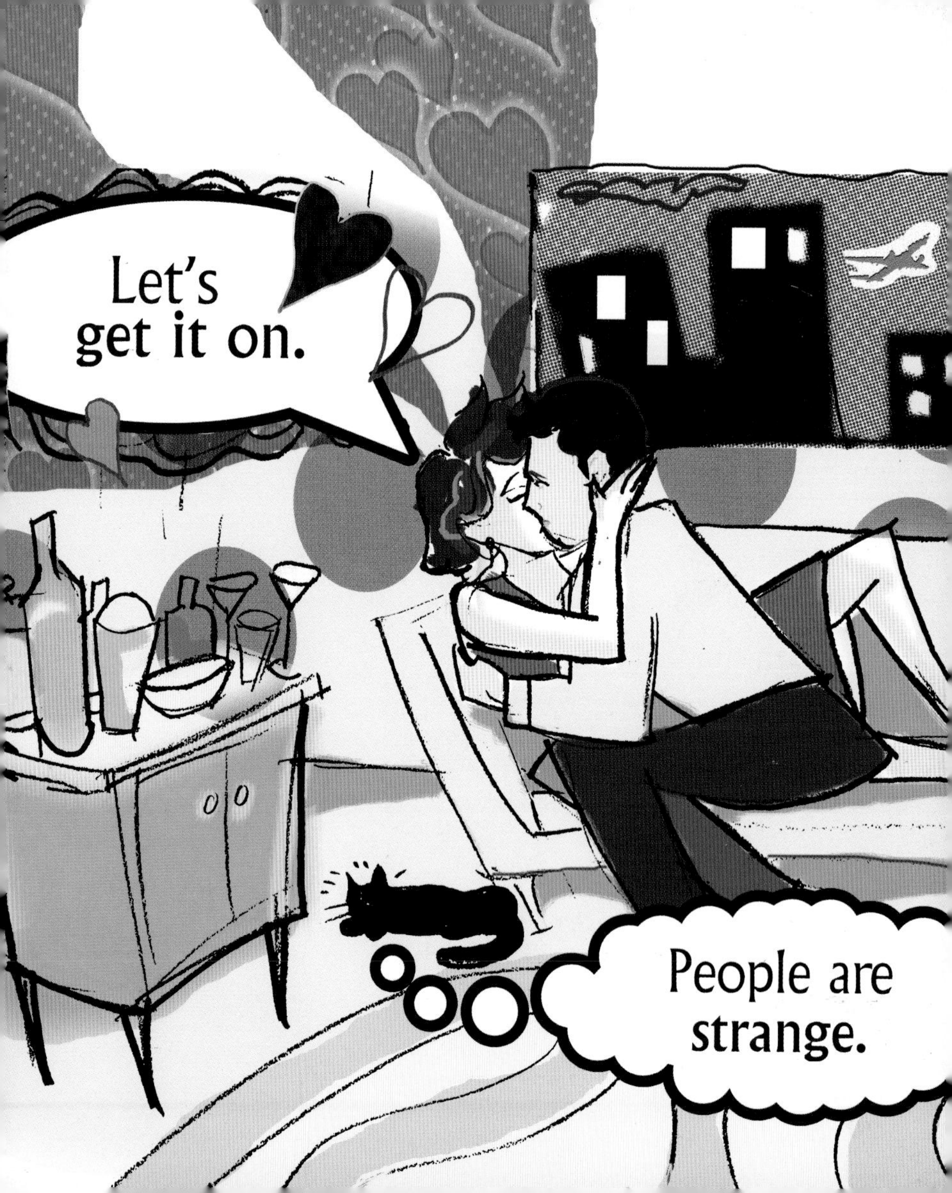
Let's get it on.
People are strange.

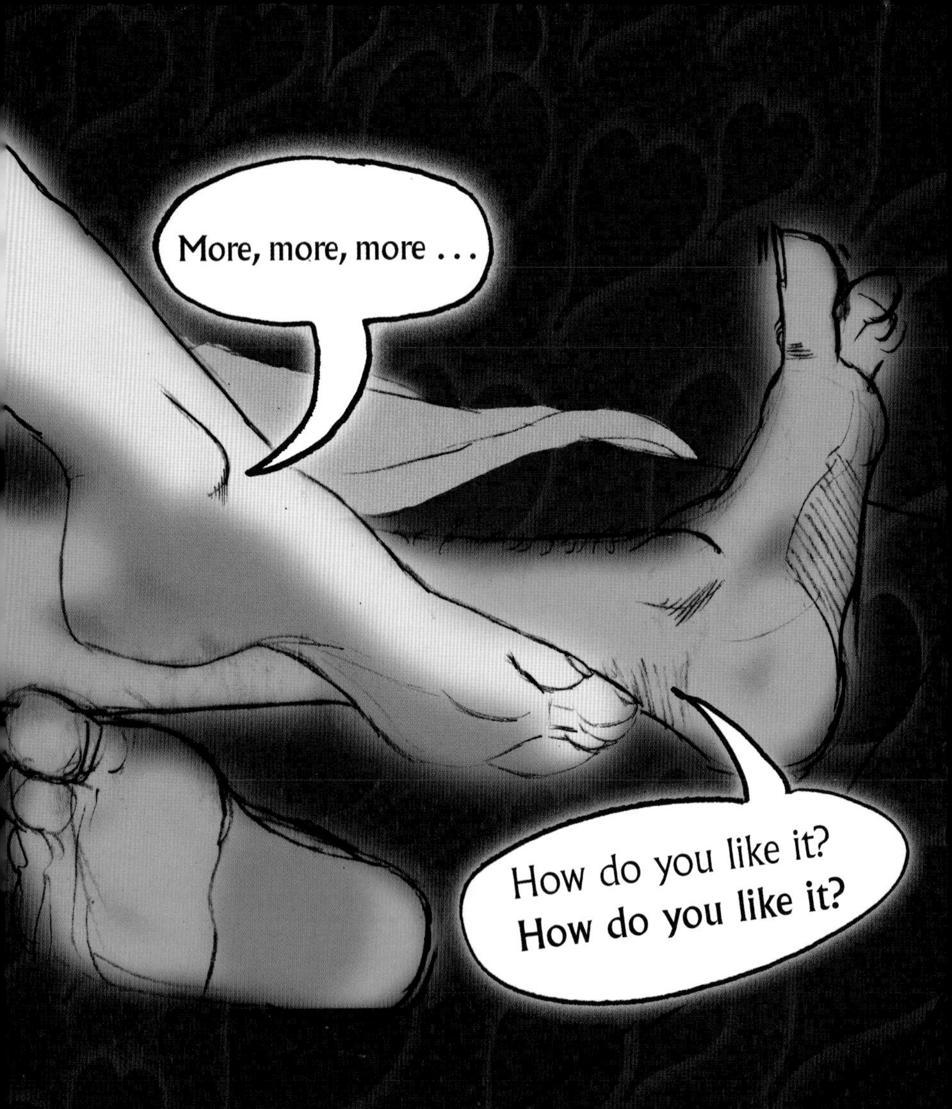
More, more, more . . .
How do you like it? How do you like it?

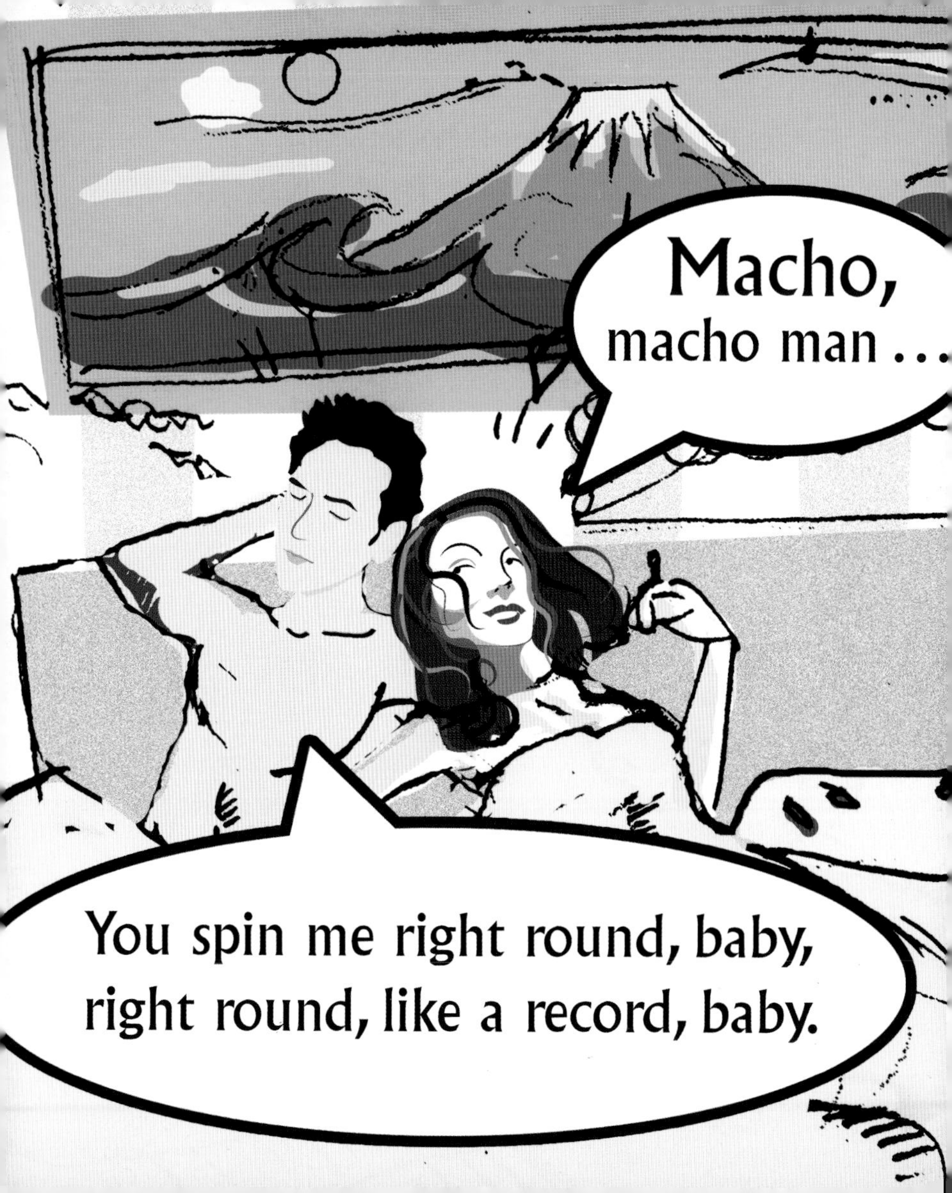
Macho, macho man . . .
You spin me right round, baby, right round, like a record, baby.

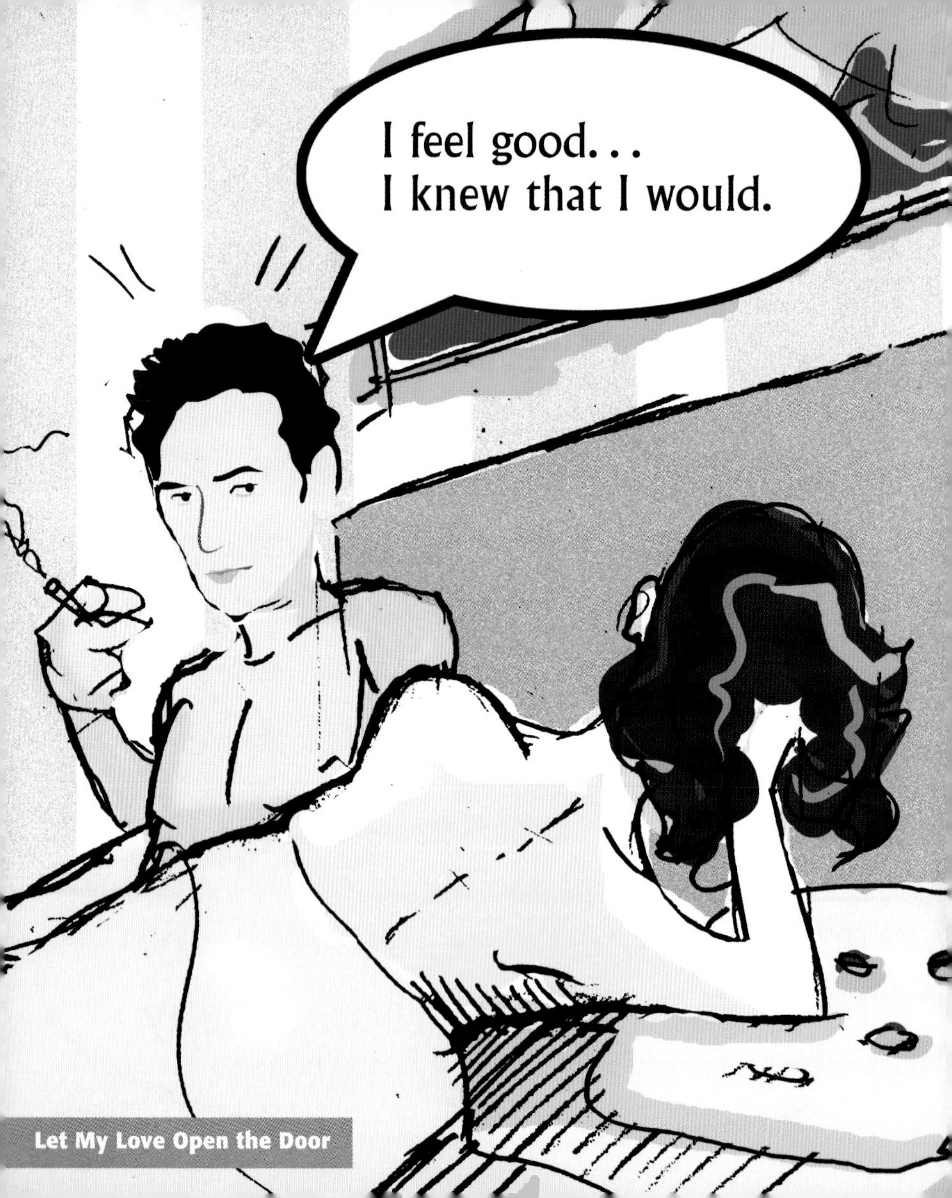
I feel good...
I knew that I would.

Let My Love Open the Door

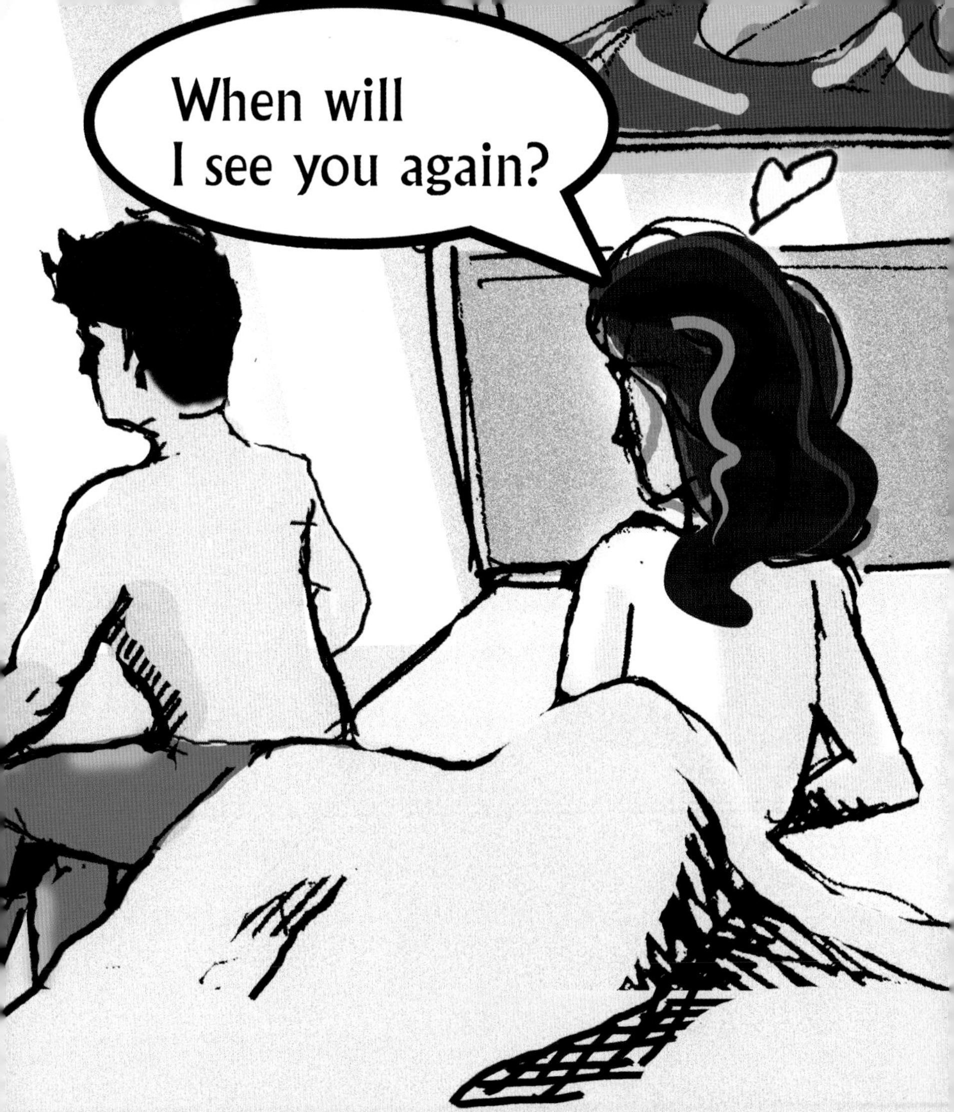
When will I see you again?

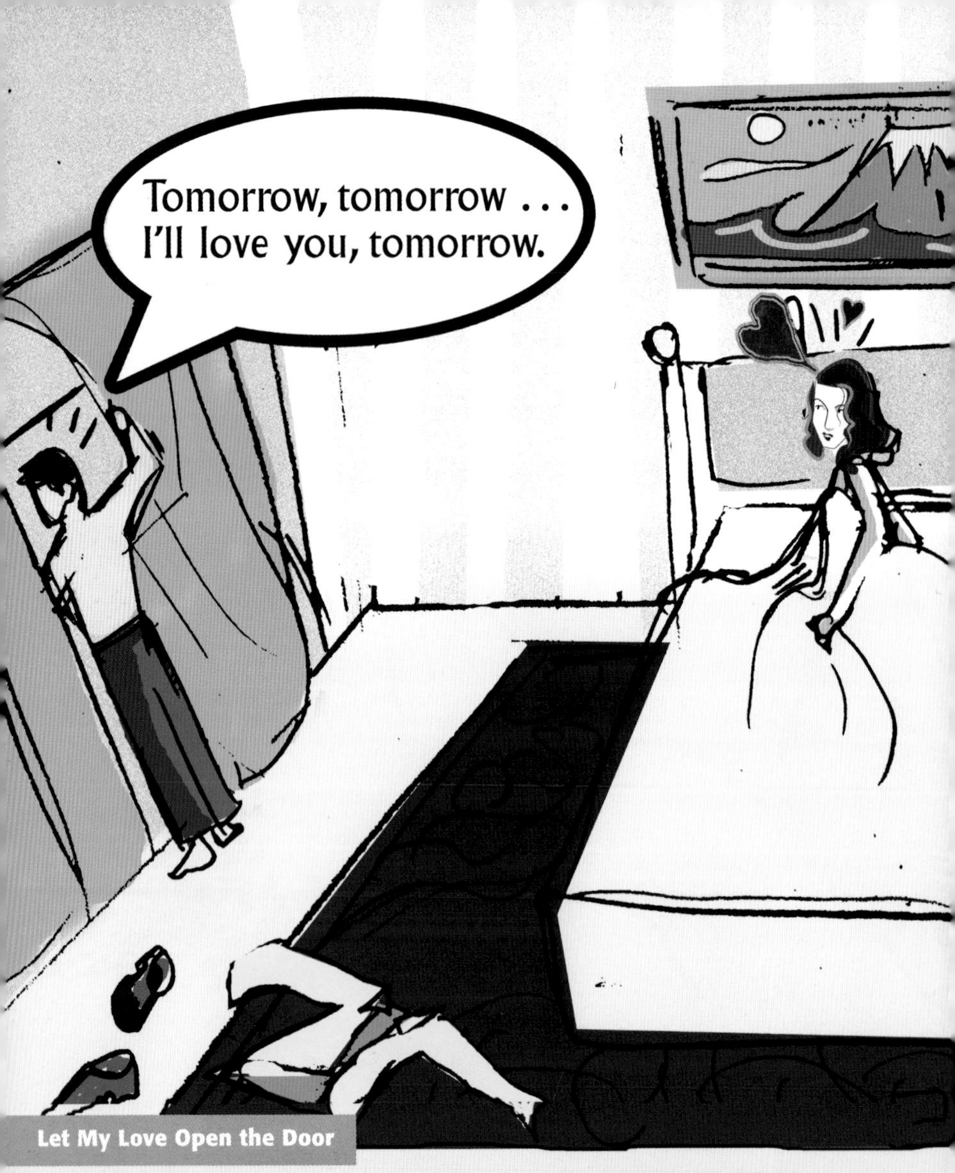
Tomorrow, tomorrow . . .
I'll love you, tomorrow.

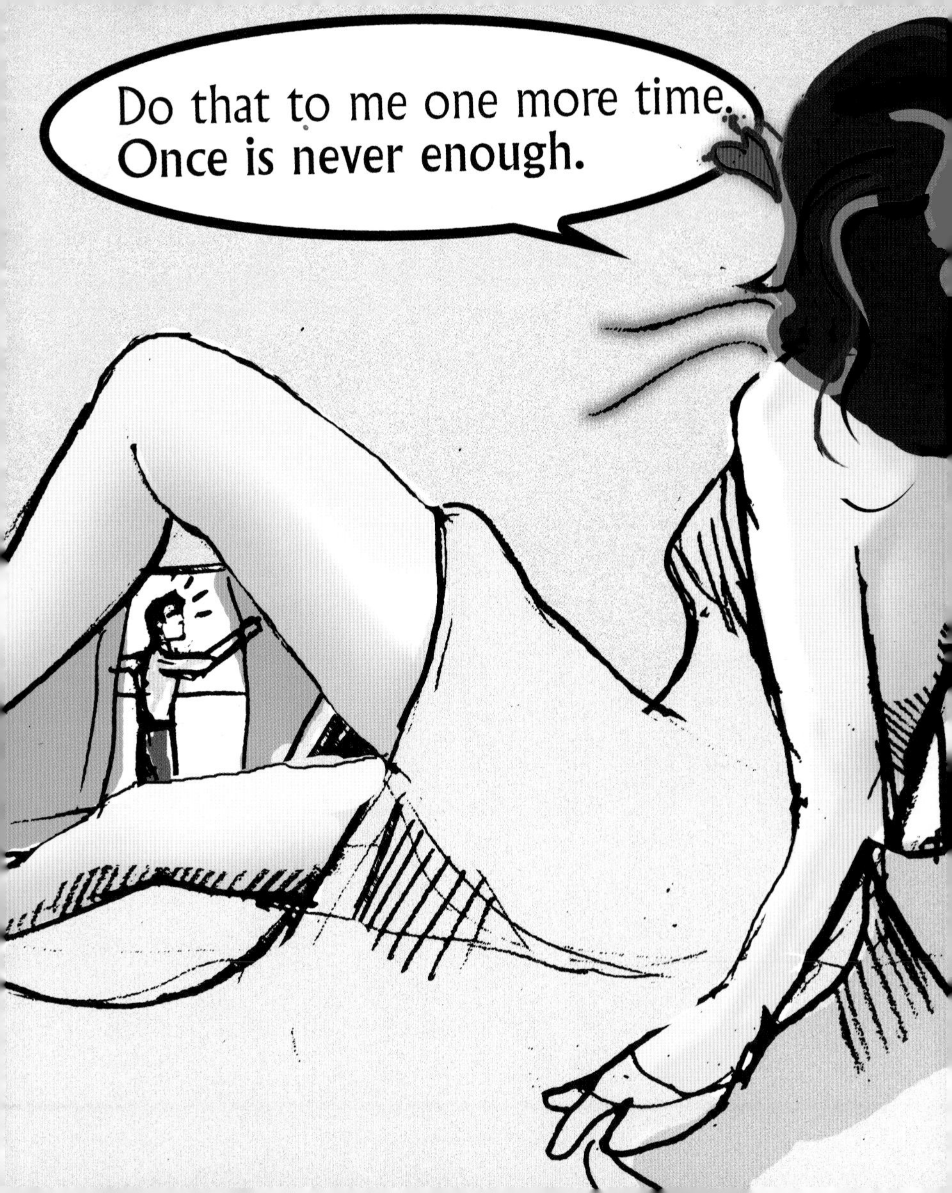
Do that to me one more time.
Once is never enough.

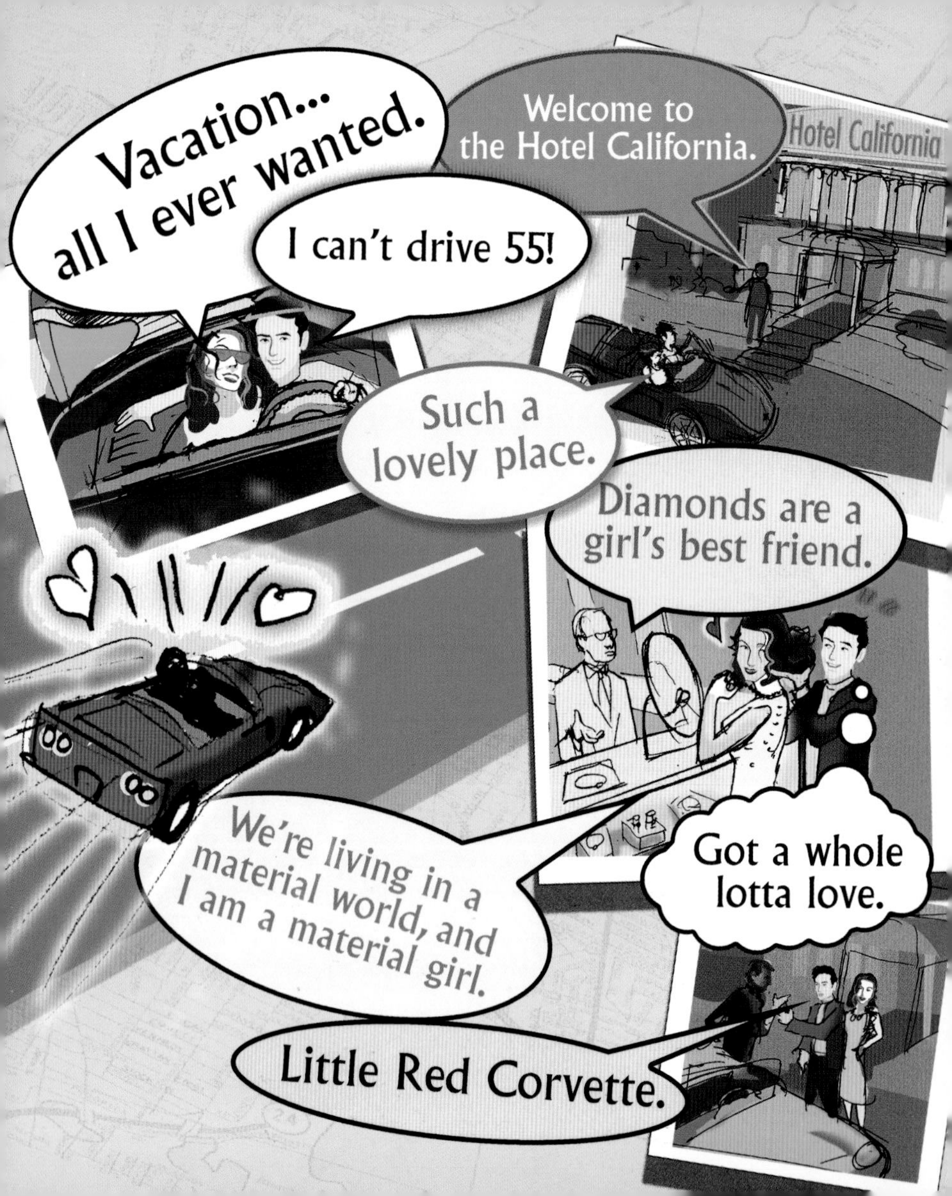
Vacation... all I ever wanted.
I can't drive 55!
Welcome to the Hotel California.
Hotel California
Such a lovely place.
Diamonds are a girl's best friend.
We're living in a material world, and I am a material girl.
Got a whole lotta love.
Little Red Corvette.

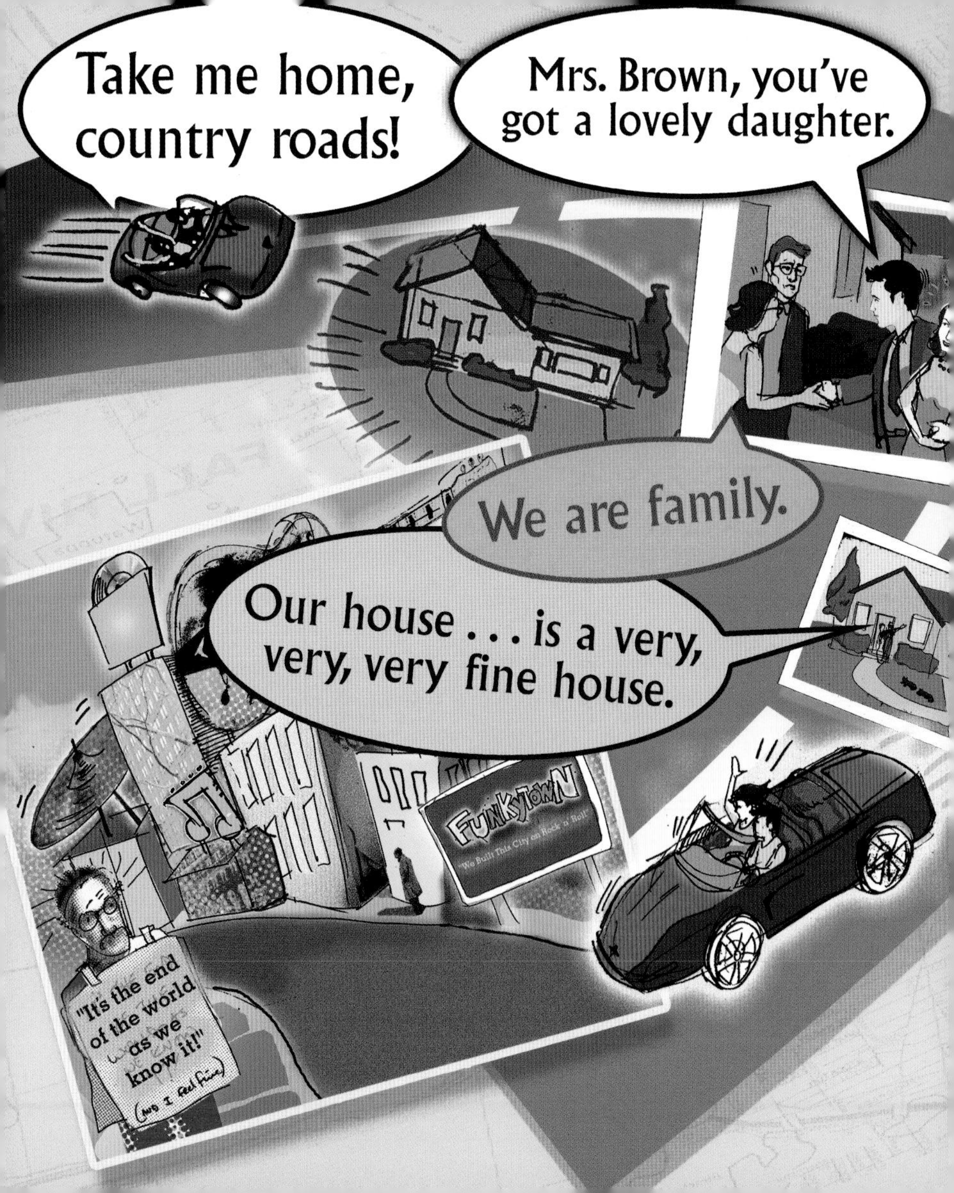
Take me home, country roads!
Mrs. Brown, you've got a lovely daughter.
We are family.
Our house . . . is a very, very, very fine house.
FUNKYTOWN
"We Built This City on Rock 'n' Roll"
"It's the end of the world as we know it!"
(And I Feel Fine)

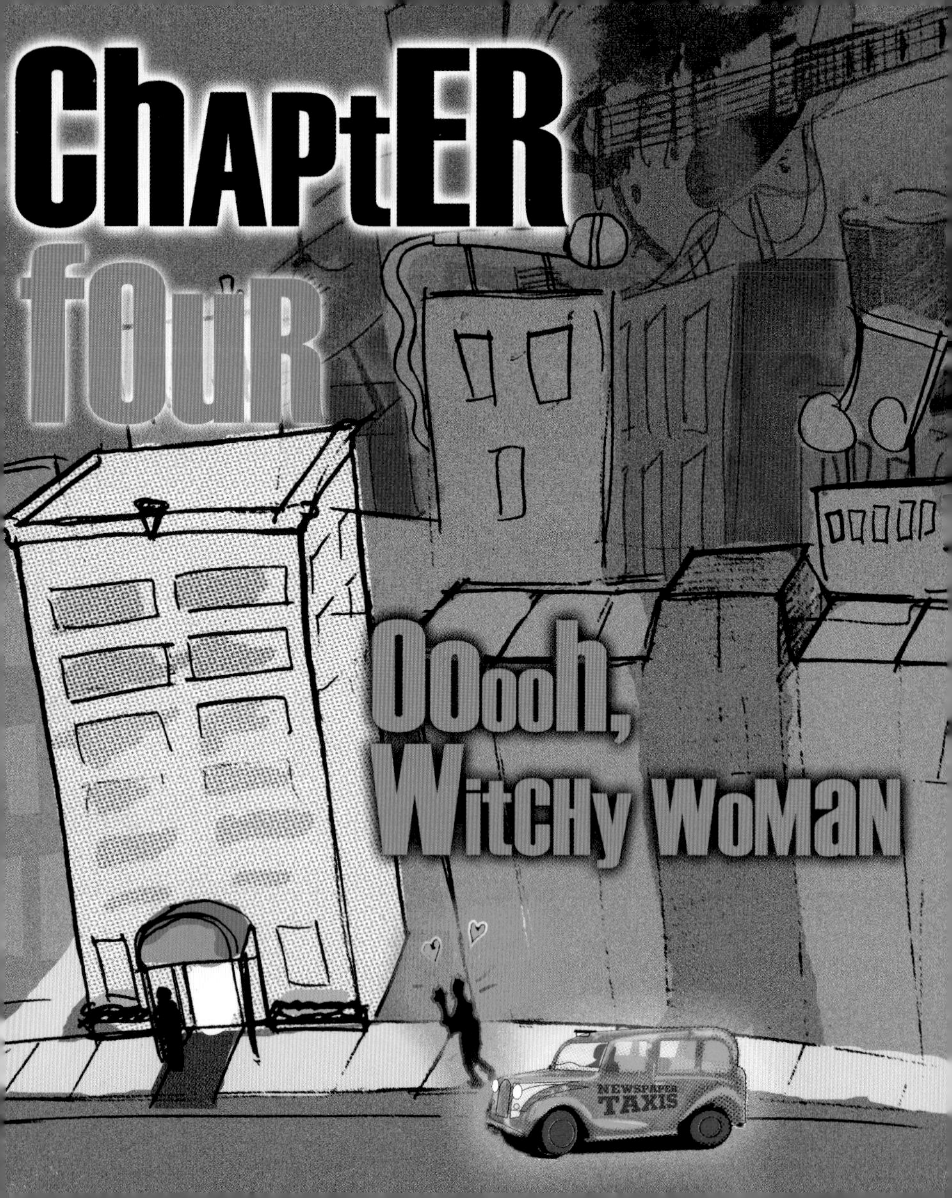
ChAptER
fOuR
OOooh,
WitcHy WoMAN
NEWSPAPER
TAXIS

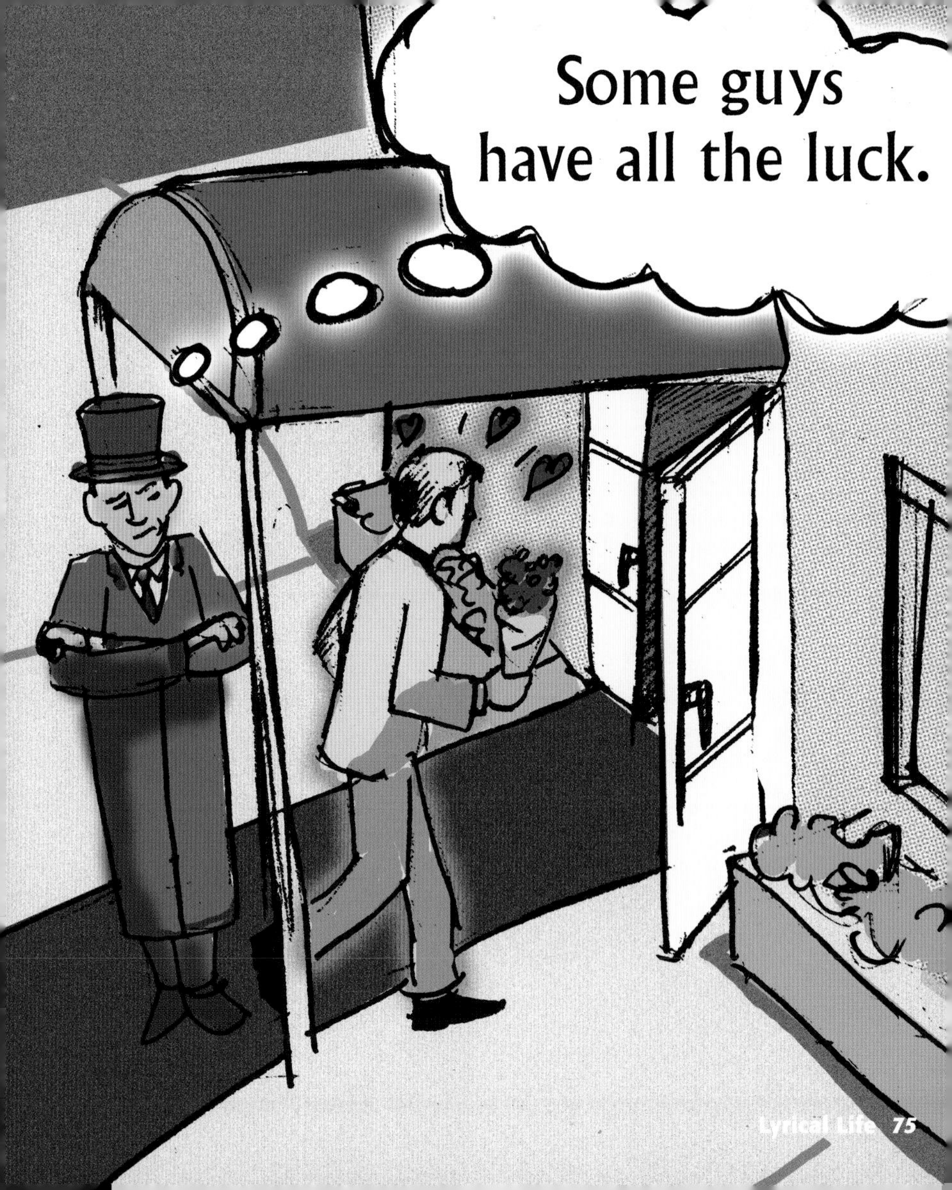
Some guys have all the luck.

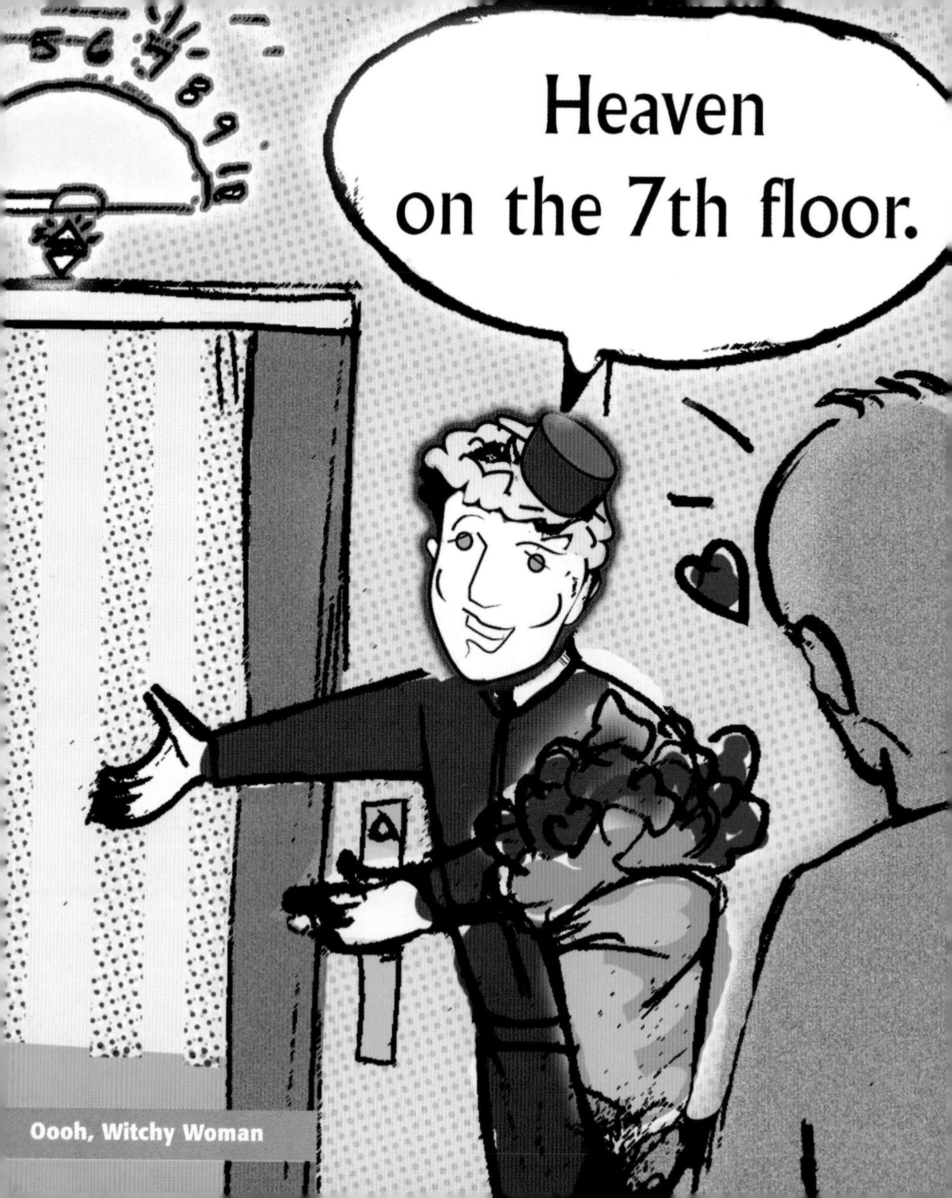
Heaven on the 7th floor.

Oooh, Witchy Woman

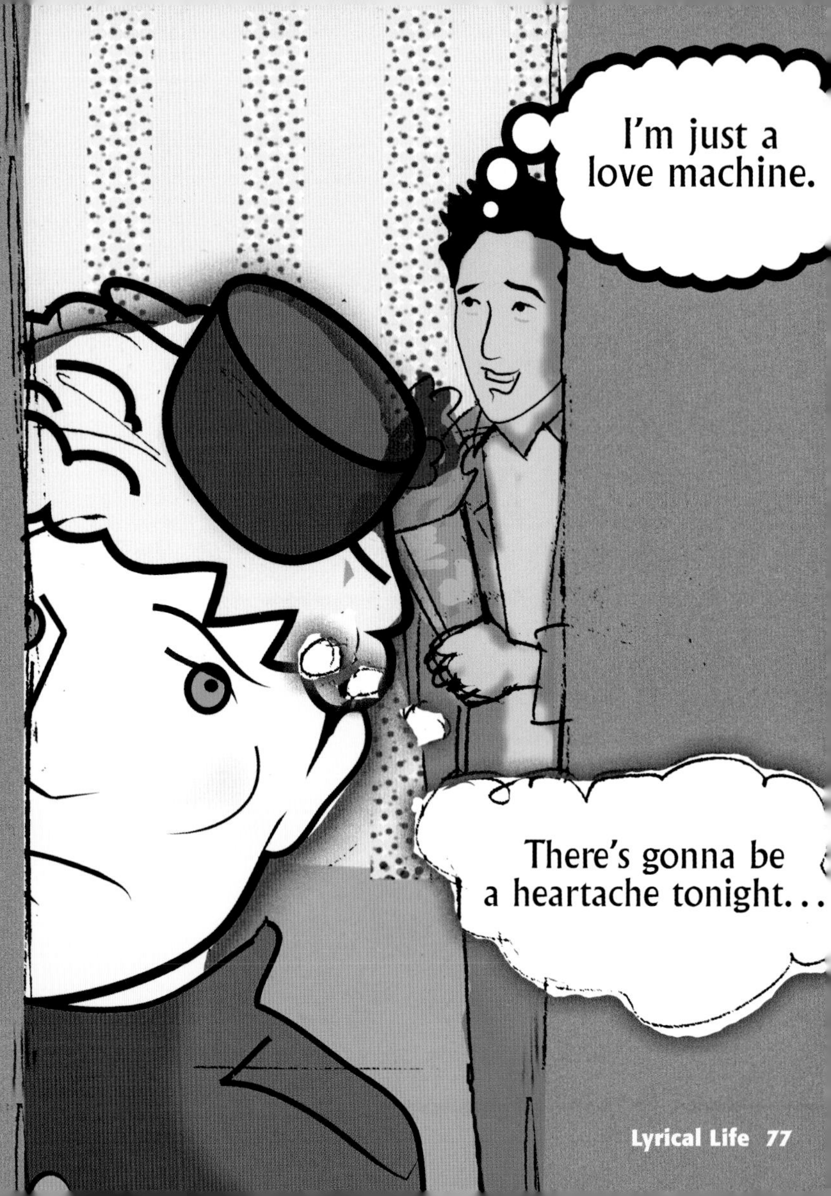
I'm just a love machine.
There's gonna be a heartache tonight…

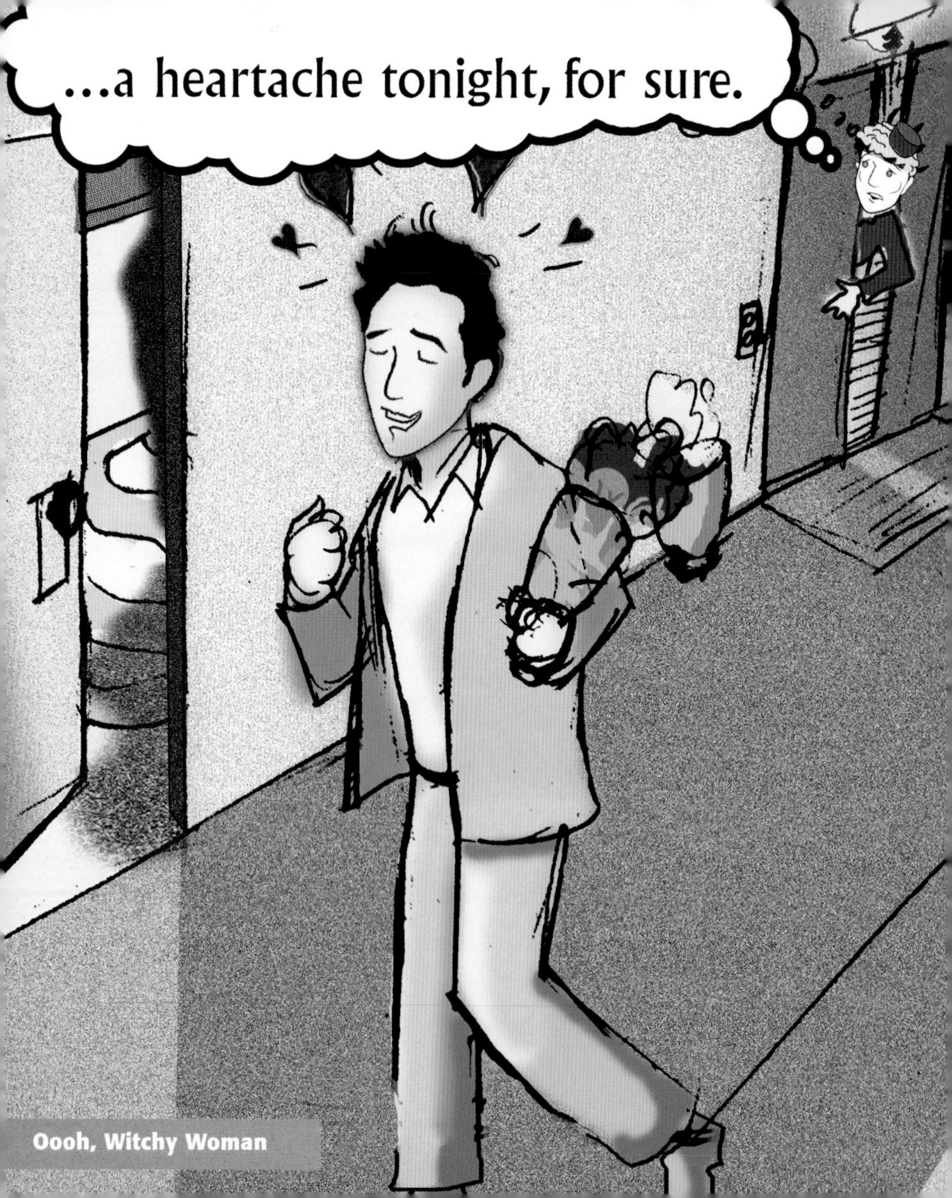
…a heartache tonight, for sure.
Oooh, Witchy Woman

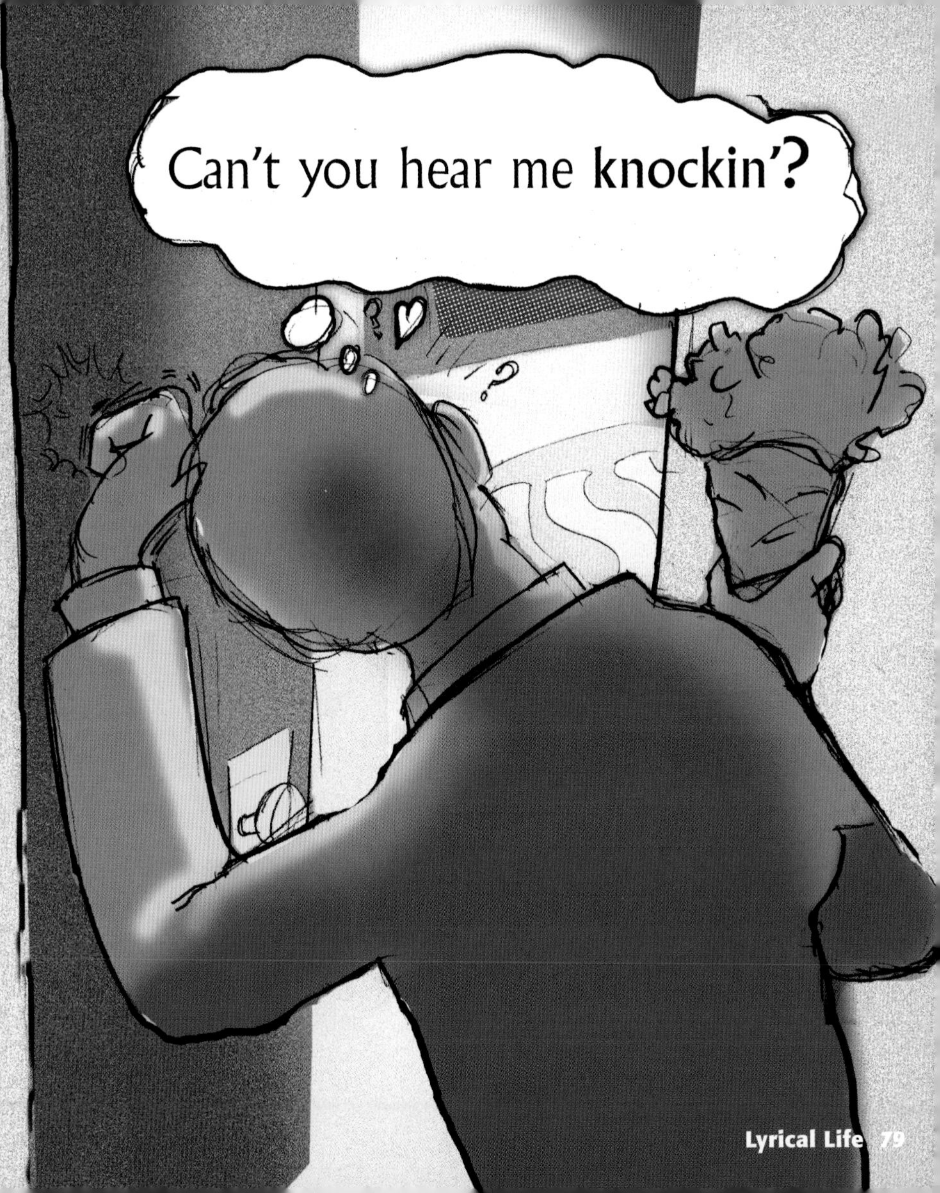
Can't you hear me knockin'?

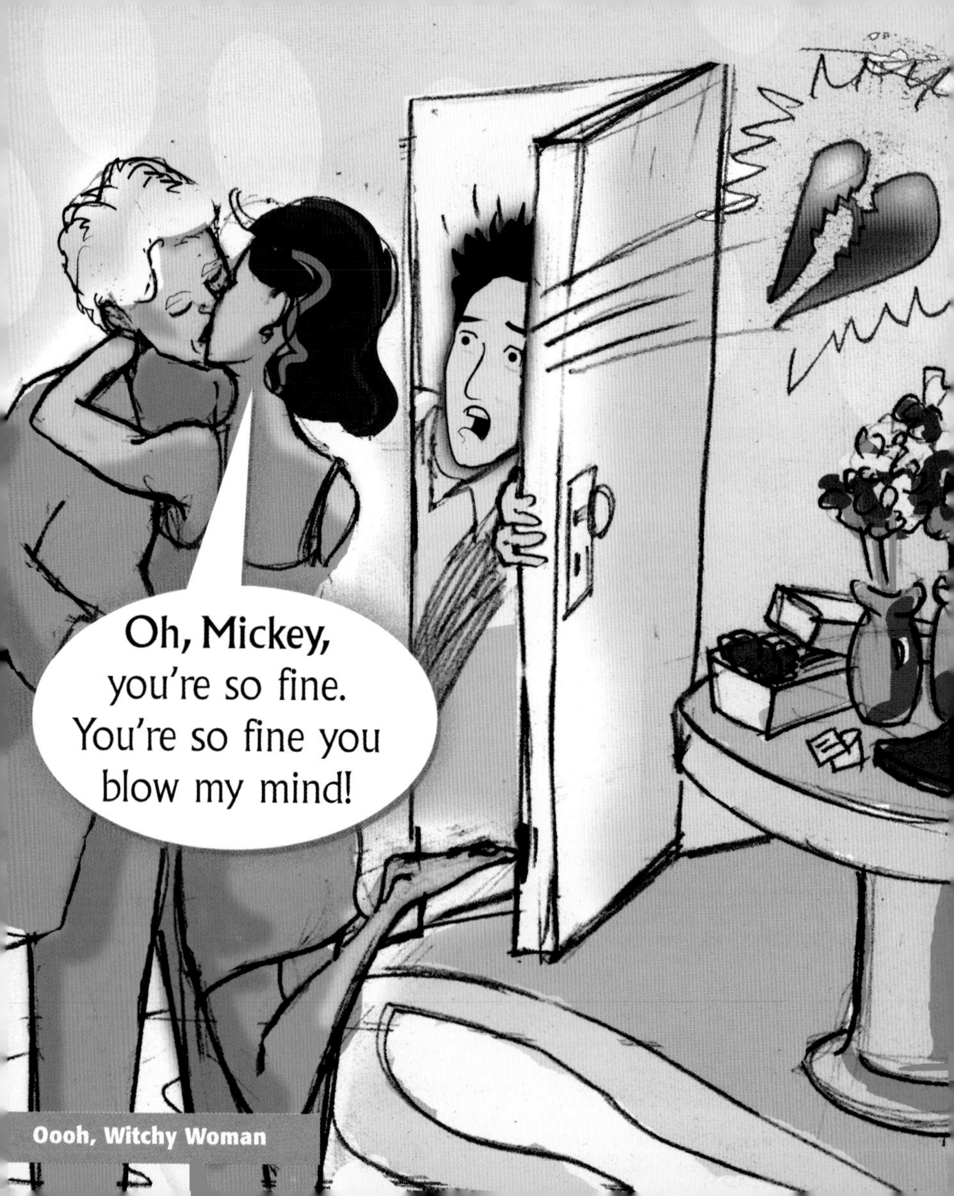
Oh, Mickey, you're so fine. You're so fine you blow my mind!

Oooh, Witchy Woman

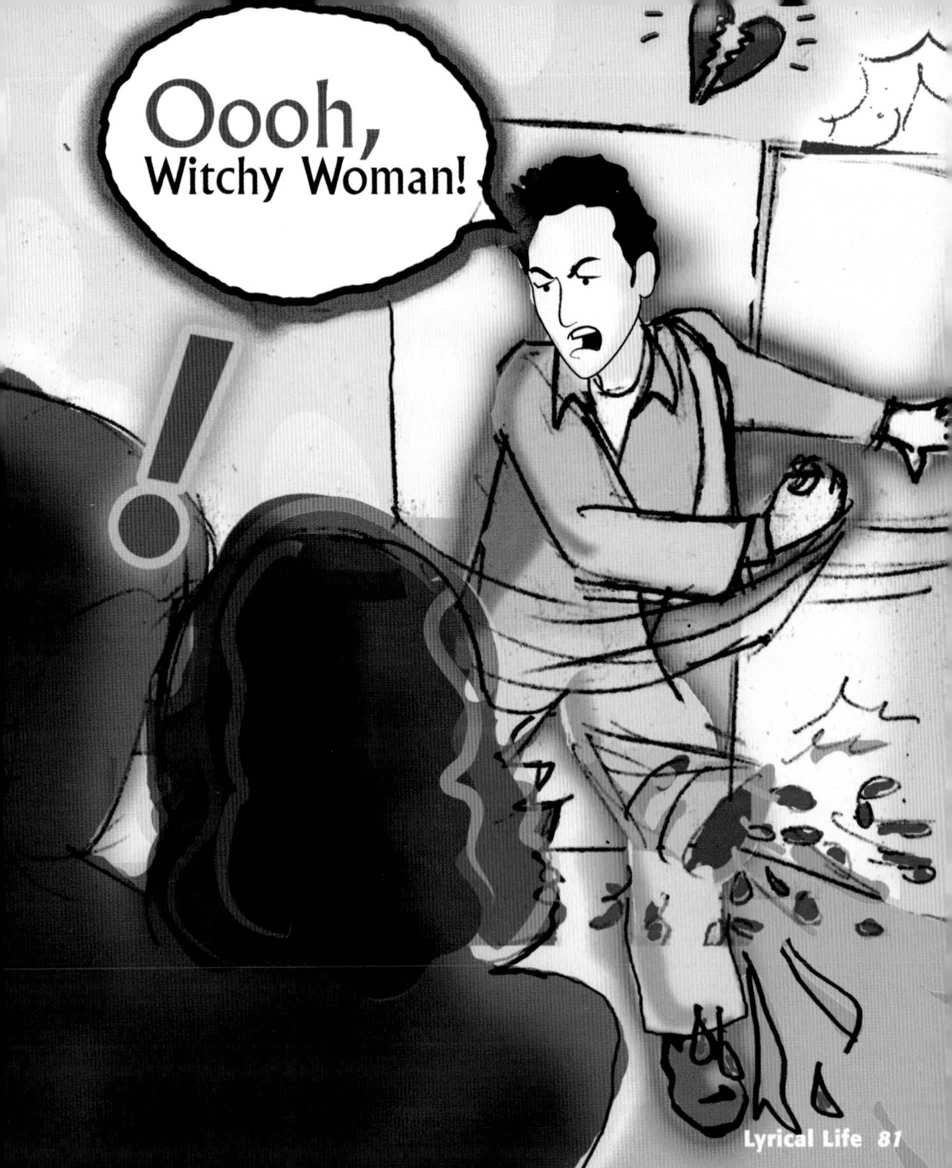
Oooh,
Witchy Woman!

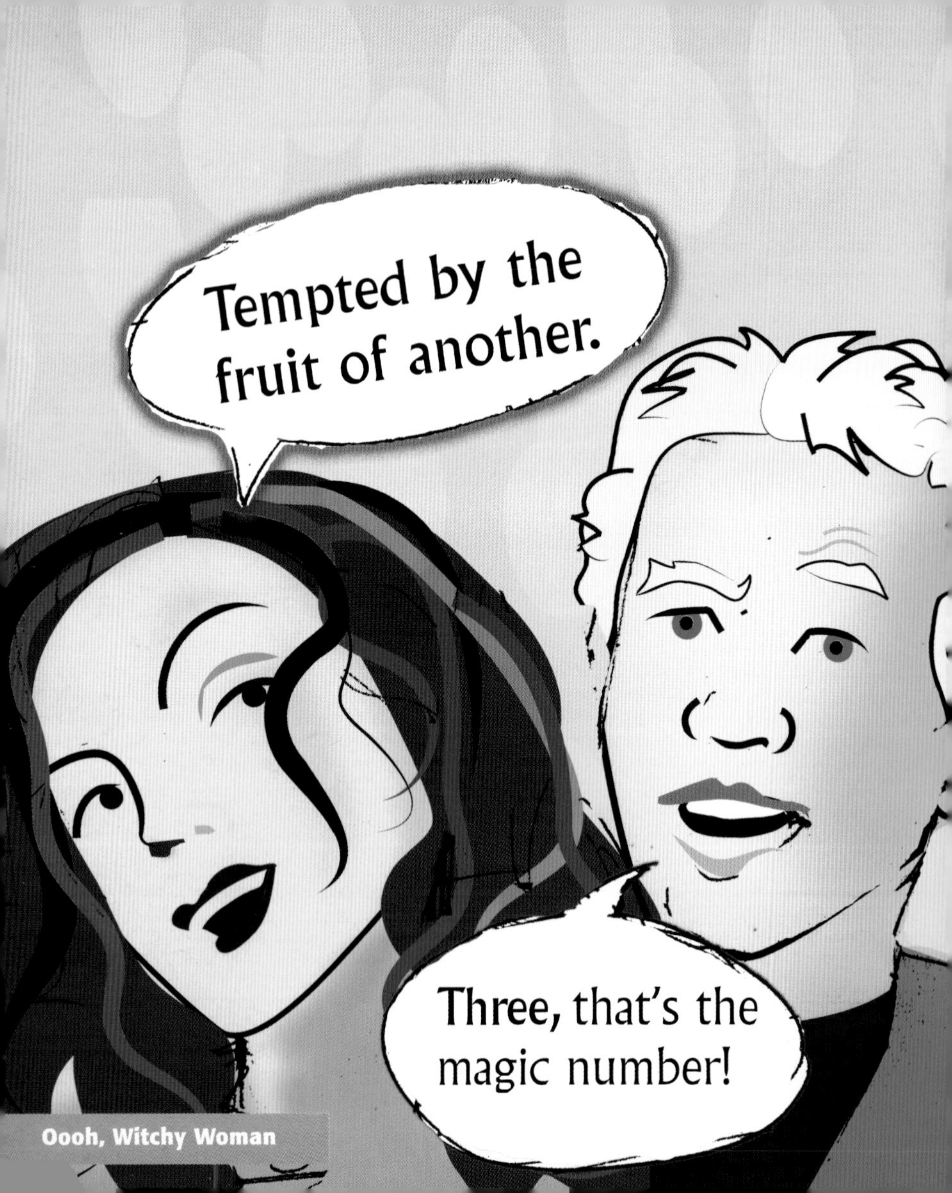
Tempted by the fruit of another.
Three, that's the magic number!

Oooh, Witchy Woman

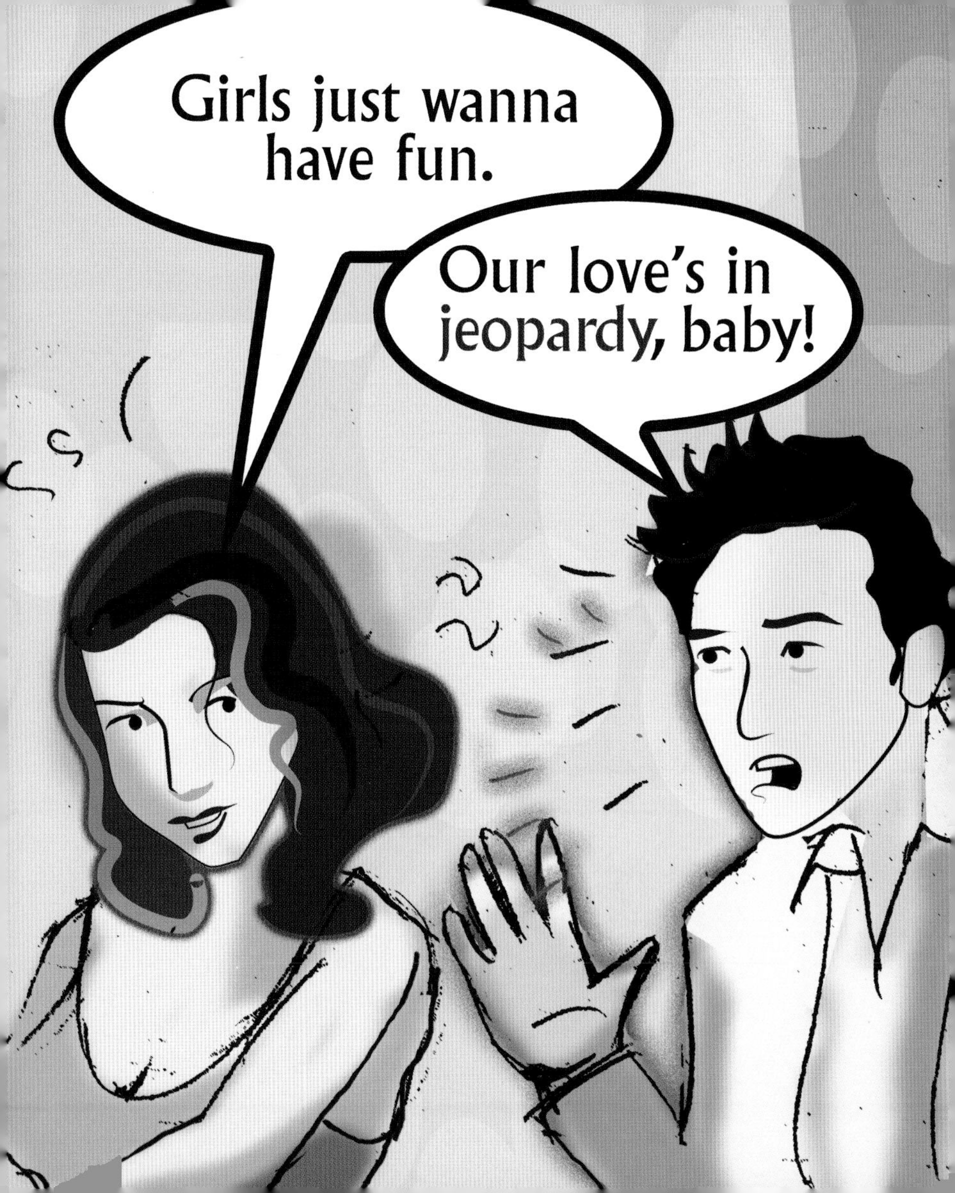
Girls just wanna have fun.
Our love's in jeopardy, baby!

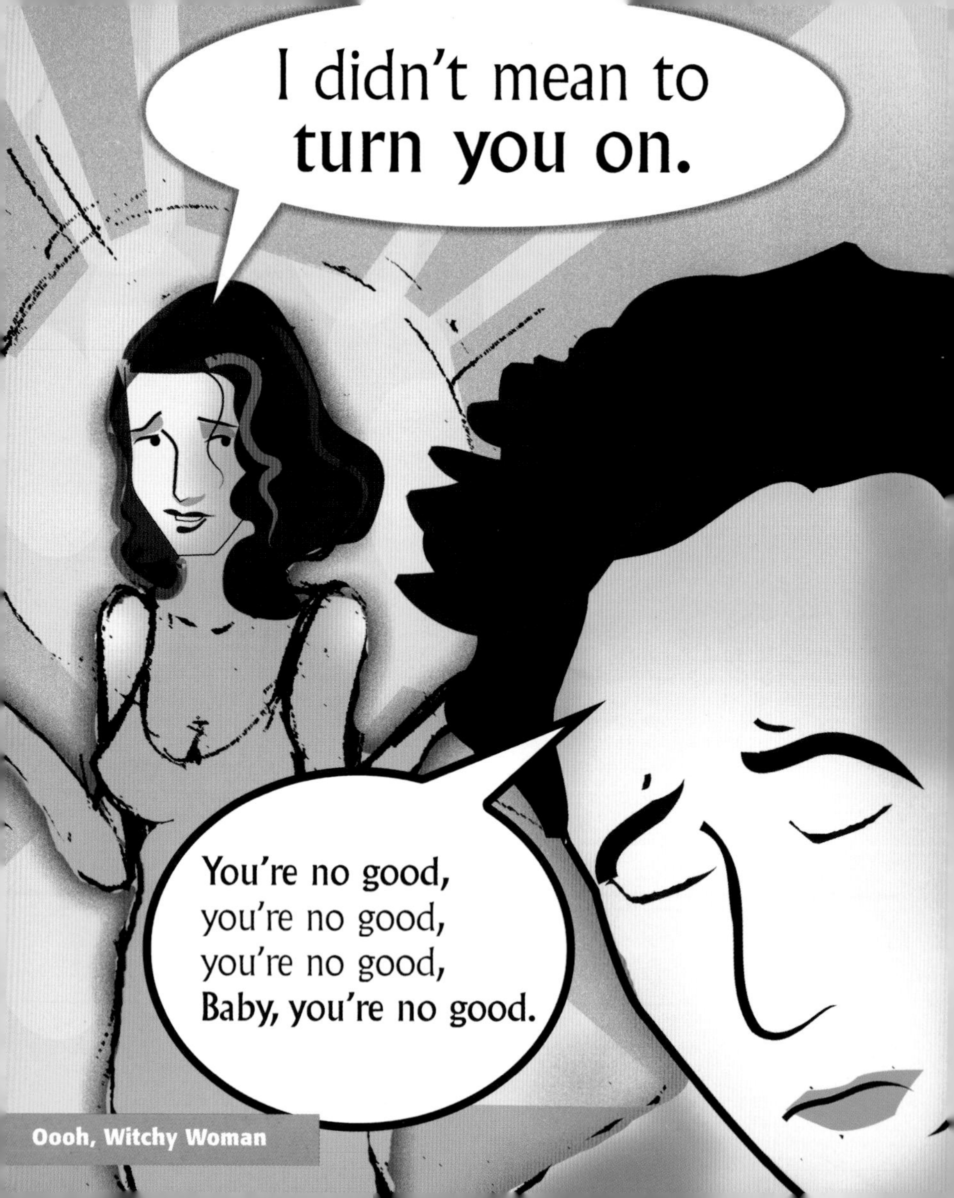
I didn't mean to turn you on.
You're no good, you're no good, you're no good, Baby, you're no good.

Oooh, Witchy Woman

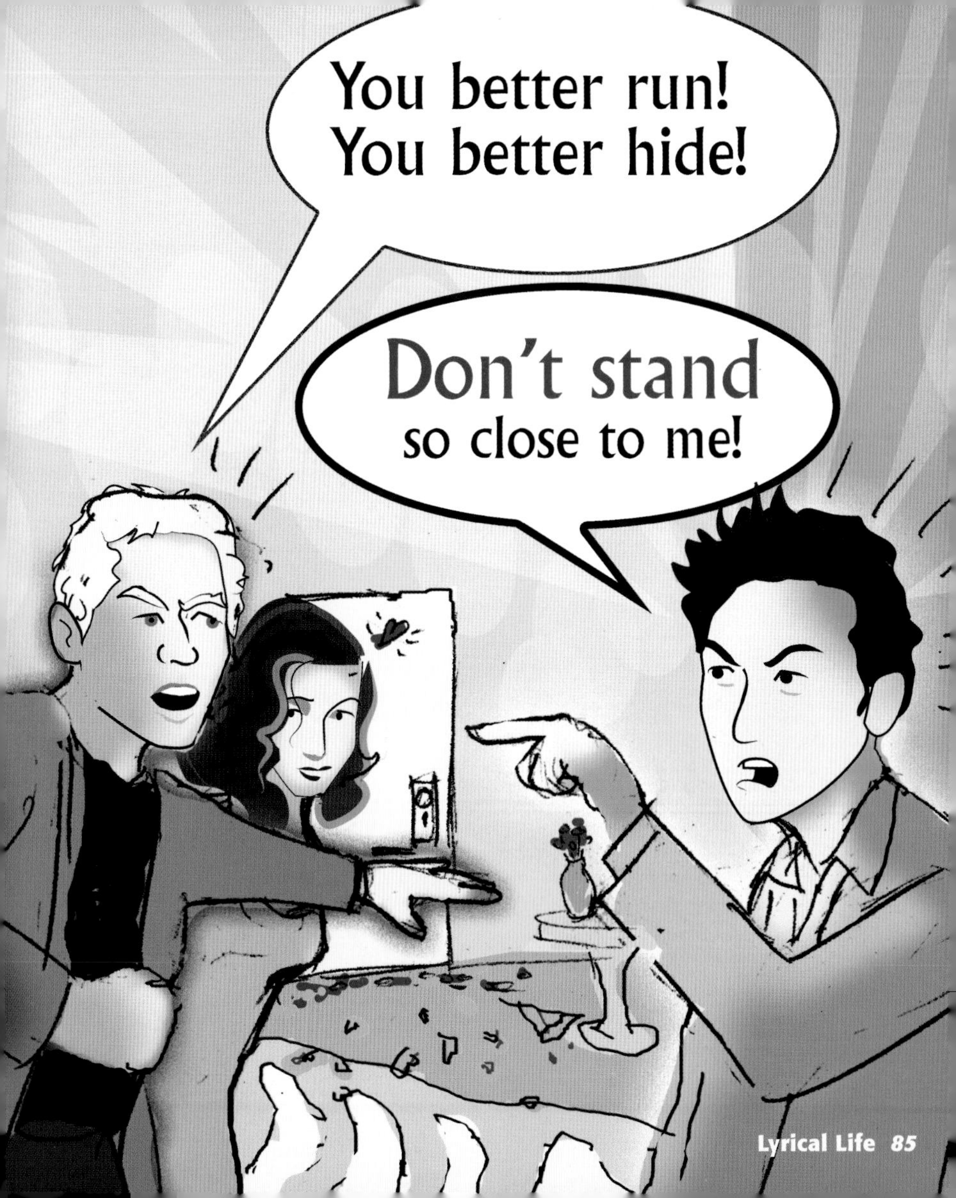
You better run! You better hide!
Don't stand so close to me!

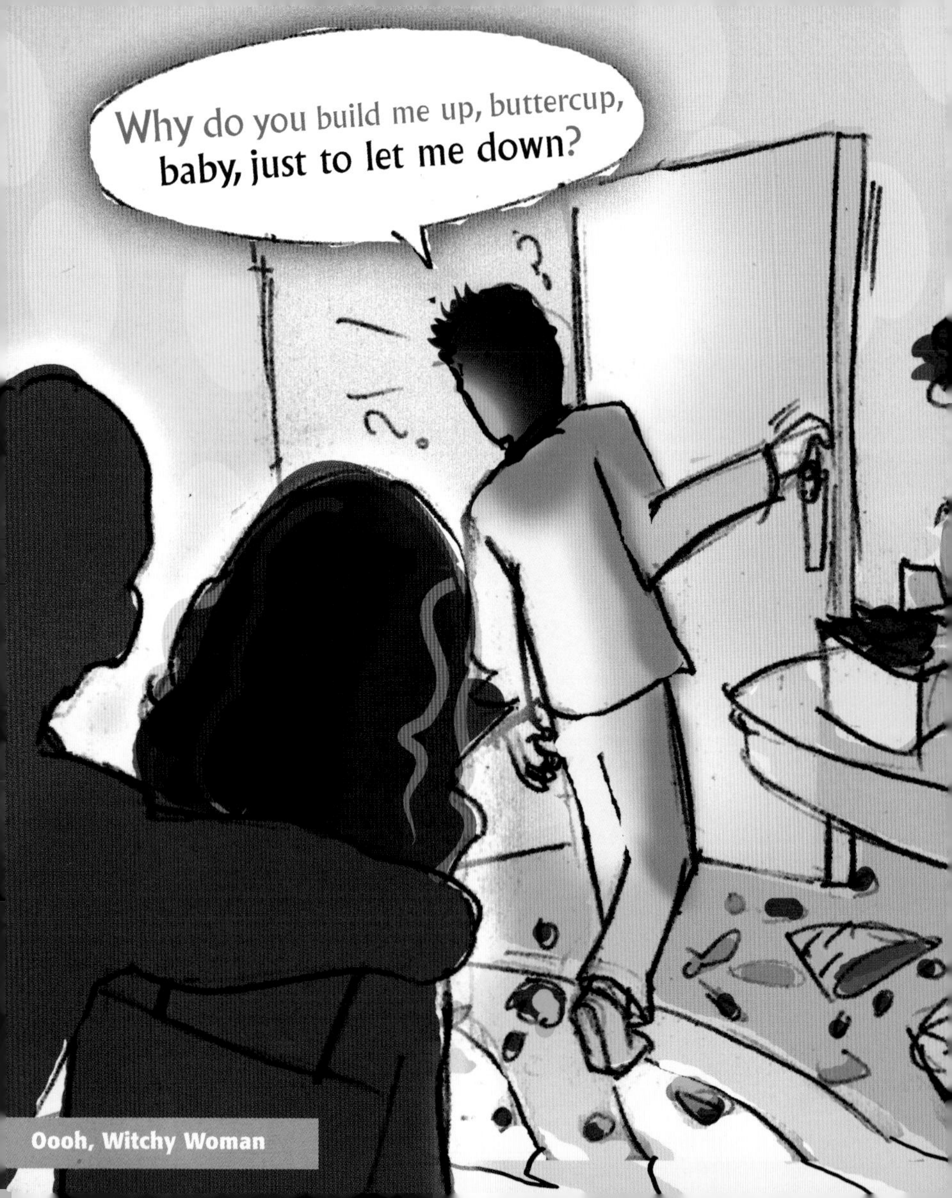
Why do you build me up, buttercup, baby, just to let me down?
Oooh, Witchy Woman

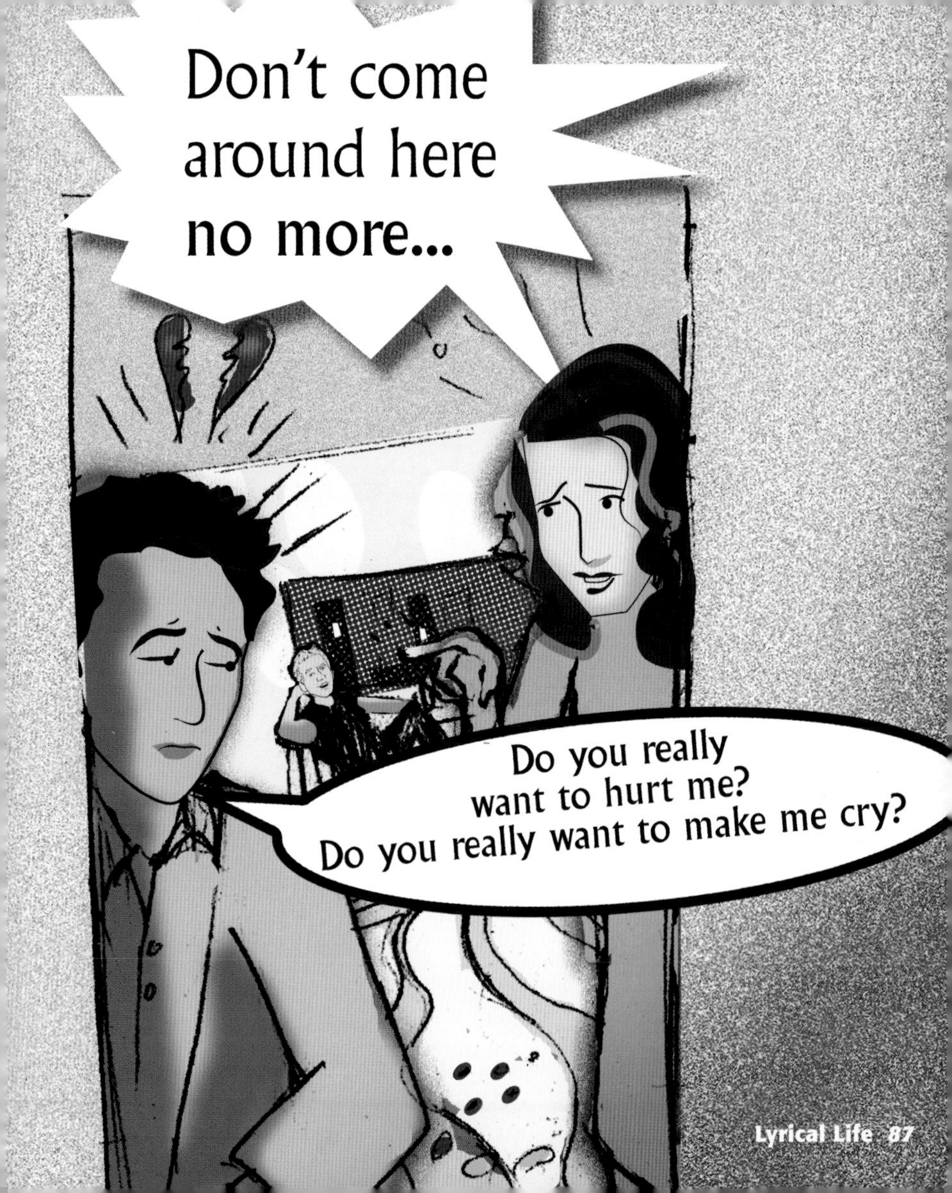
Don't come around here no more...
Do you really want to hurt me? Do you really want to make me cry?

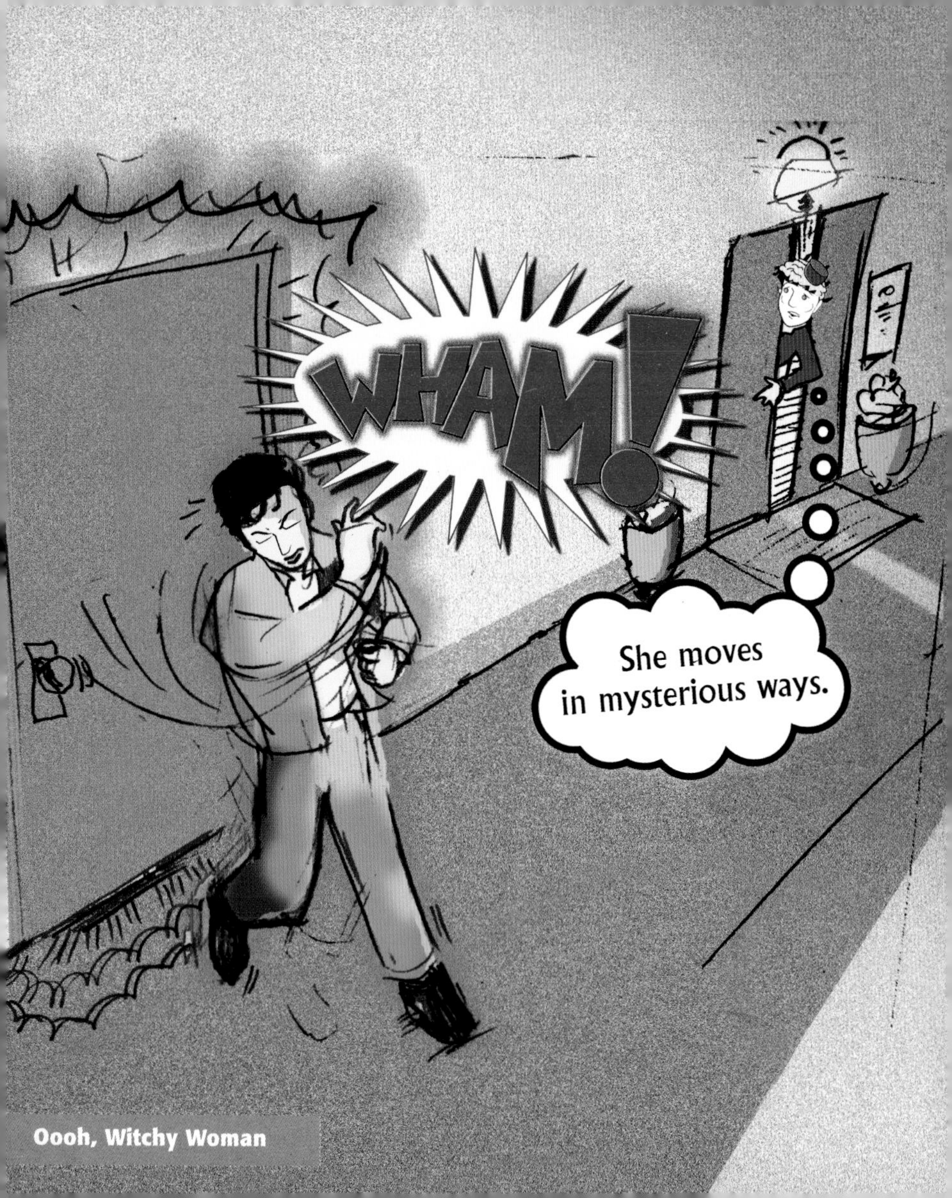
WHAM!
She moves in mysterious ways.

Oooh, Witchy Woman

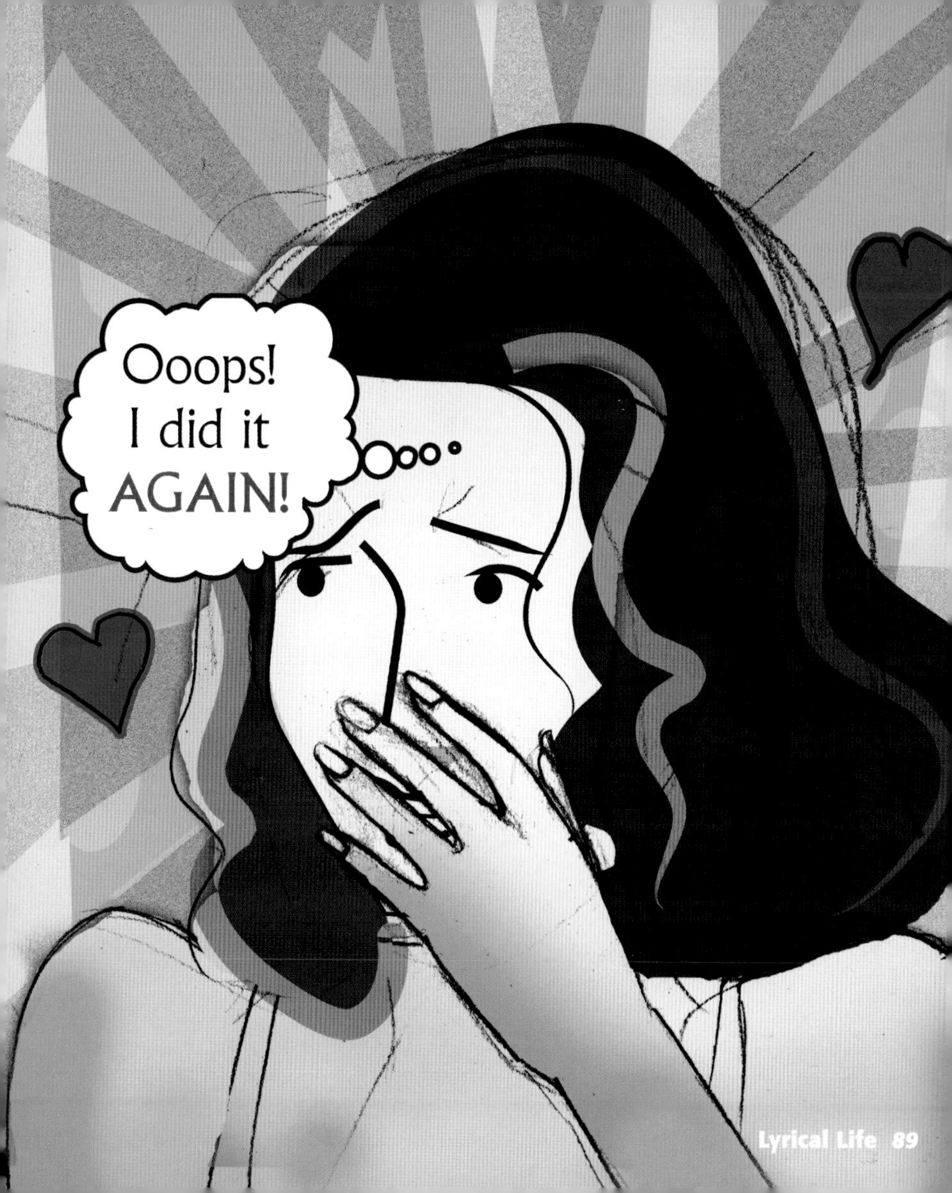
Ooops! I did it AGAIN!

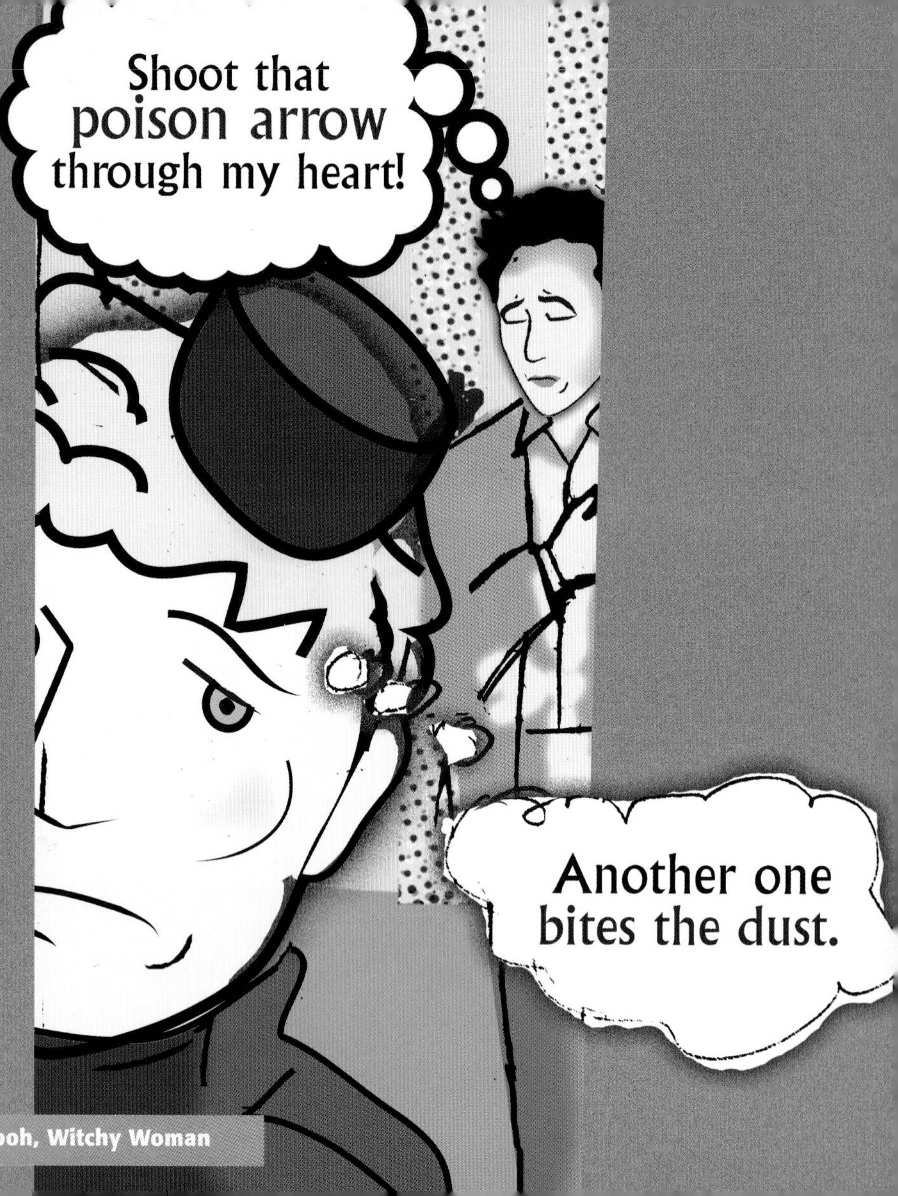
Shoot that poison arrow through my heart!
Another one bites the dust.

Chapter Five

Shout, shout, Let it all Out!

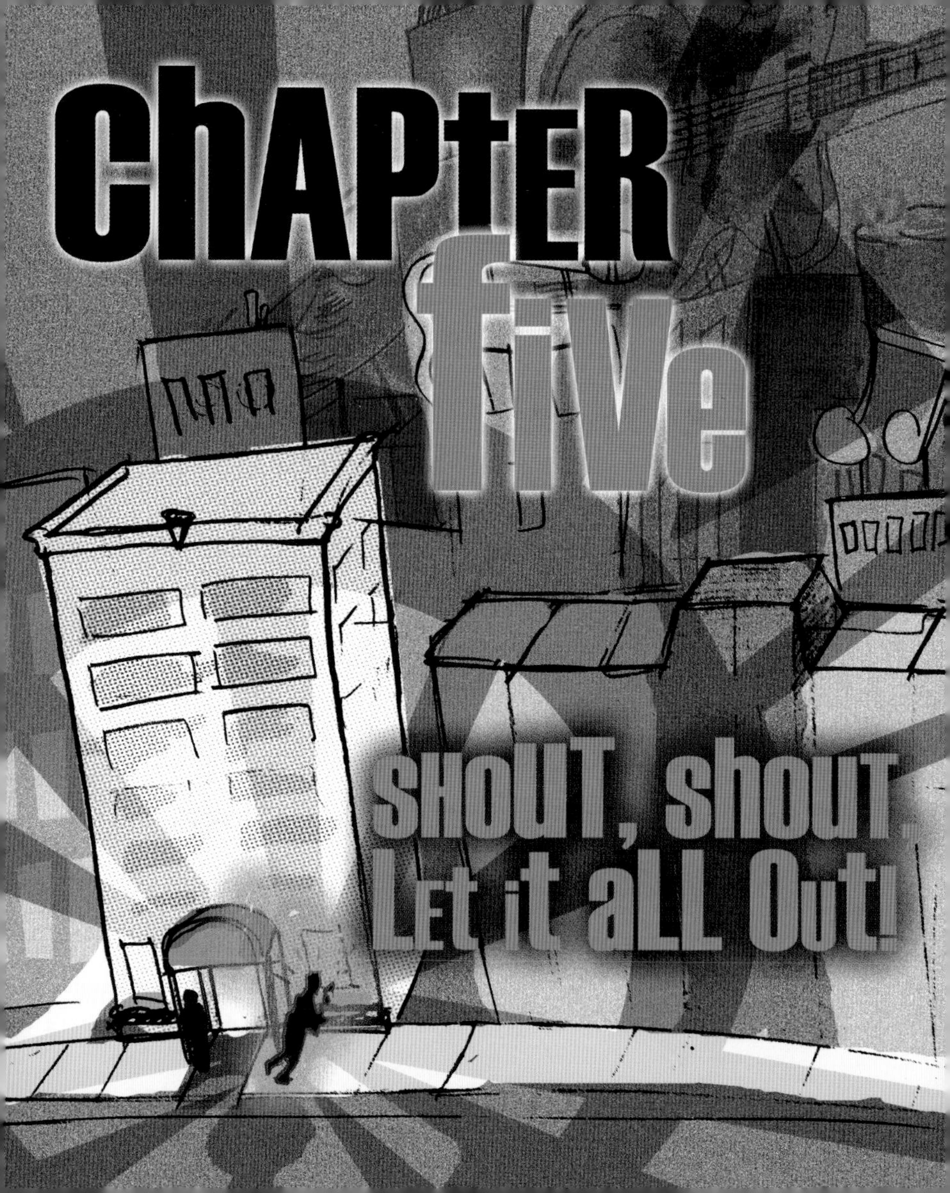

And I ran. . .I ran so far away.

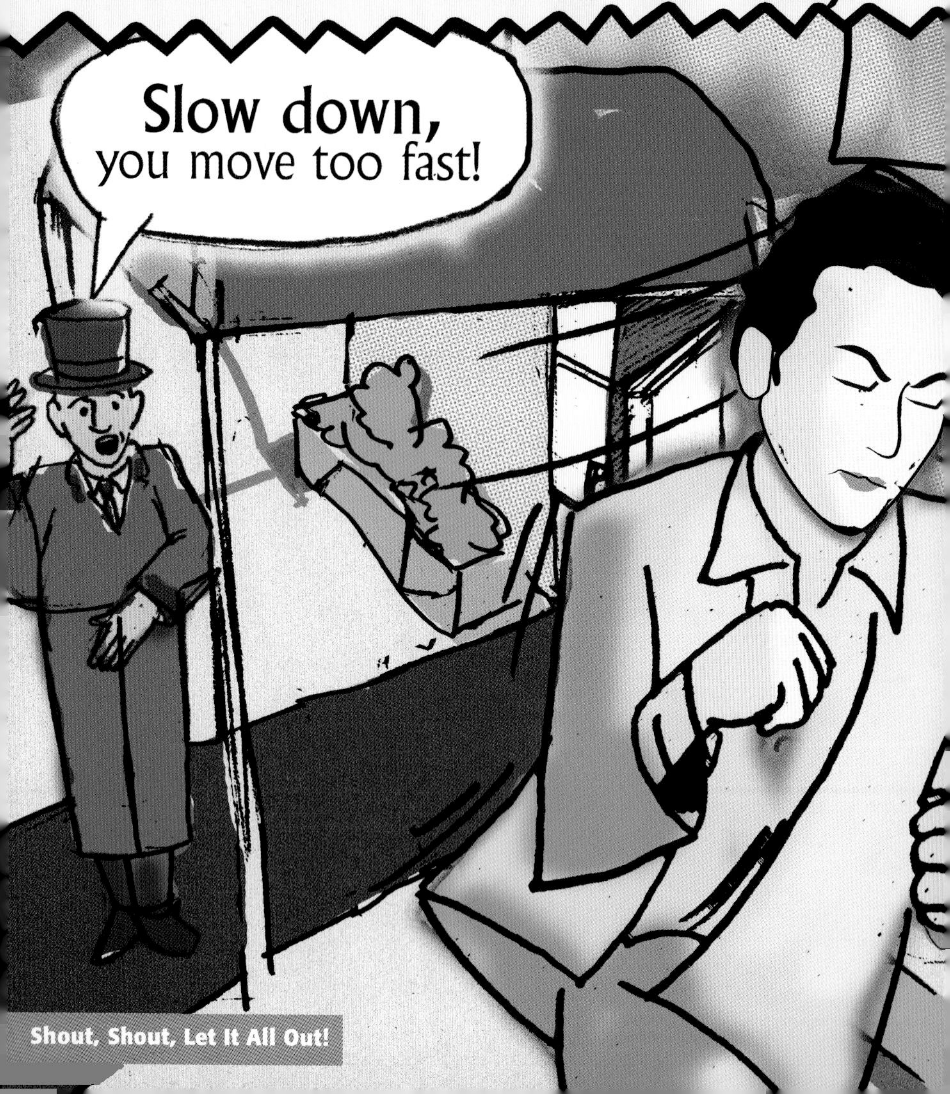
Slow down,
you move too fast!

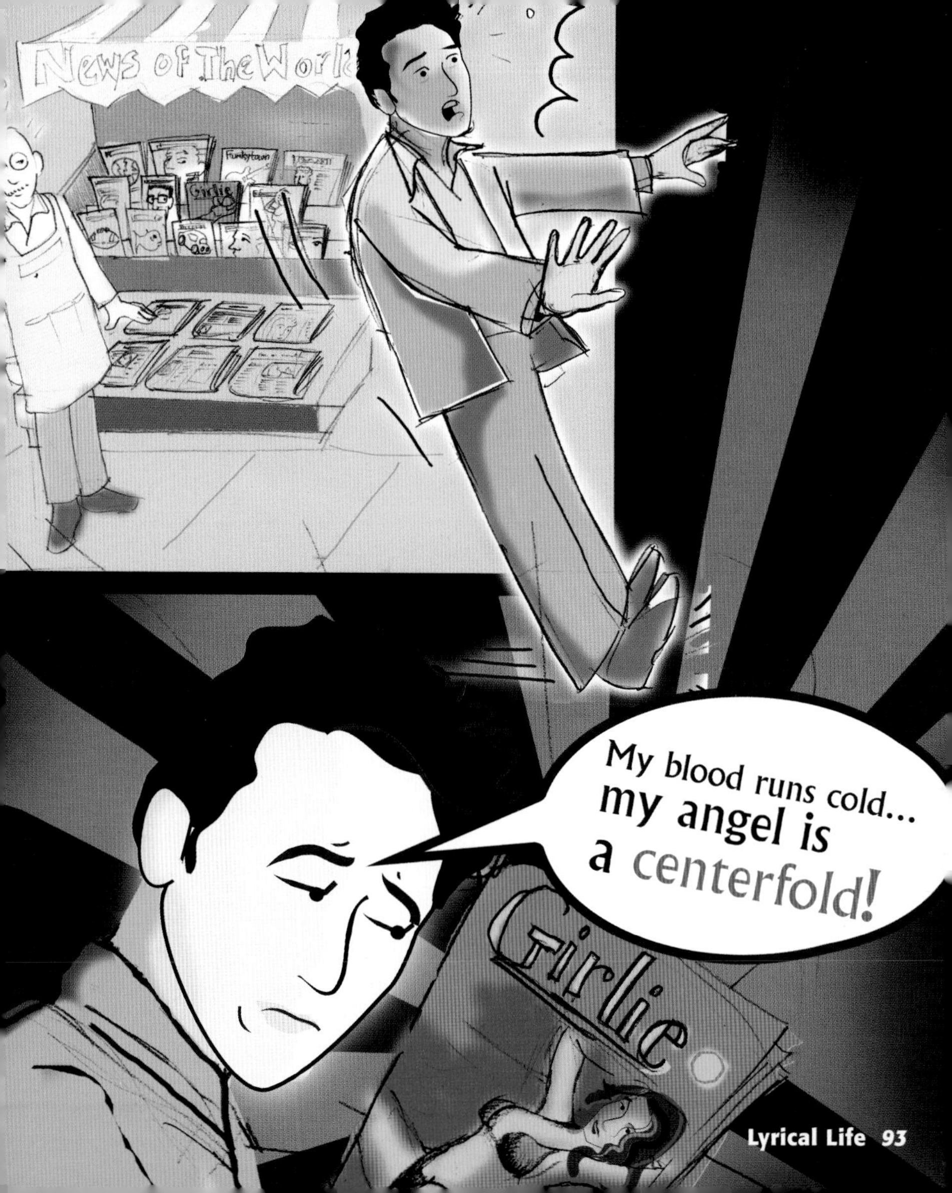
News of The World
Funkytown
Girlie
My blood runs cold... my angel is a centerfold!
Girlie

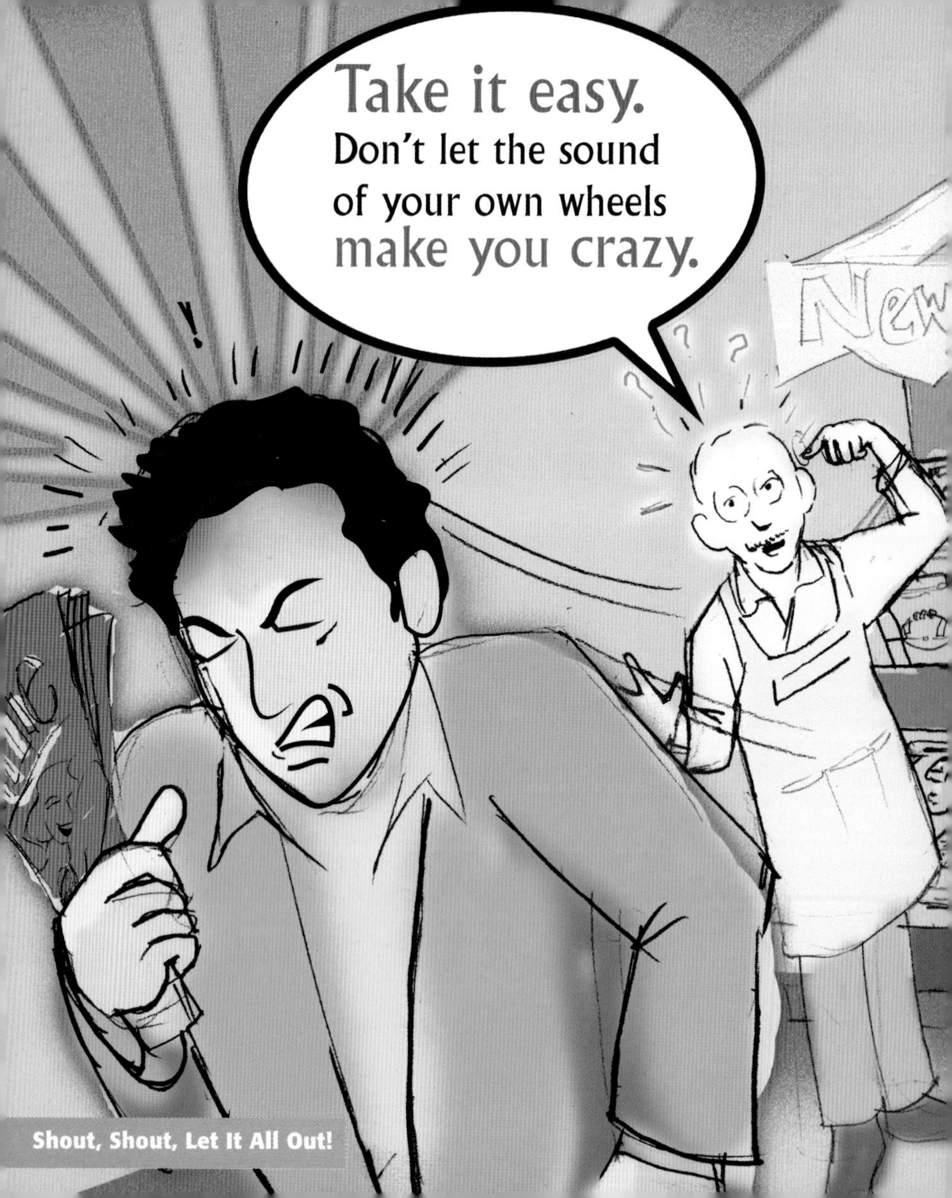
Take it easy.
Don't let the sound
of your own wheels
make you crazy.
New

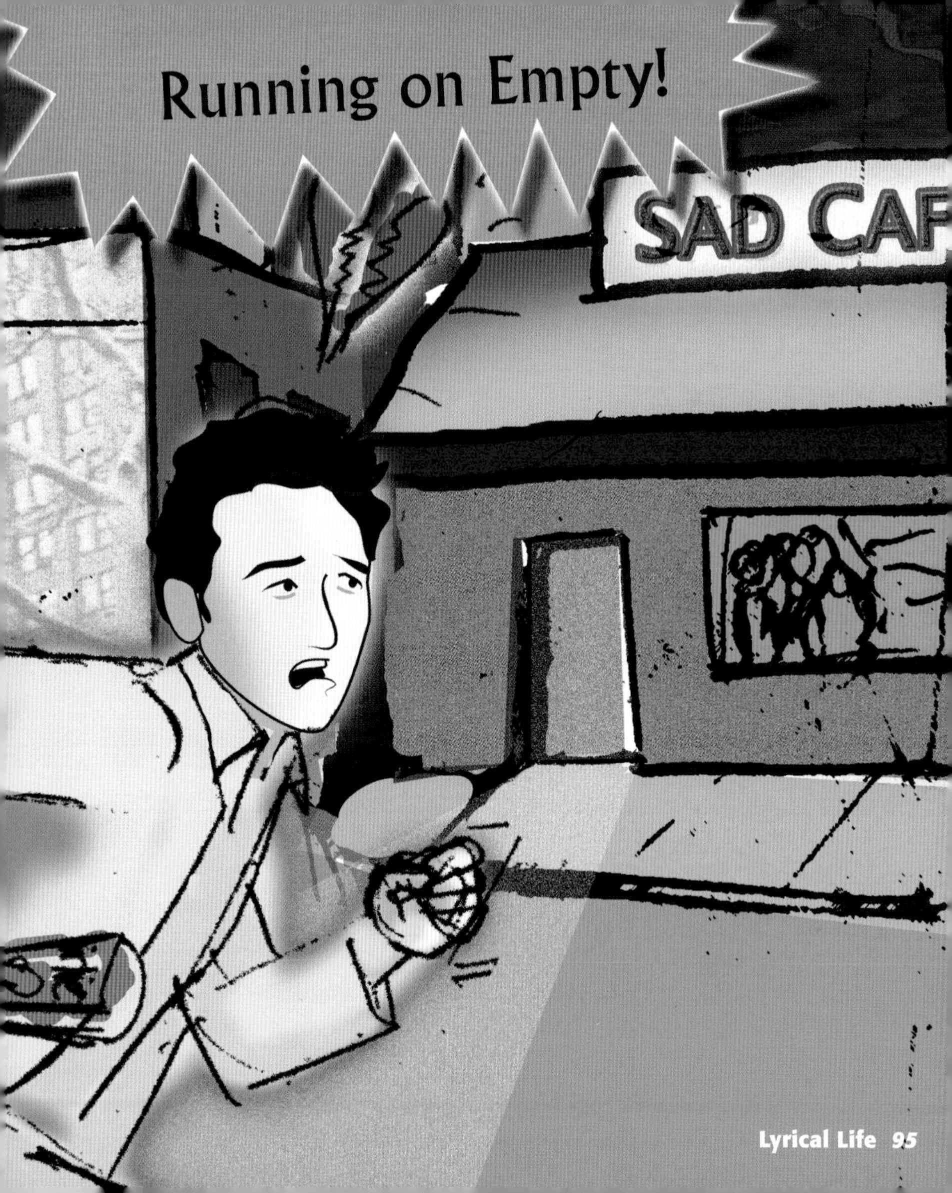
Running on Empty!
SAD CAF

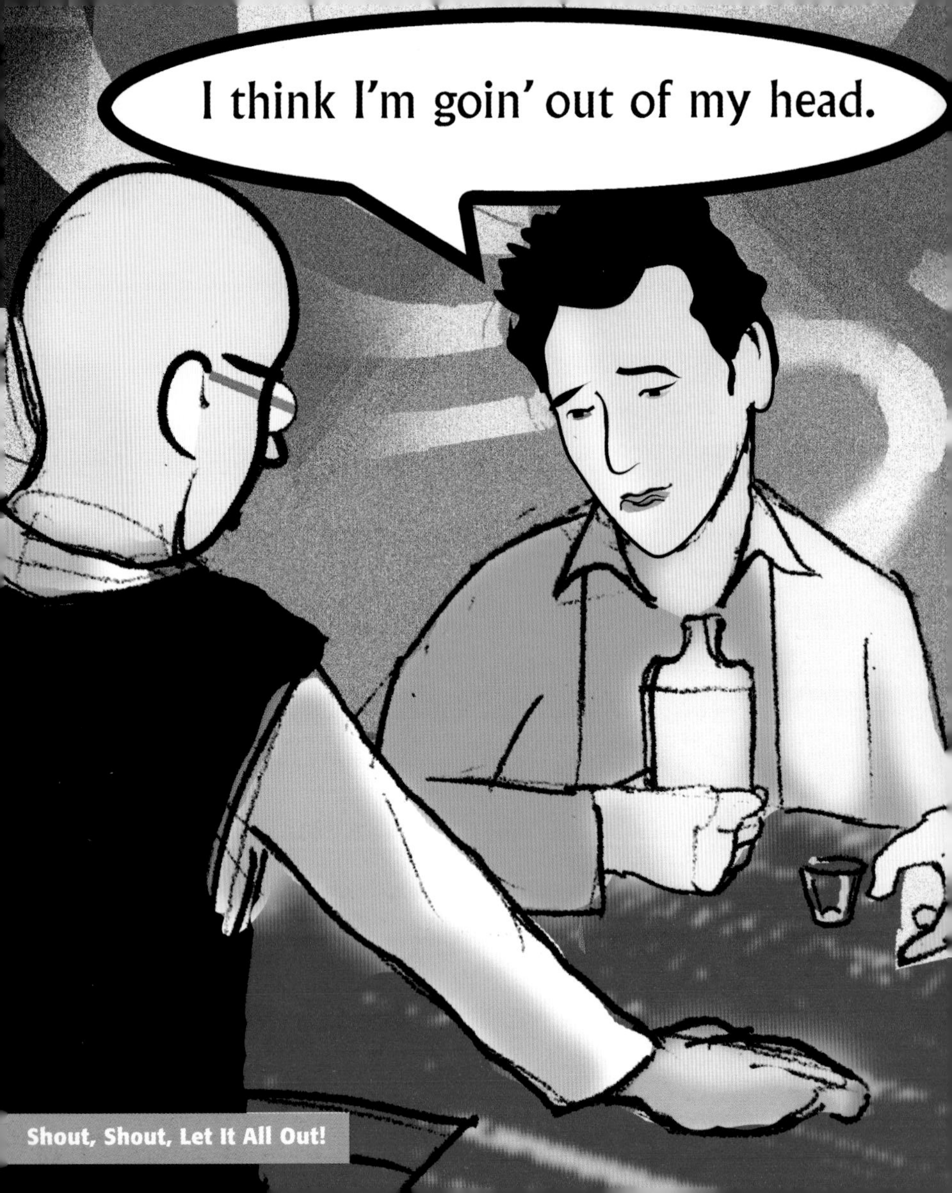
I think I'm goin' out of my head.

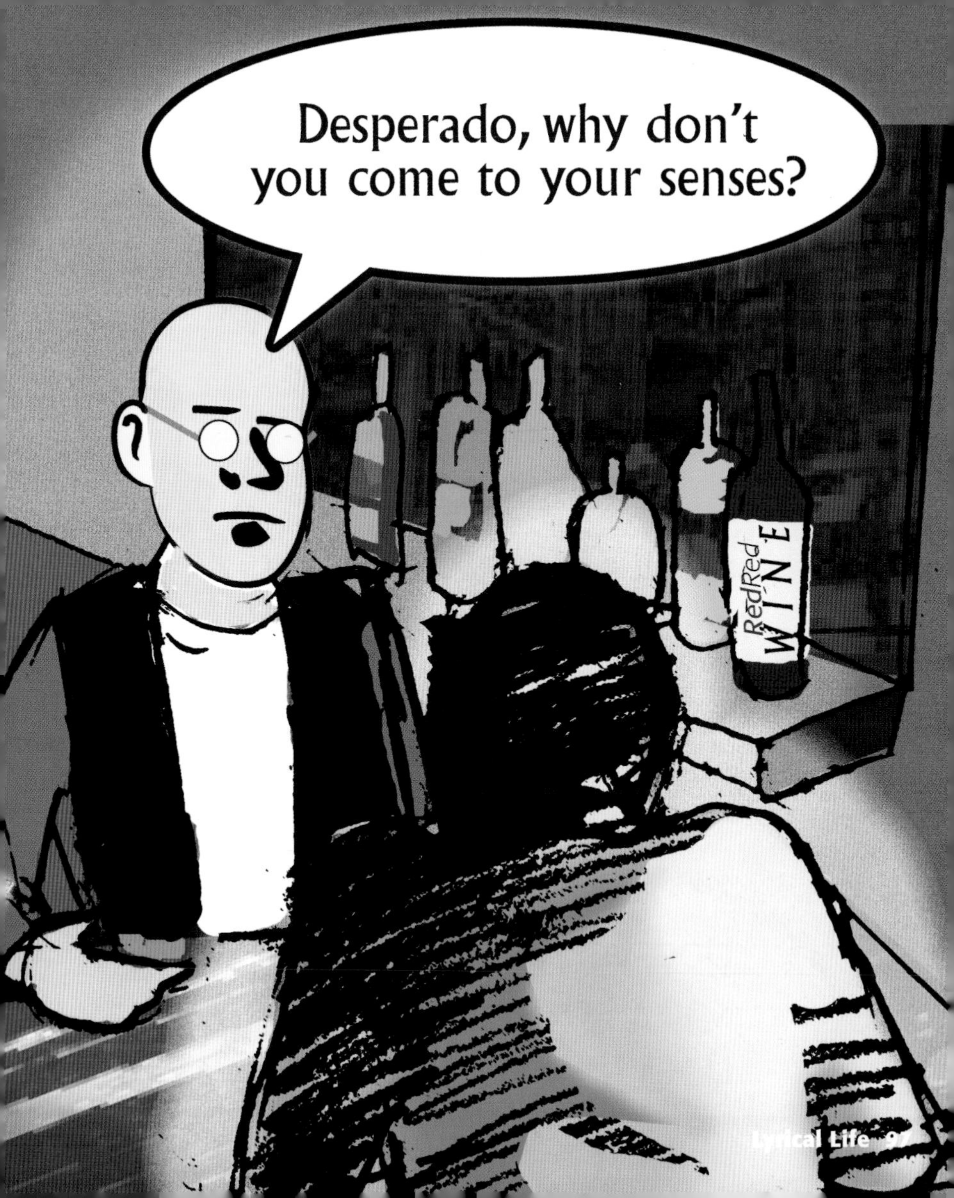
Desperado, why don't you come to your senses?
Red Red WINE

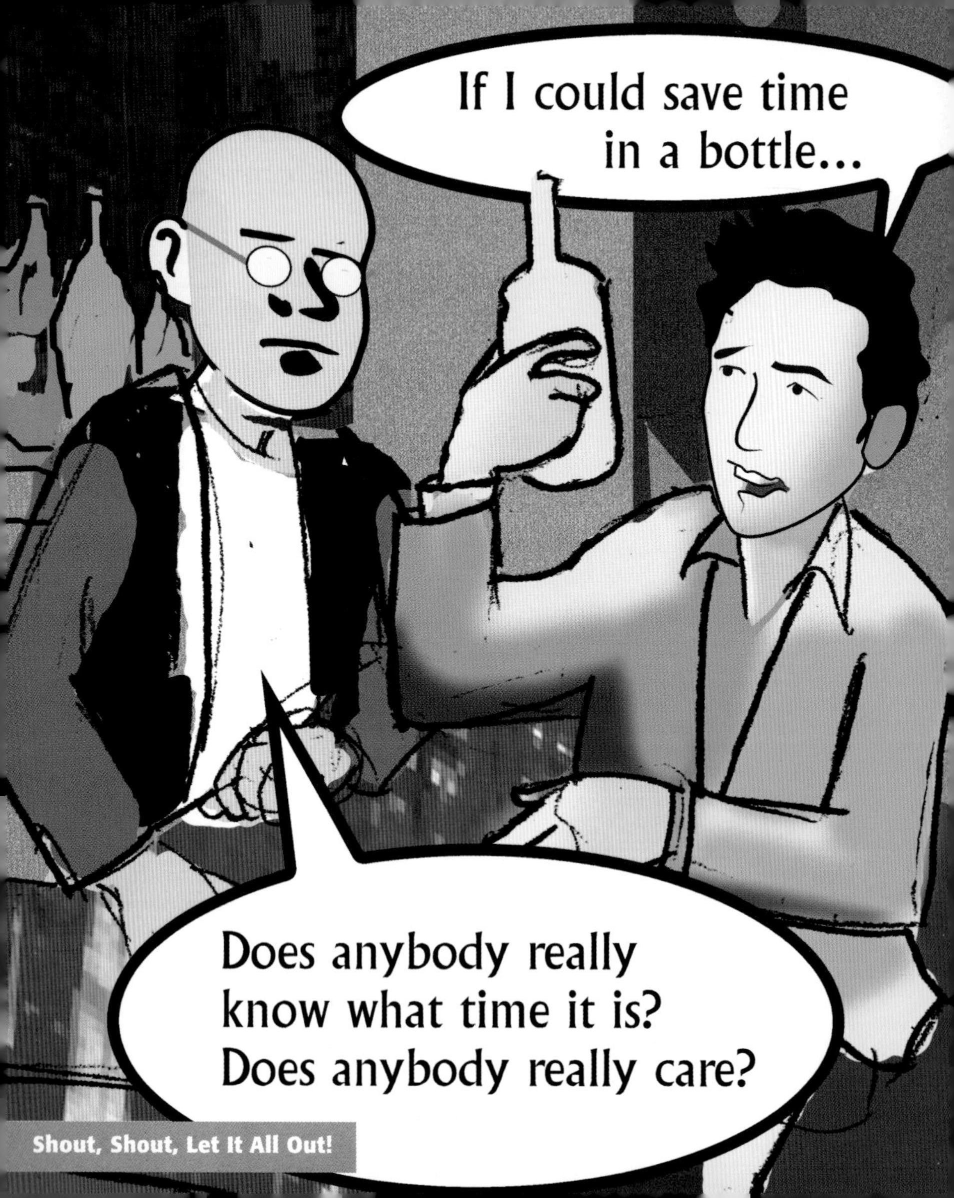
If I could save time in a bottle...
Does anybody really know what time it is? Does anybody really care?

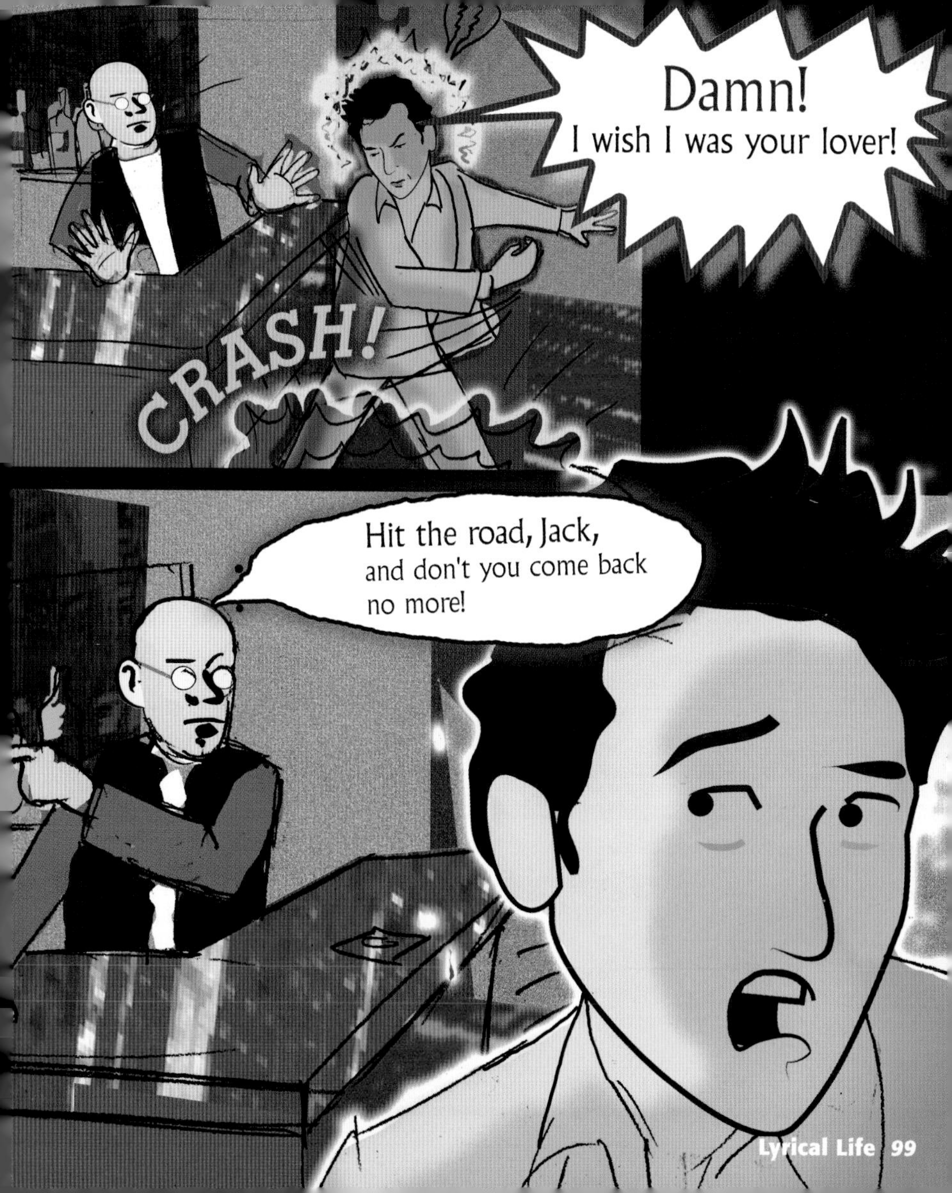
Damn!
I wish I was your lover!
CRASH!
Hit the road, Jack, and don't you come back no more!

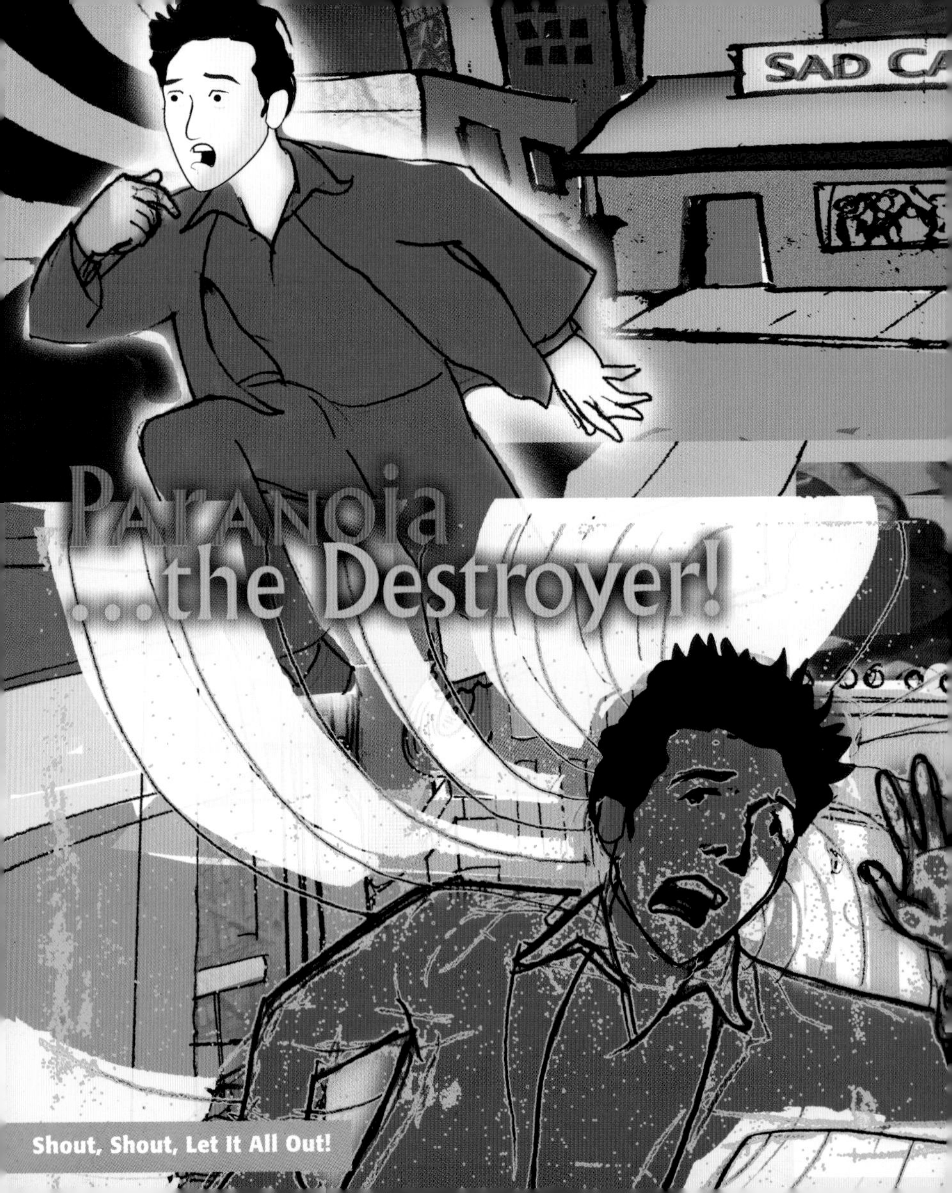

Paranoia ...the Destroyer!

Shout, Shout, Let It All Out!

Homeward Bound

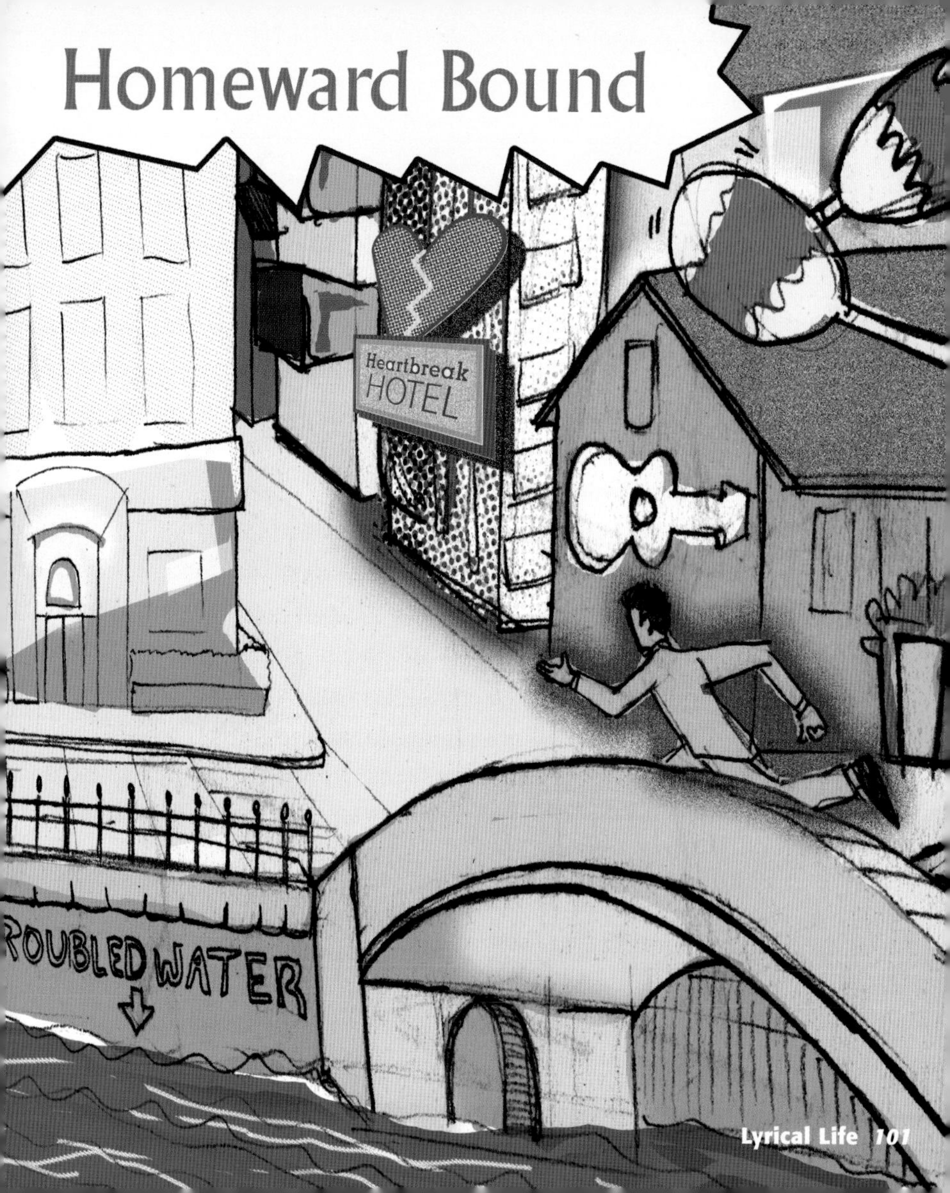
Heartbreak
HOTEL
ROUBLED WATER

Alone Again (Naturally)

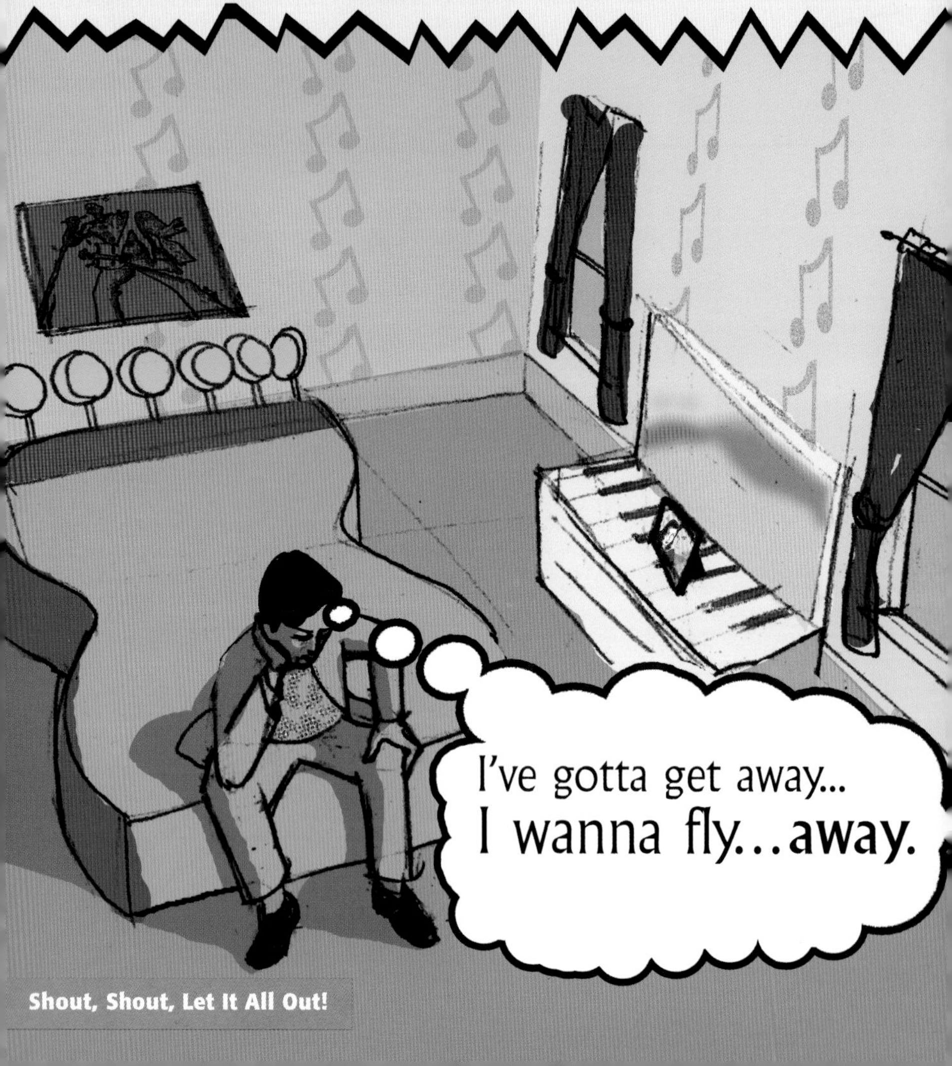
I've gotta get away...
I wanna fly...away.

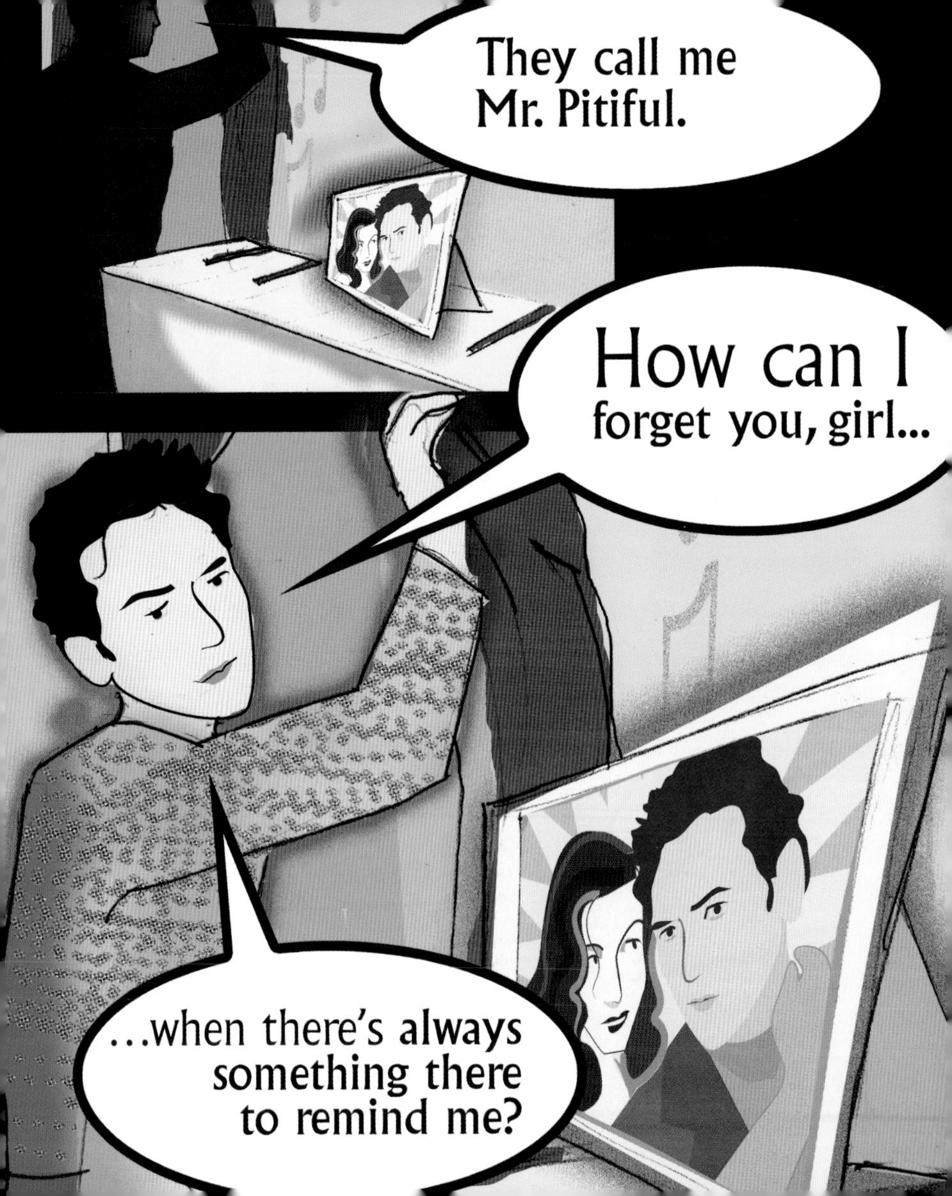

They call me Mr. Pitiful.
How can I forget you, girl...
...when there's always something there to remind me?

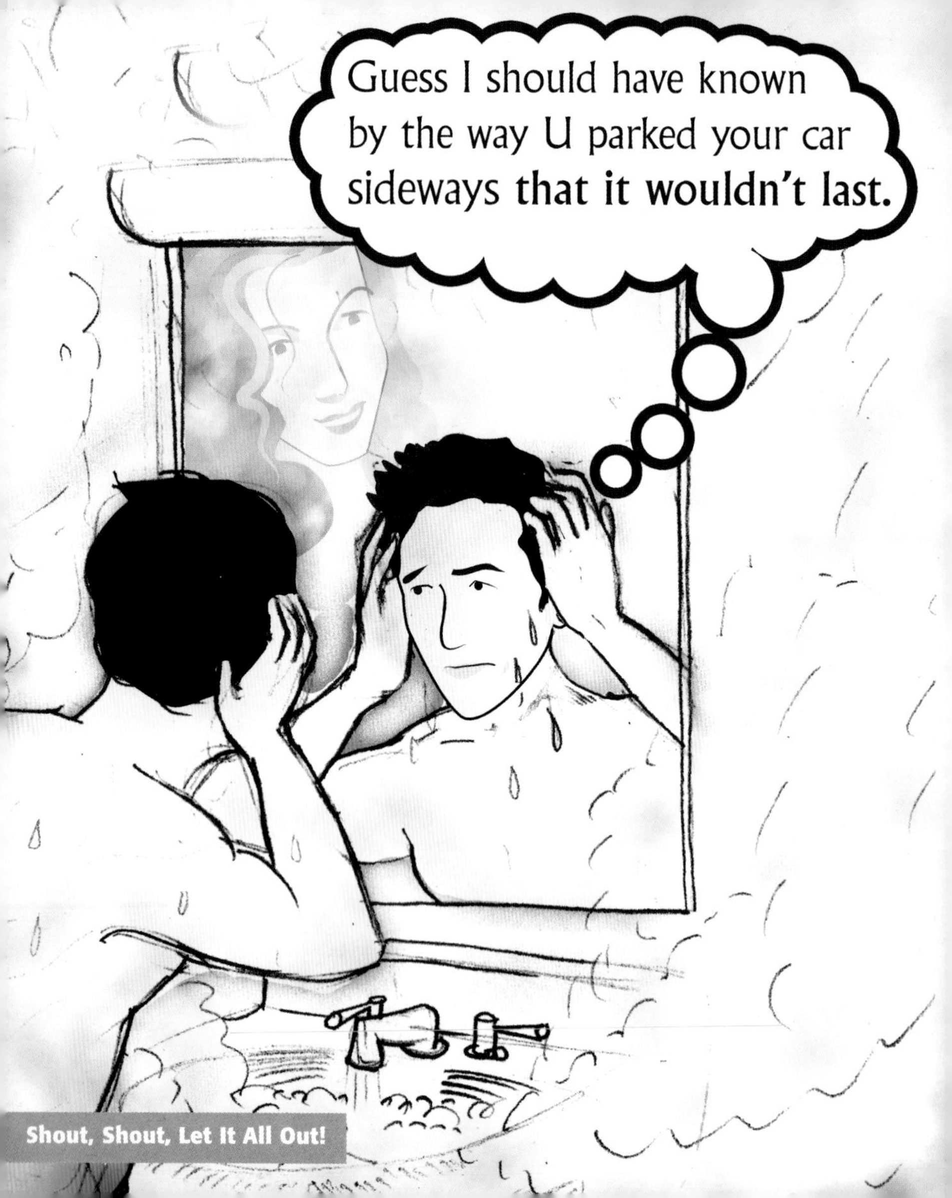
Guess I should have known by the way U parked your car sideways that it wouldn't last.

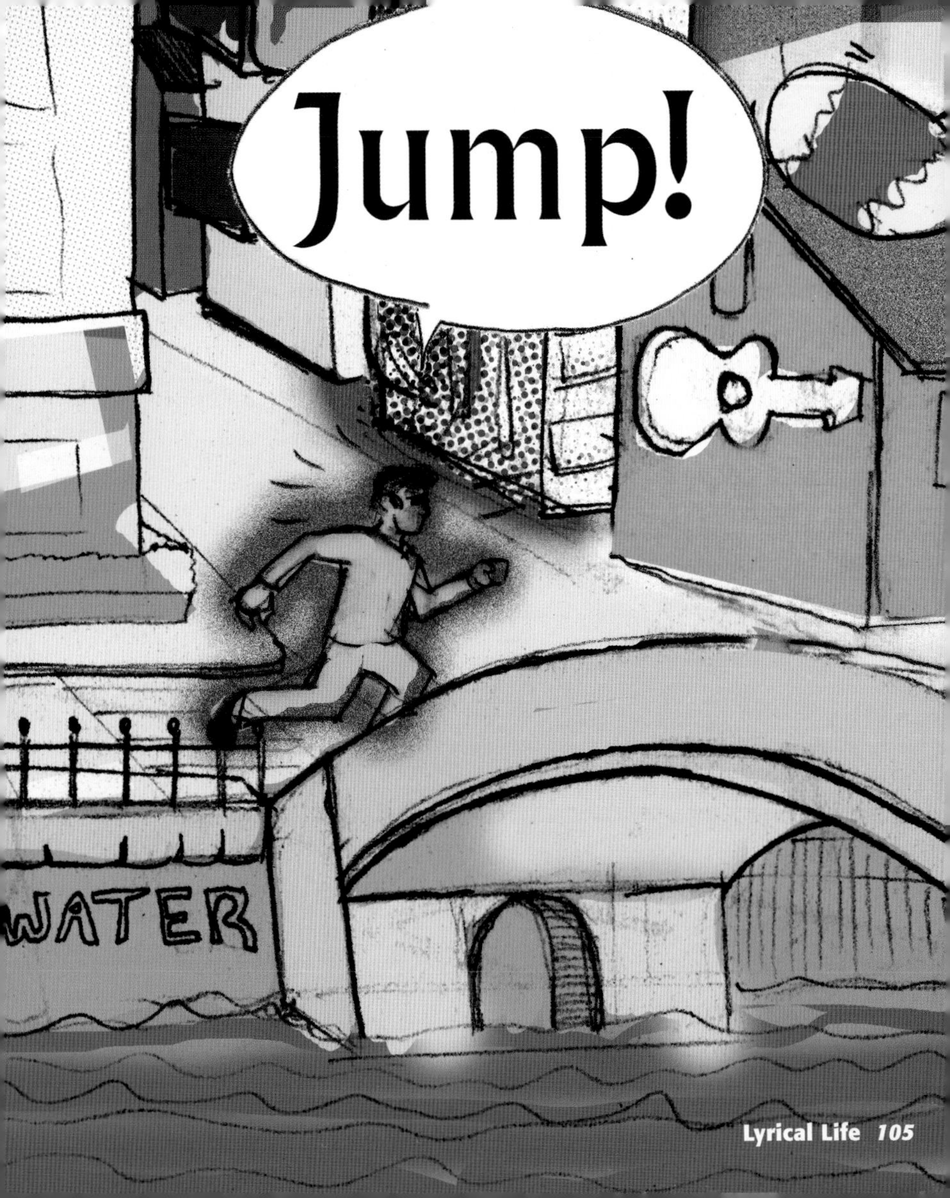
Jump!
WATER

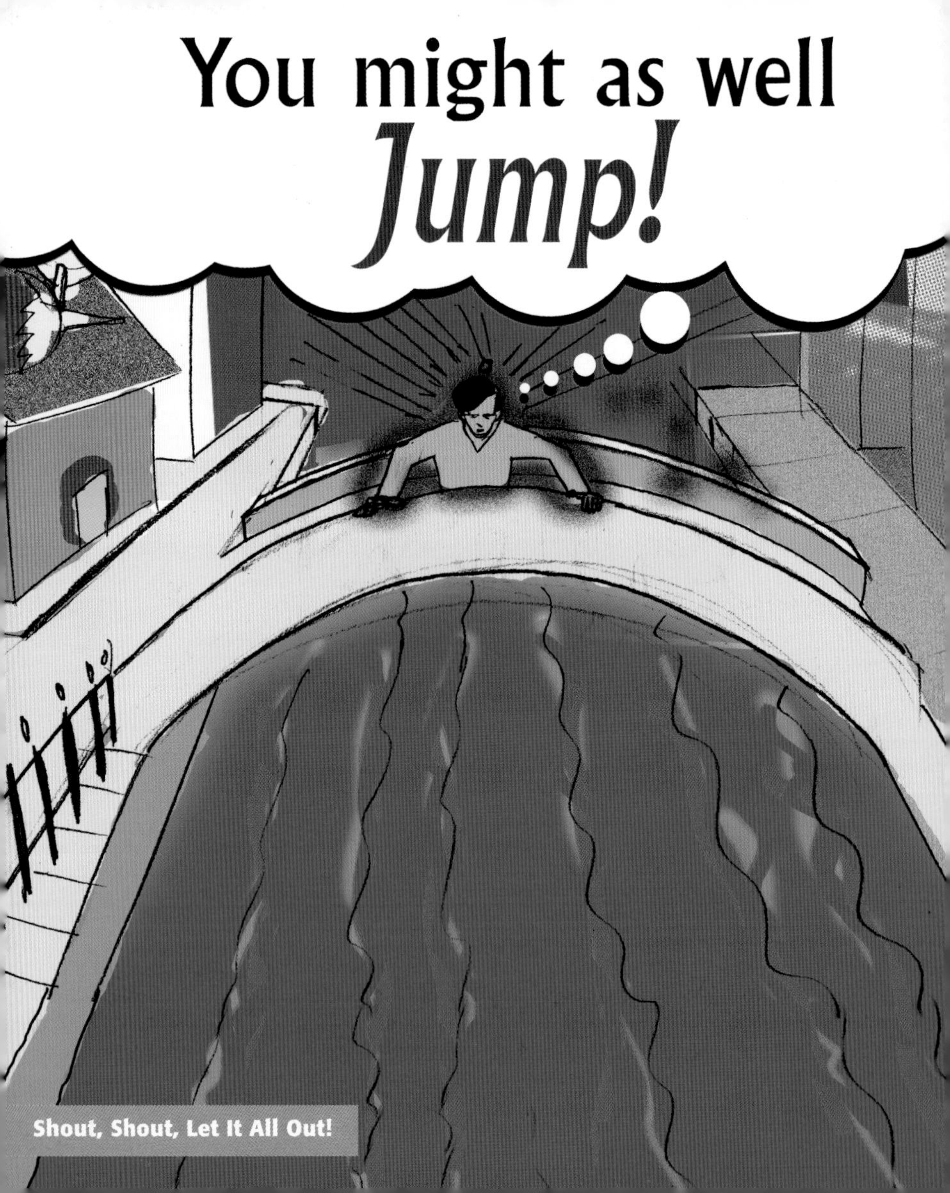
You might as well
Jump!

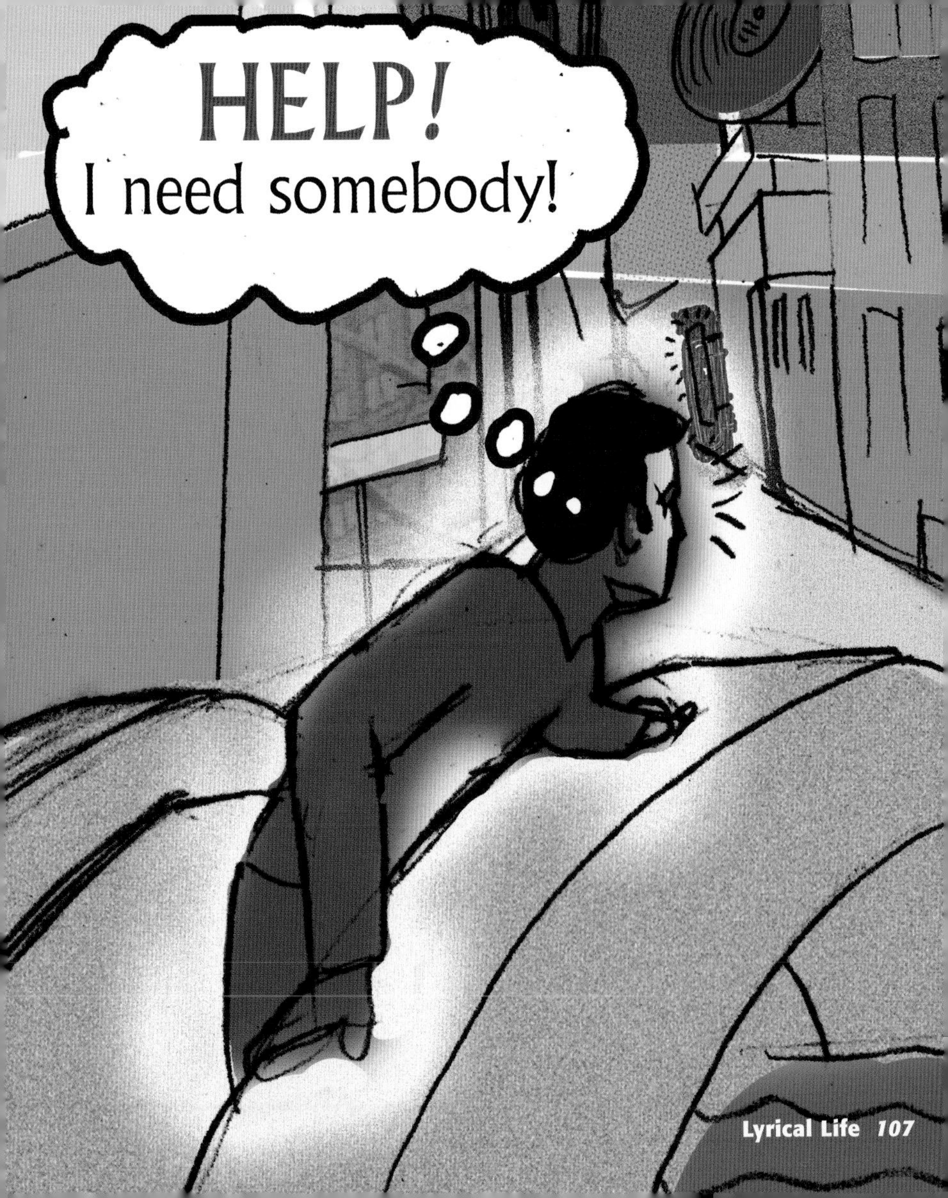
HELP!
I need somebody!

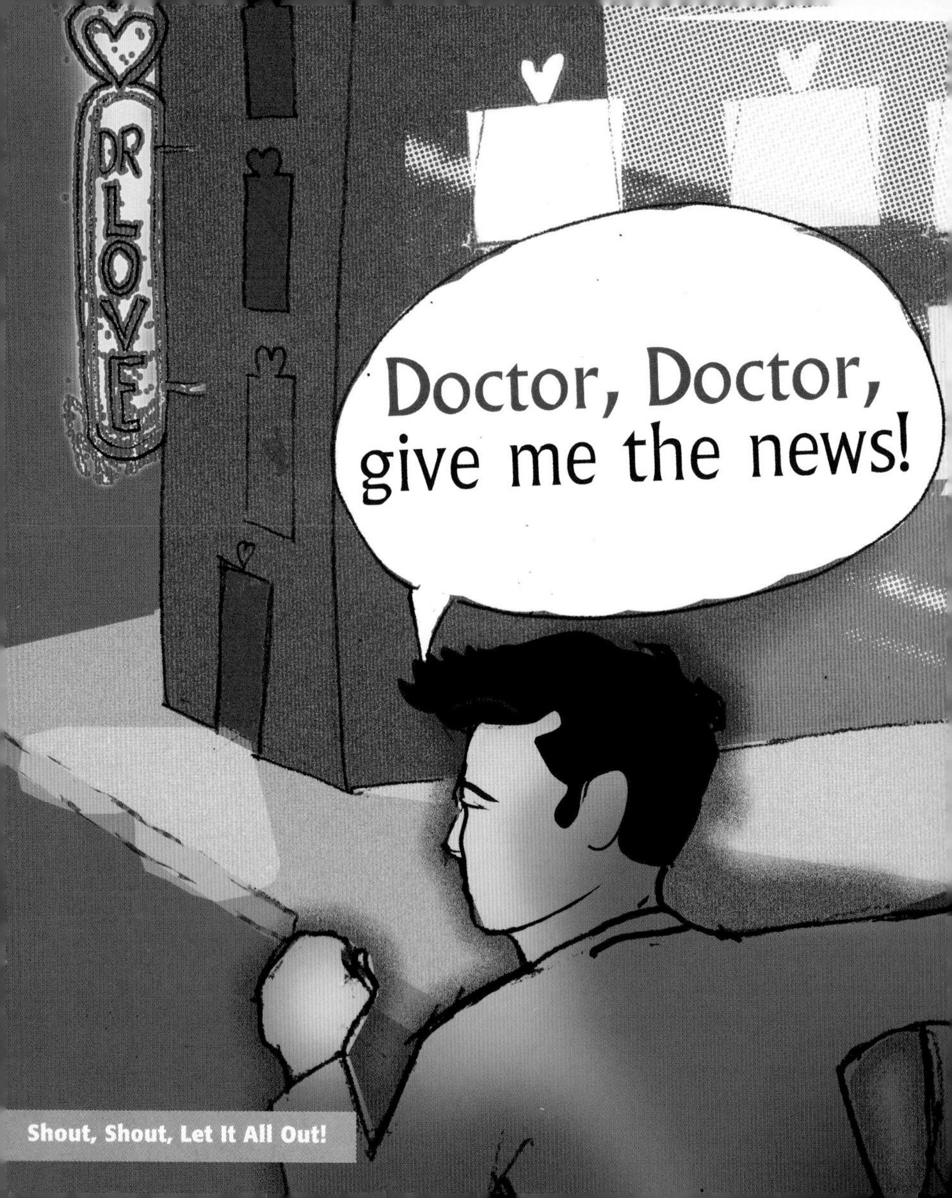
DR LOVE
Doctor, Doctor, give me the news!

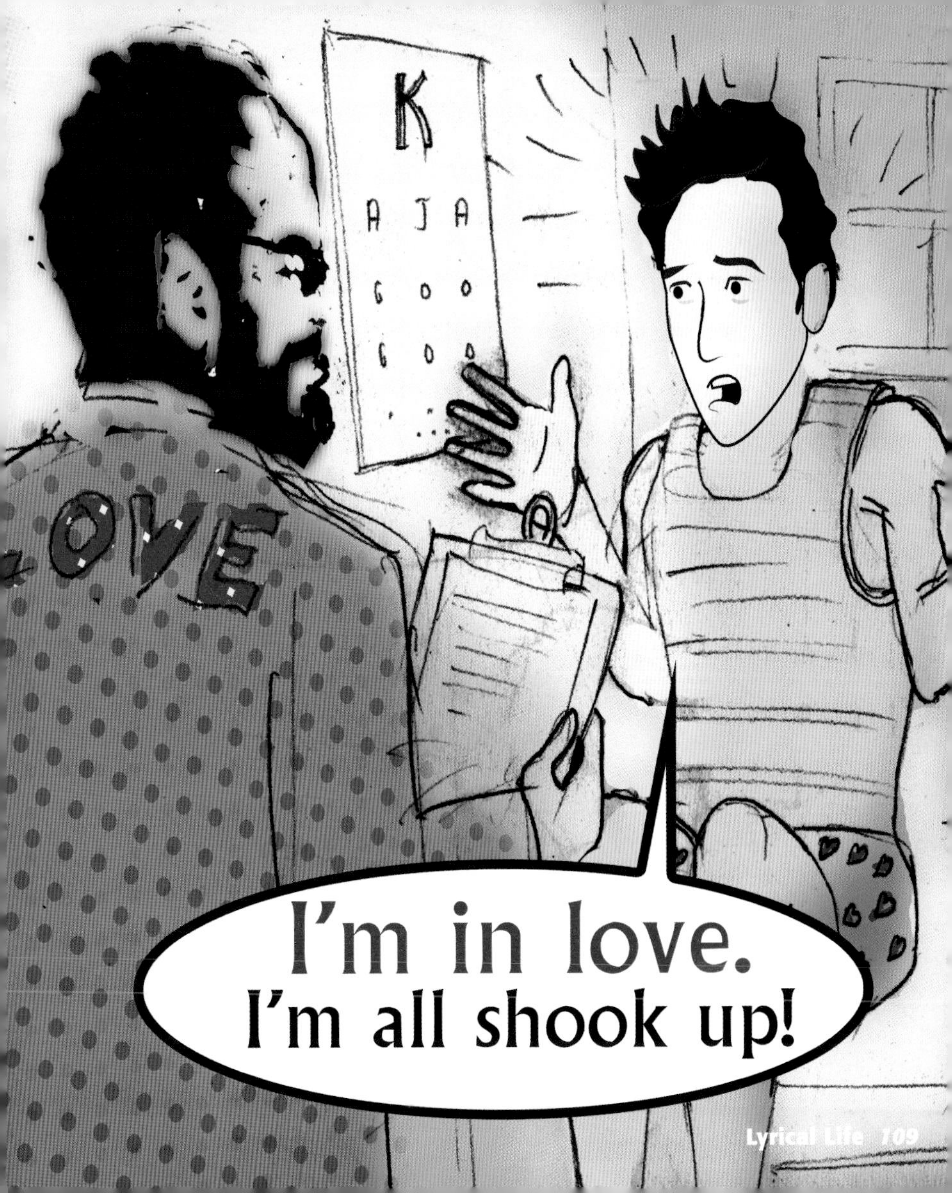
K
A J A
G O O
G O D
LOVE
I'm in love.
I'm all shook up!

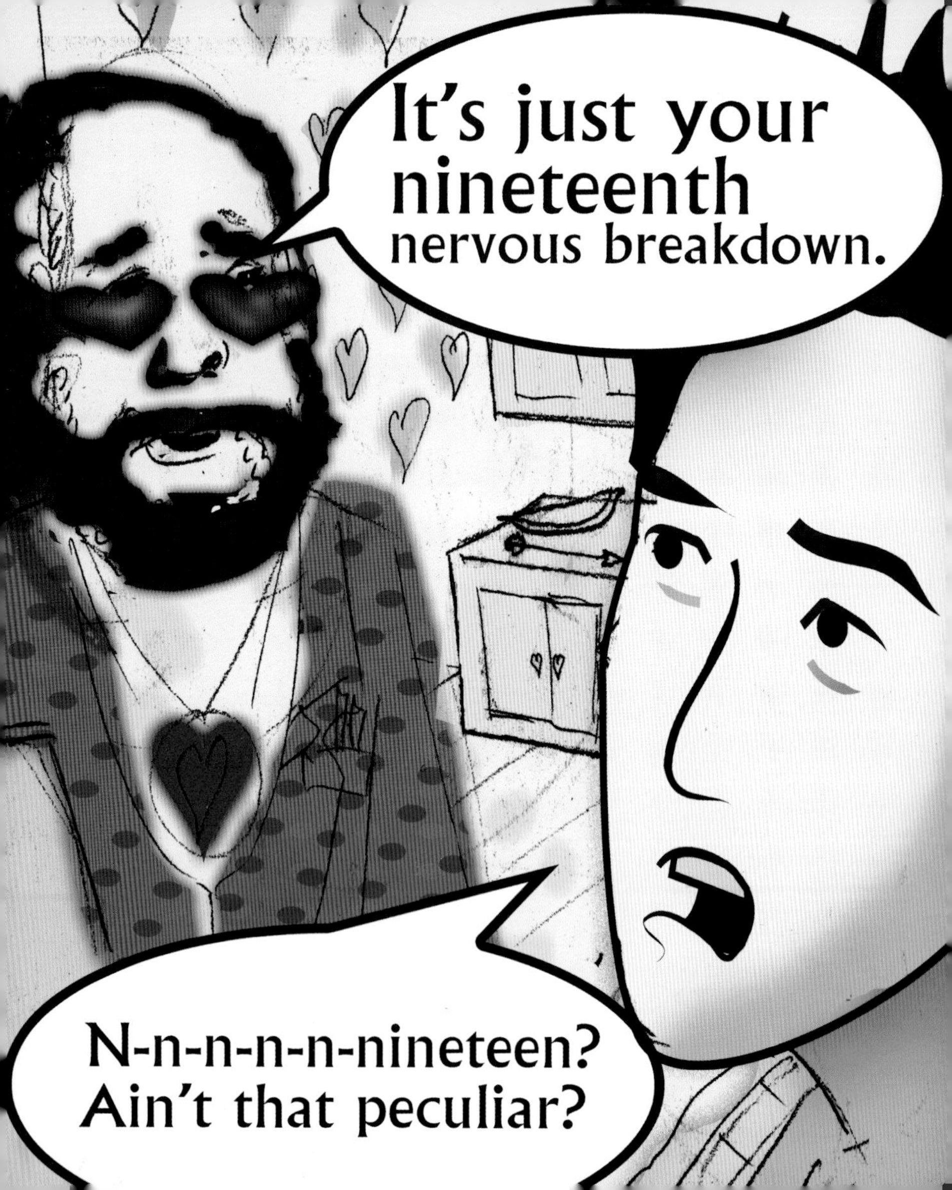
It's just your nineteenth nervous breakdown.
N-n-n-n-n-nineteen? Ain't that peculiar?

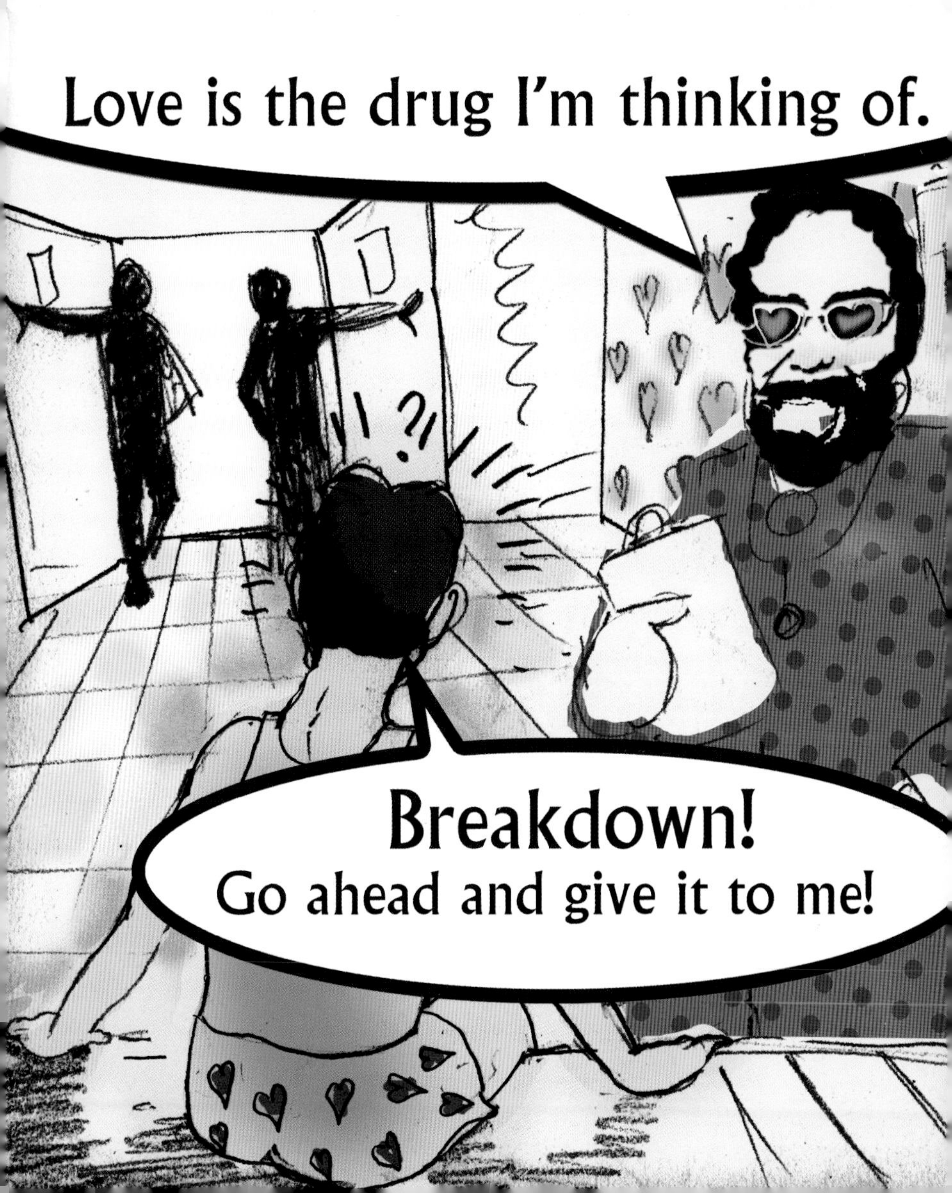
Love is the drug I'm thinking of.
?!
Breakdown!
Go ahead and give it to me!

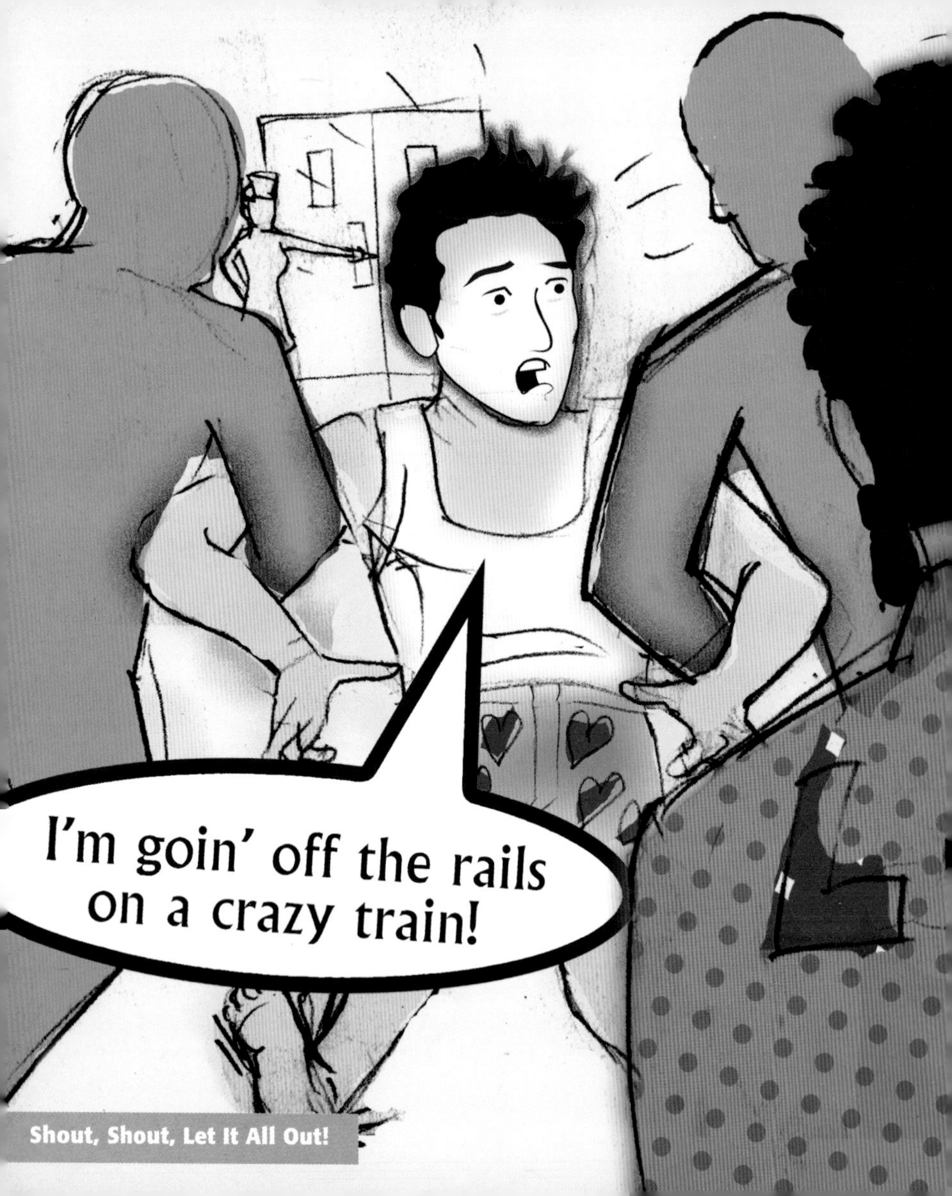
I'm goin' off the rails on a crazy train!

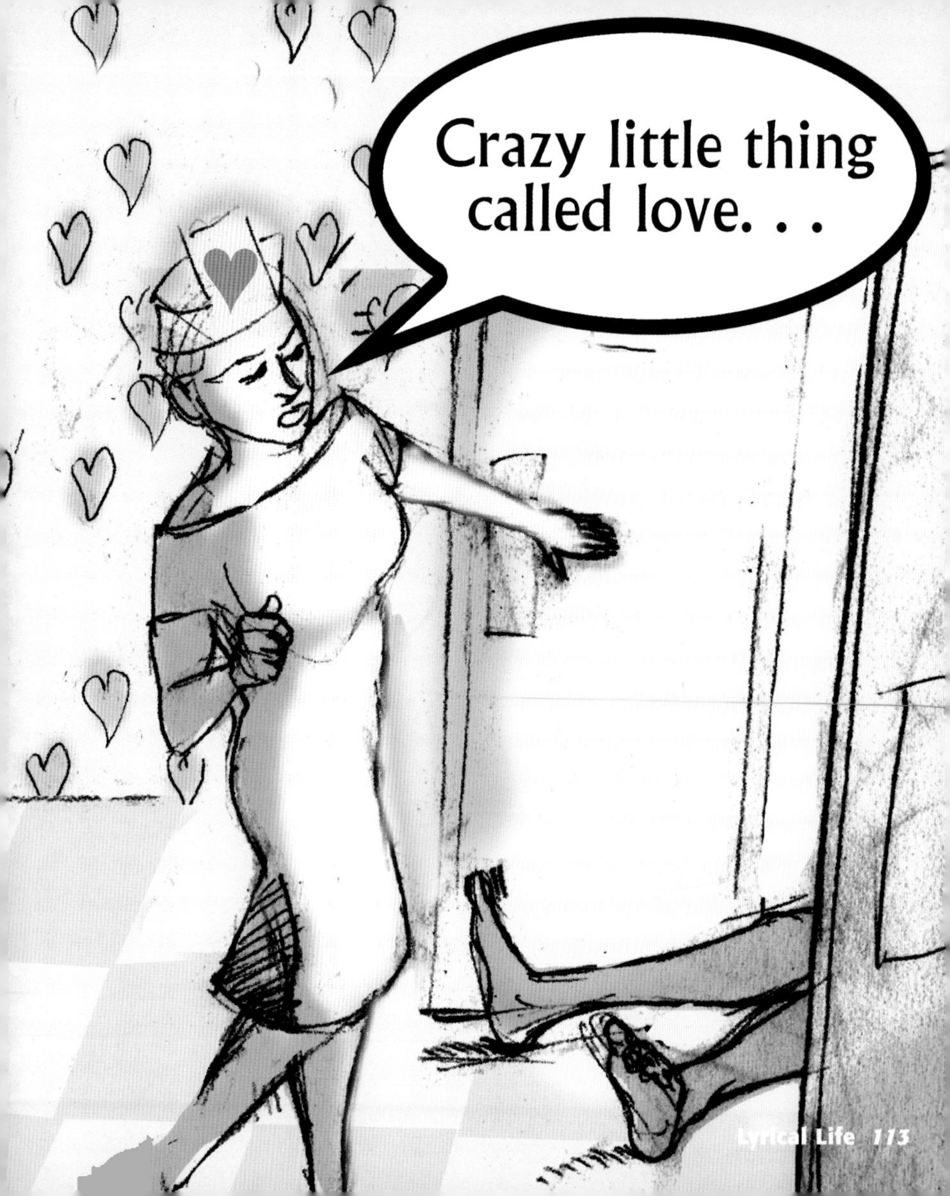
Crazy little thing called love. . .

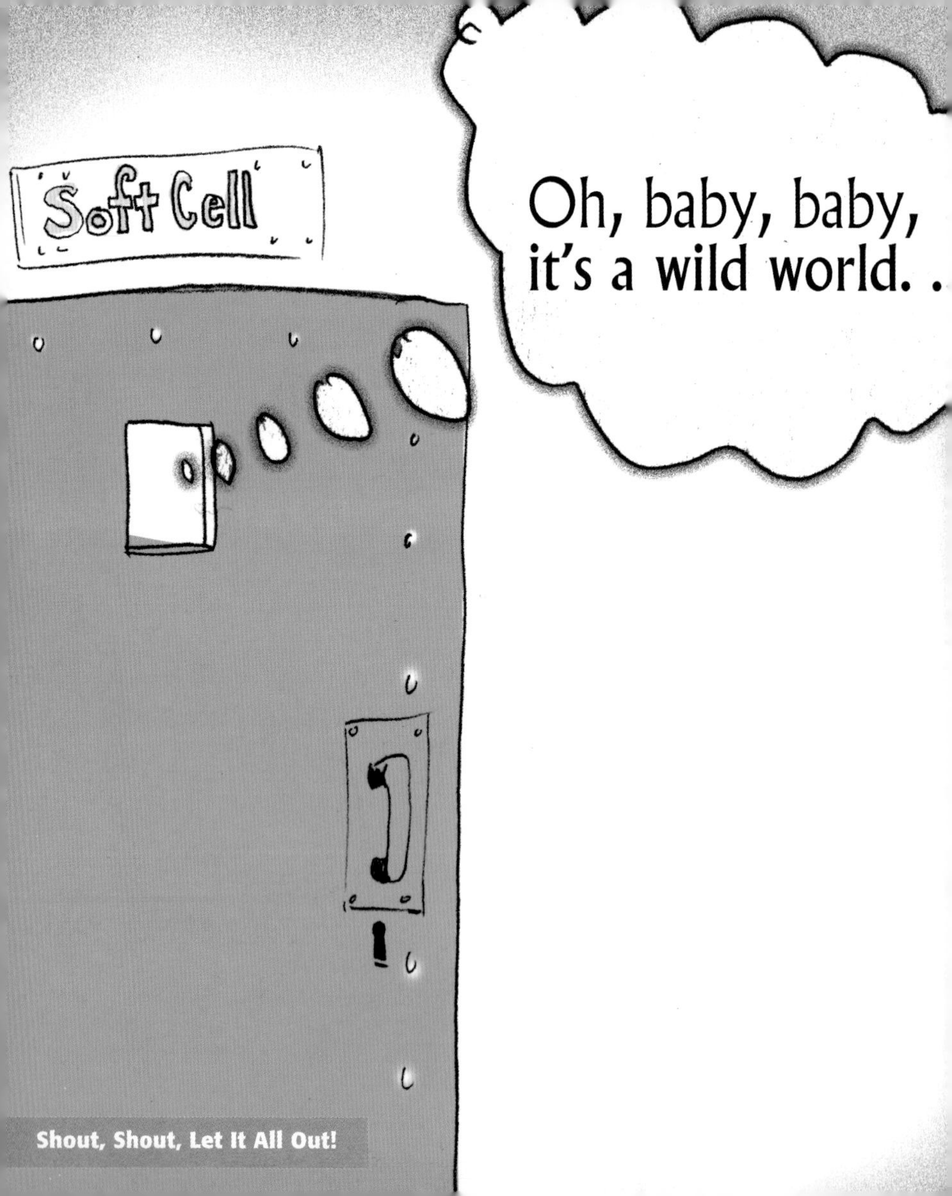
Soft Cell
Oh, baby, baby, it's a wild world. .

Shout, Shout, Let It All Out!

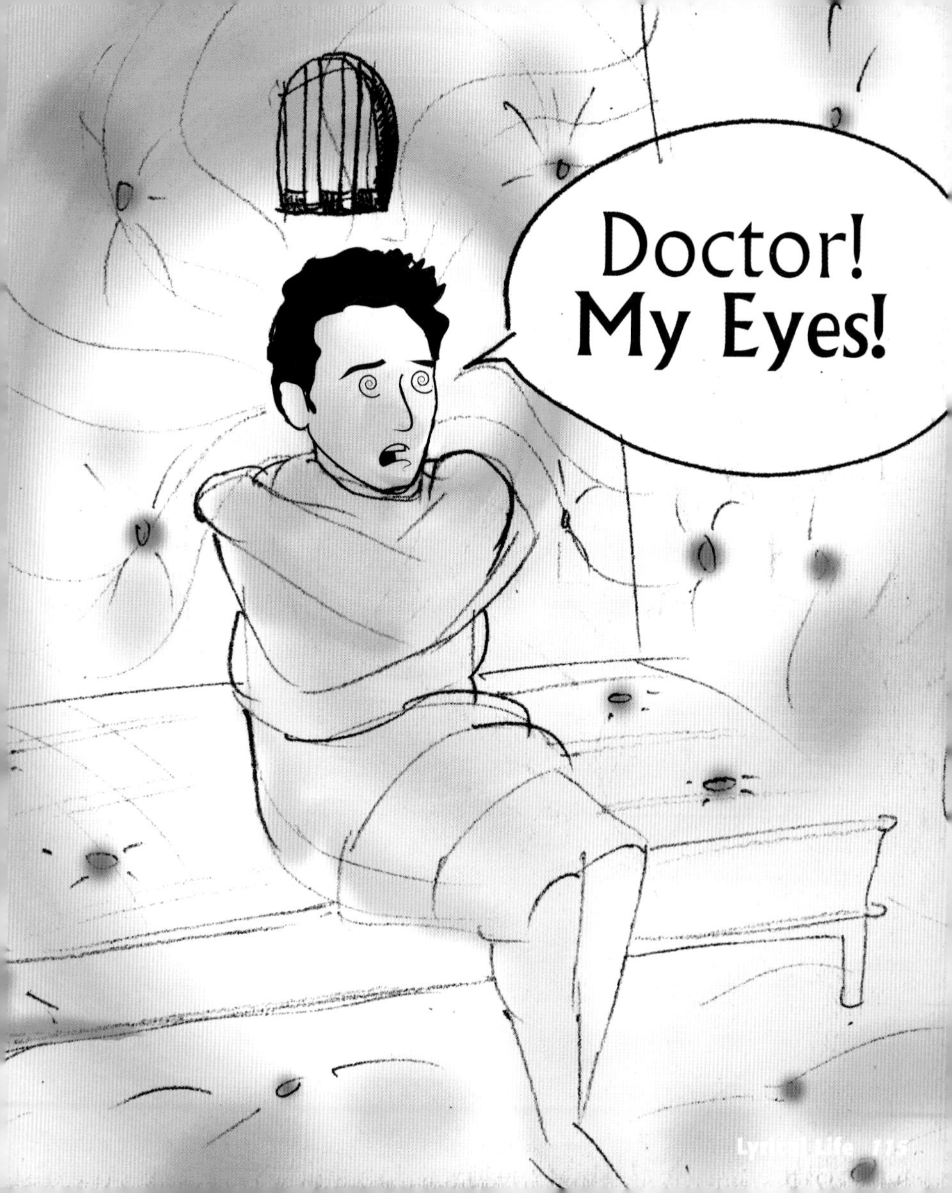
Doctor! My Eyes!

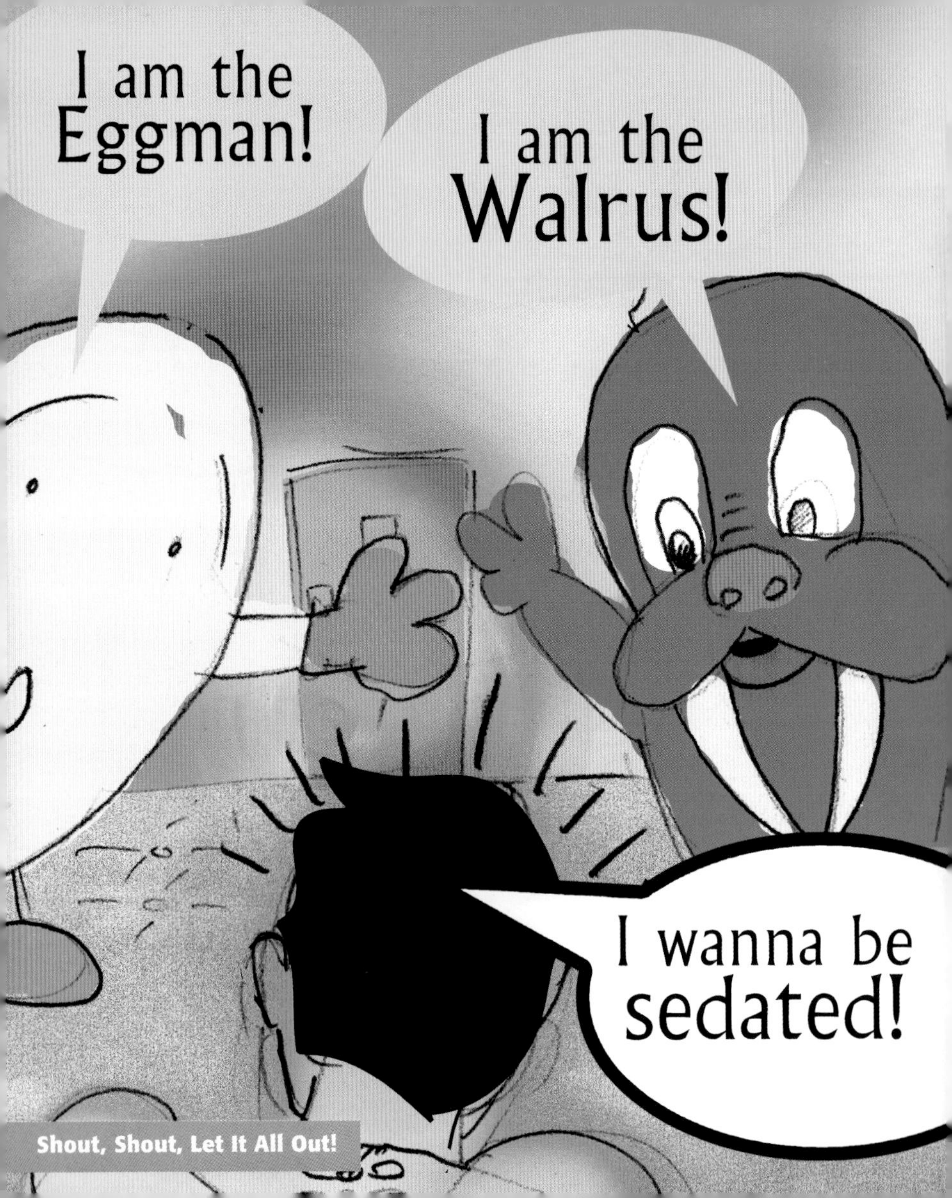
I am the Eggman!
I am the Walrus!
I wanna be sedated!

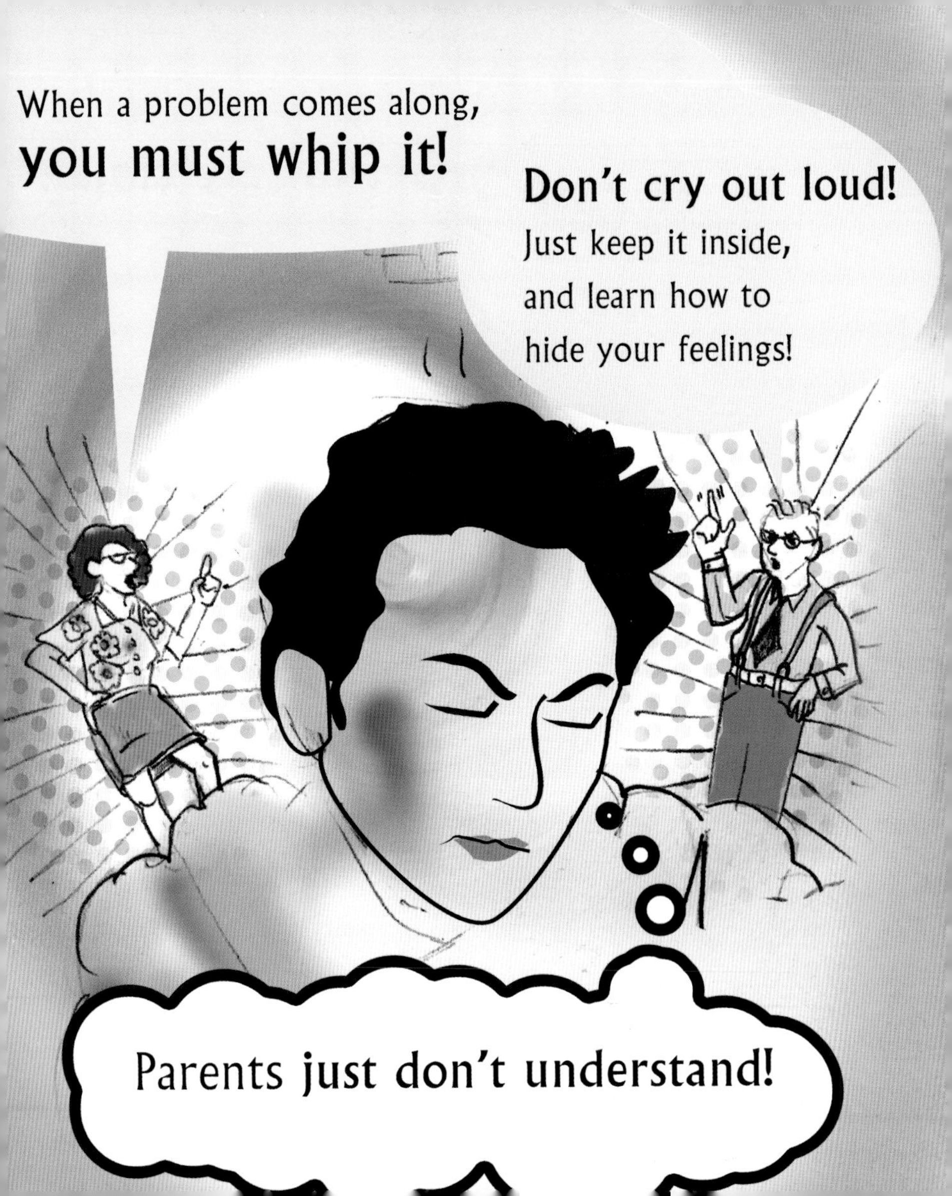
When a problem comes along, you must whip it!
Don't cry out loud! Just keep it inside, and learn how to hide your feelings!
Parents just don't understand!

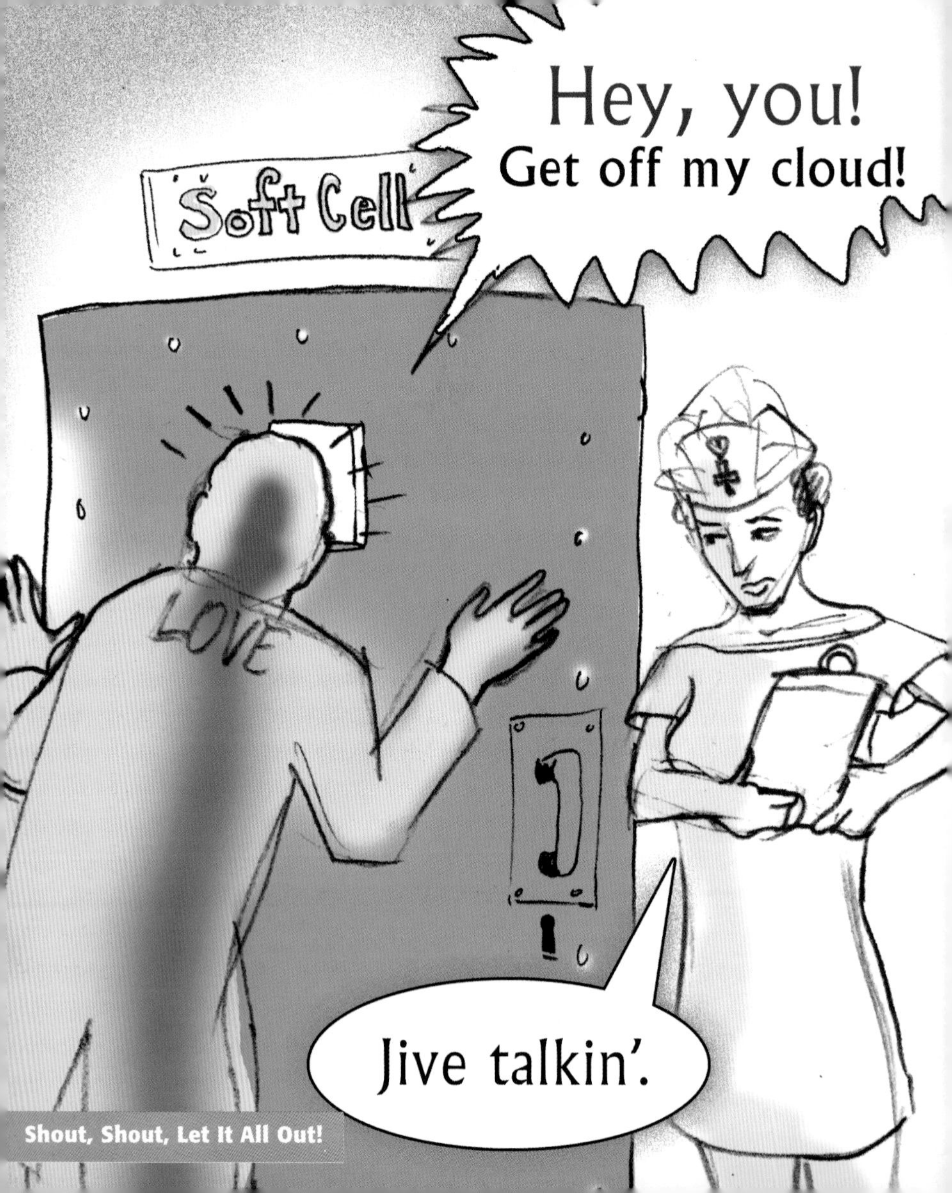
Soft Cell
Hey, you! Get off my cloud!
LOVE
Jive talkin'.

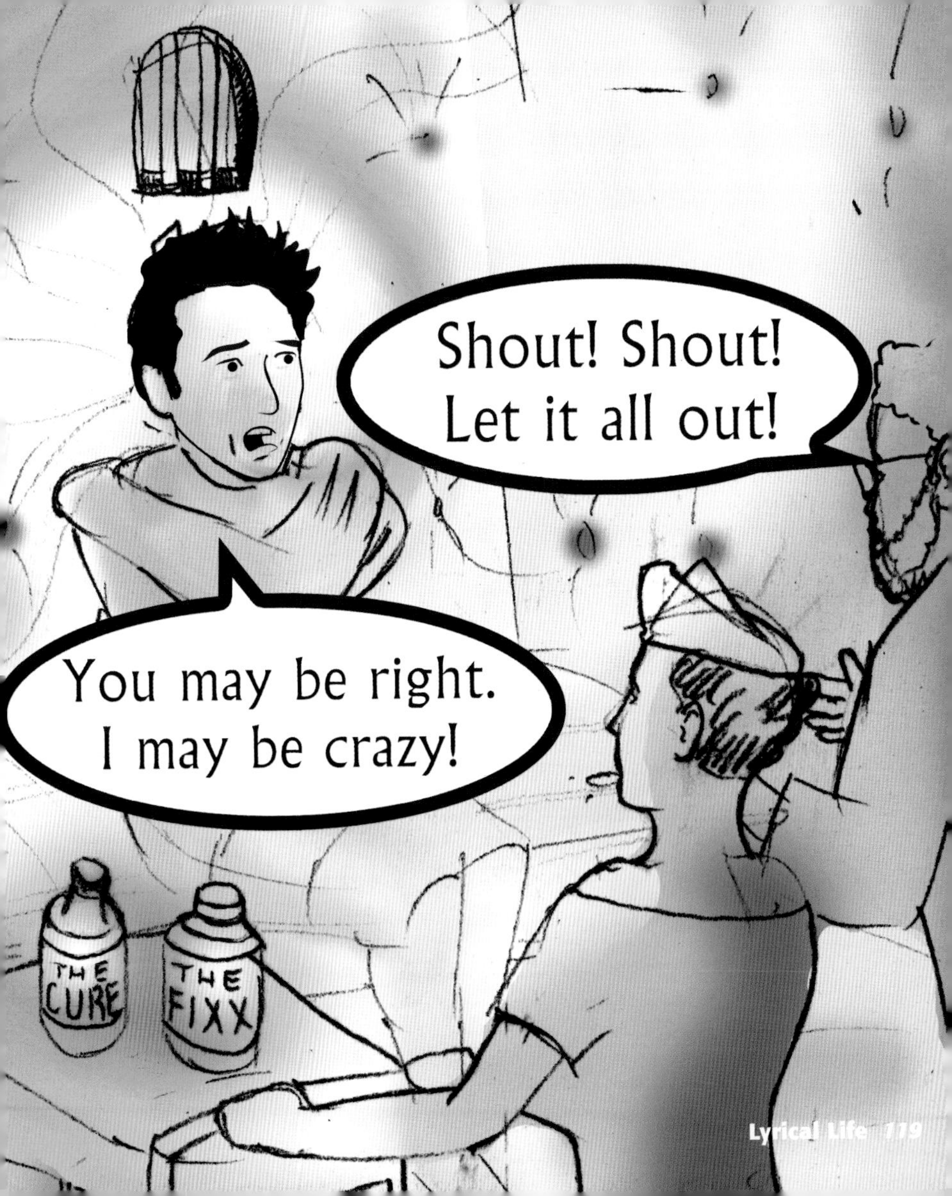
Shout! Shout! Let it all out!
You may be right. I may be crazy!
THE CURE
THE FIXX

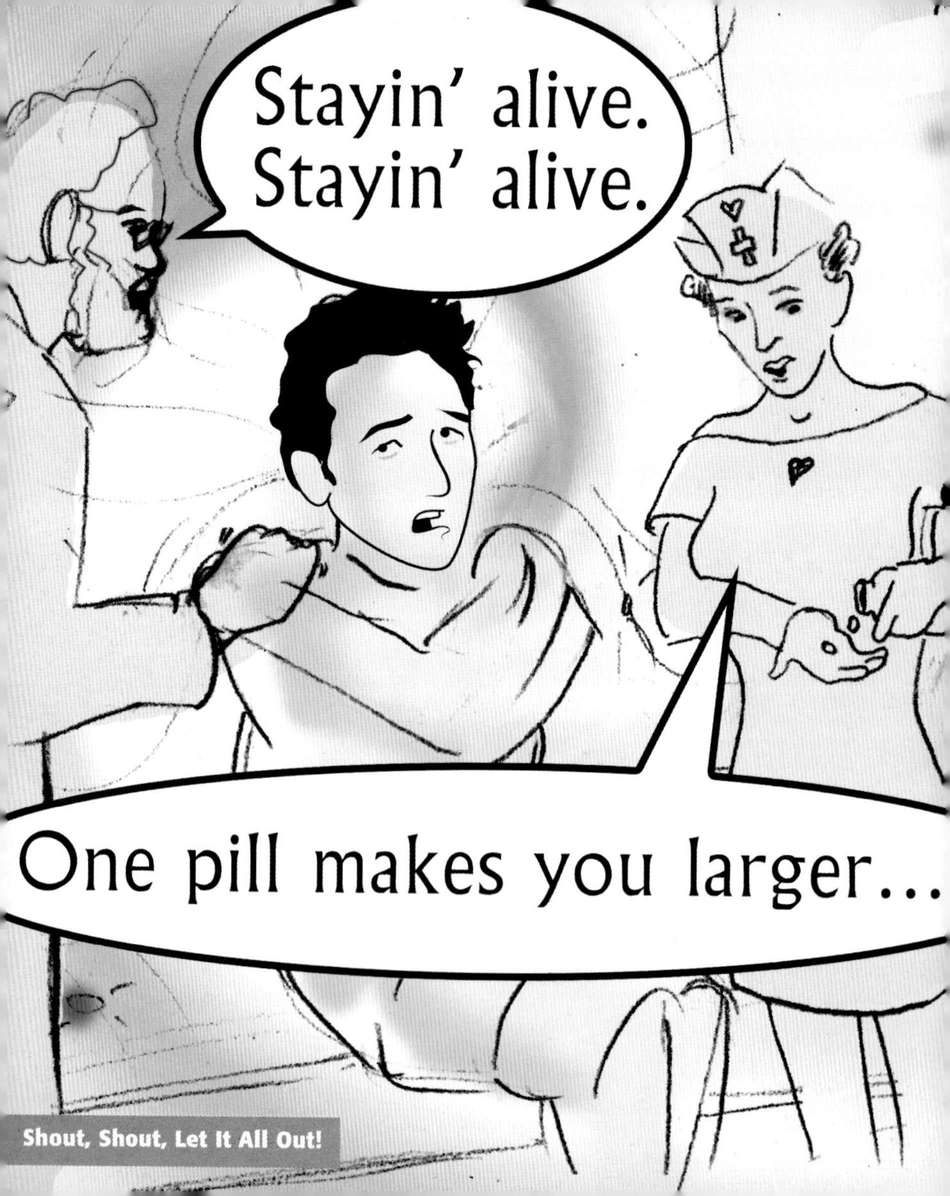
Stayin' alive. Stayin' alive.
One pill makes you larger...
Shout, Shout, Let It All Out!

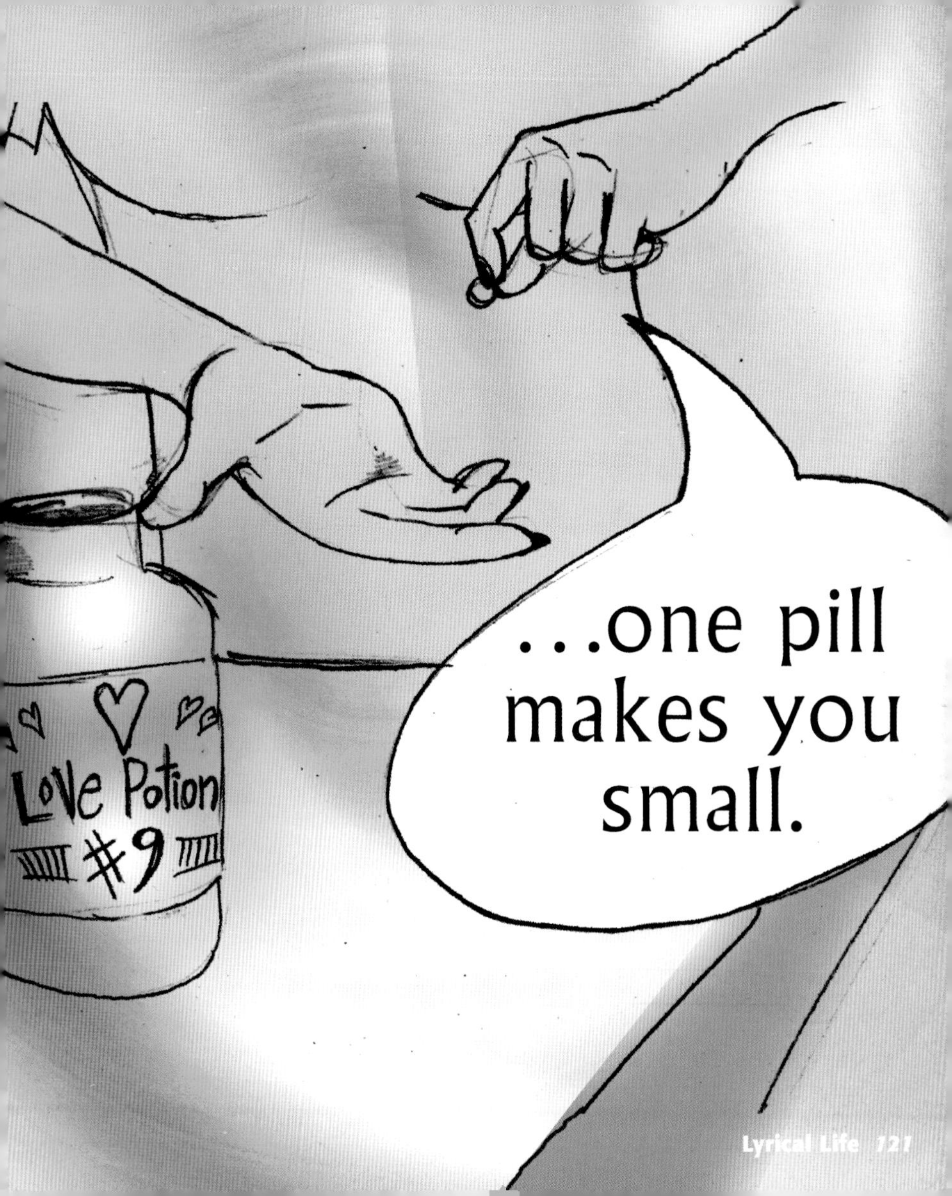
Love Potion
#9
...one pill
makes you
small.

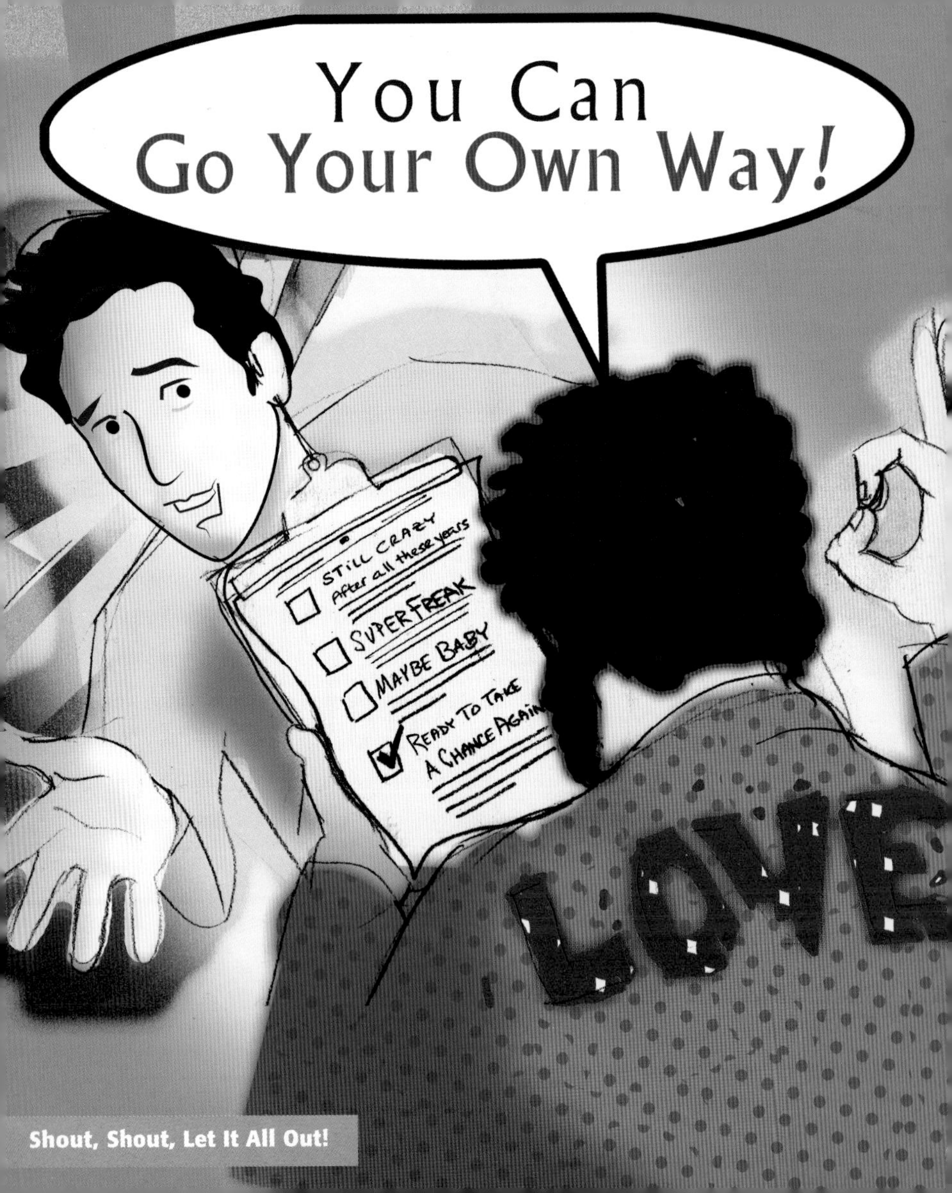
You Can Go Your Own Way!
STILL CRAZY After all these years
SUPERFREAK
MAYBE BABY
READY TO TAKE A CHANCE AGAIN
LOVE

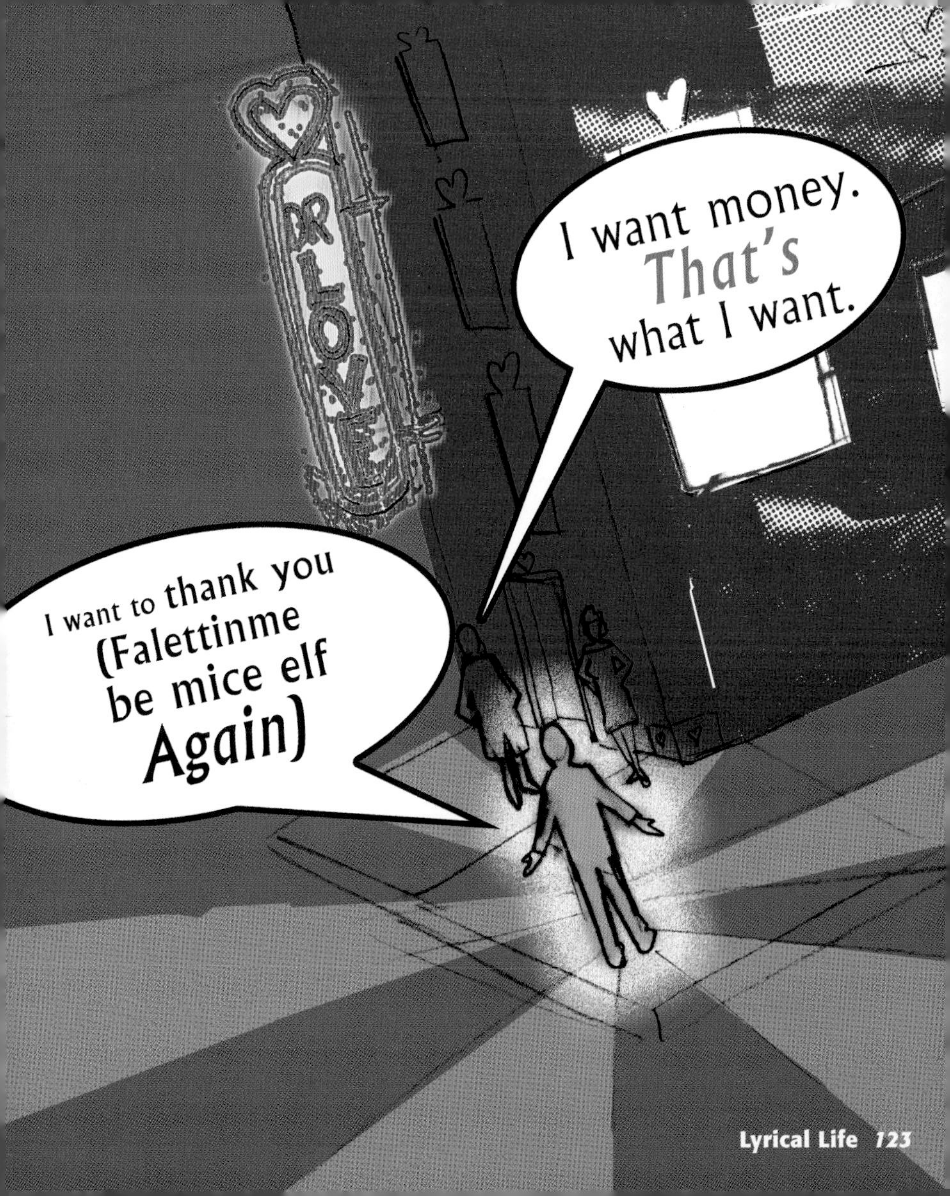
I want money. That's what I want.
I want to thank you (Falettinme be mice elf Again)
DR LOVE

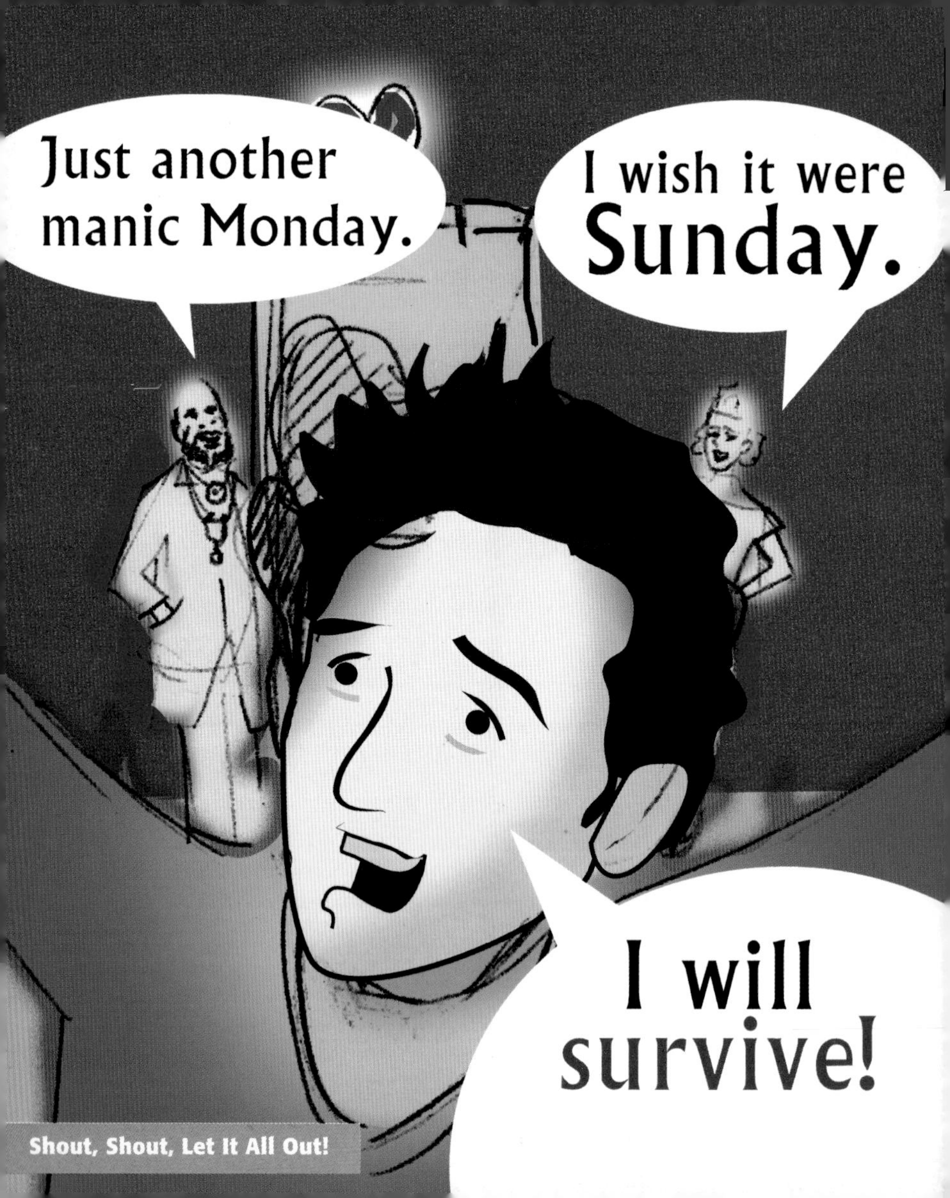
Just another manic Monday.
I wish it were Sunday.
I will survive!
Shout, Shout, Let It All Out!

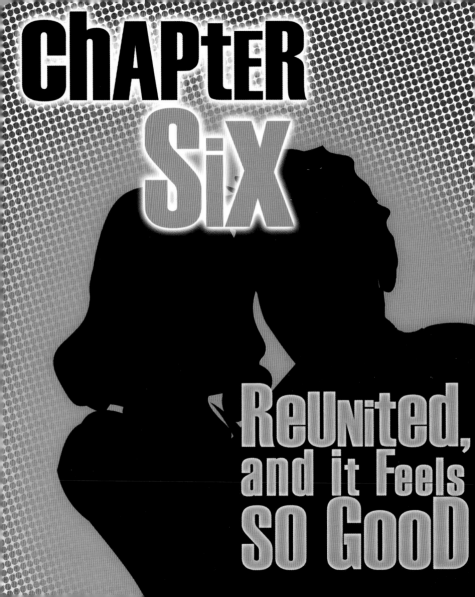

CHAPTER SIX

ReUnited, and it Feels SO GooD

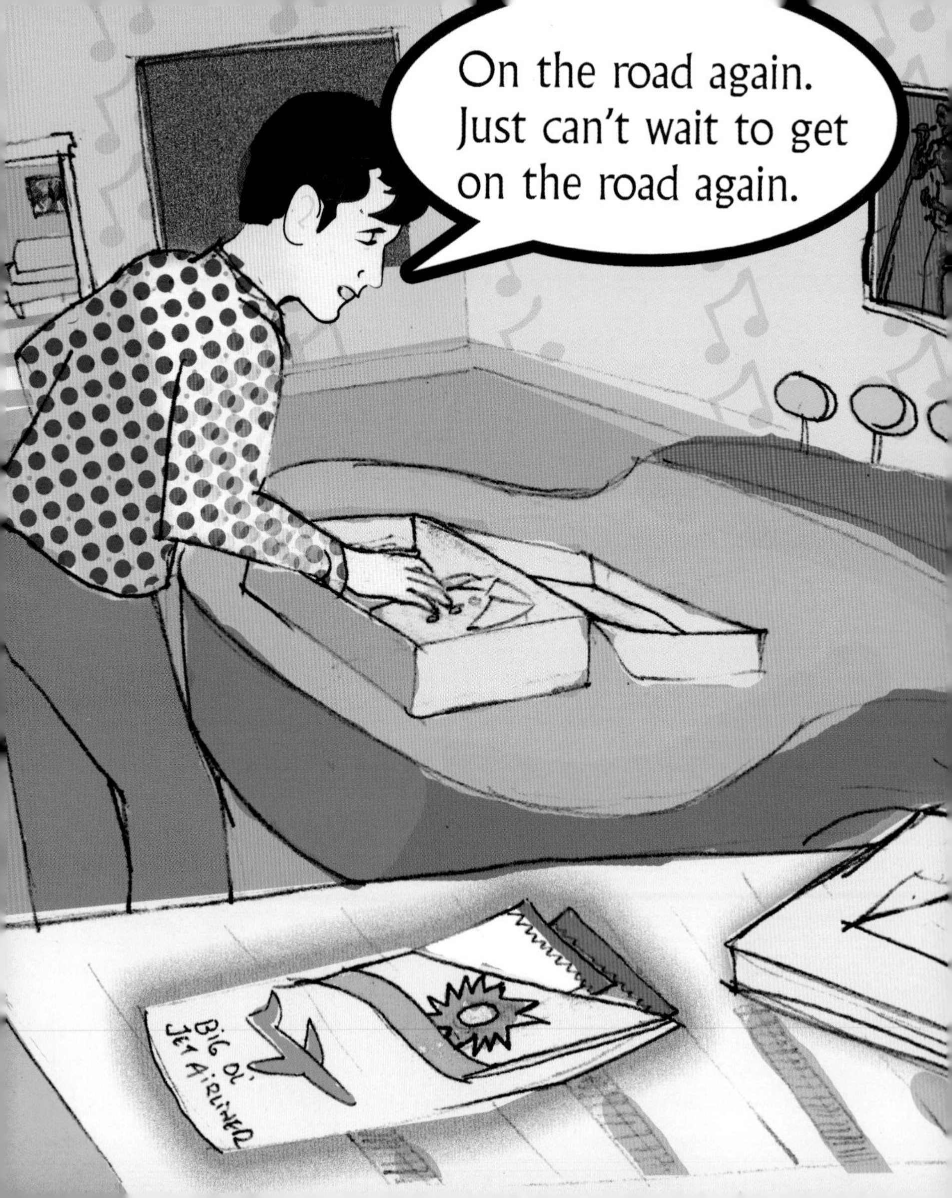
On the road again. Just can't wait to get on the road again.
BIG OL' JET AIRLINER

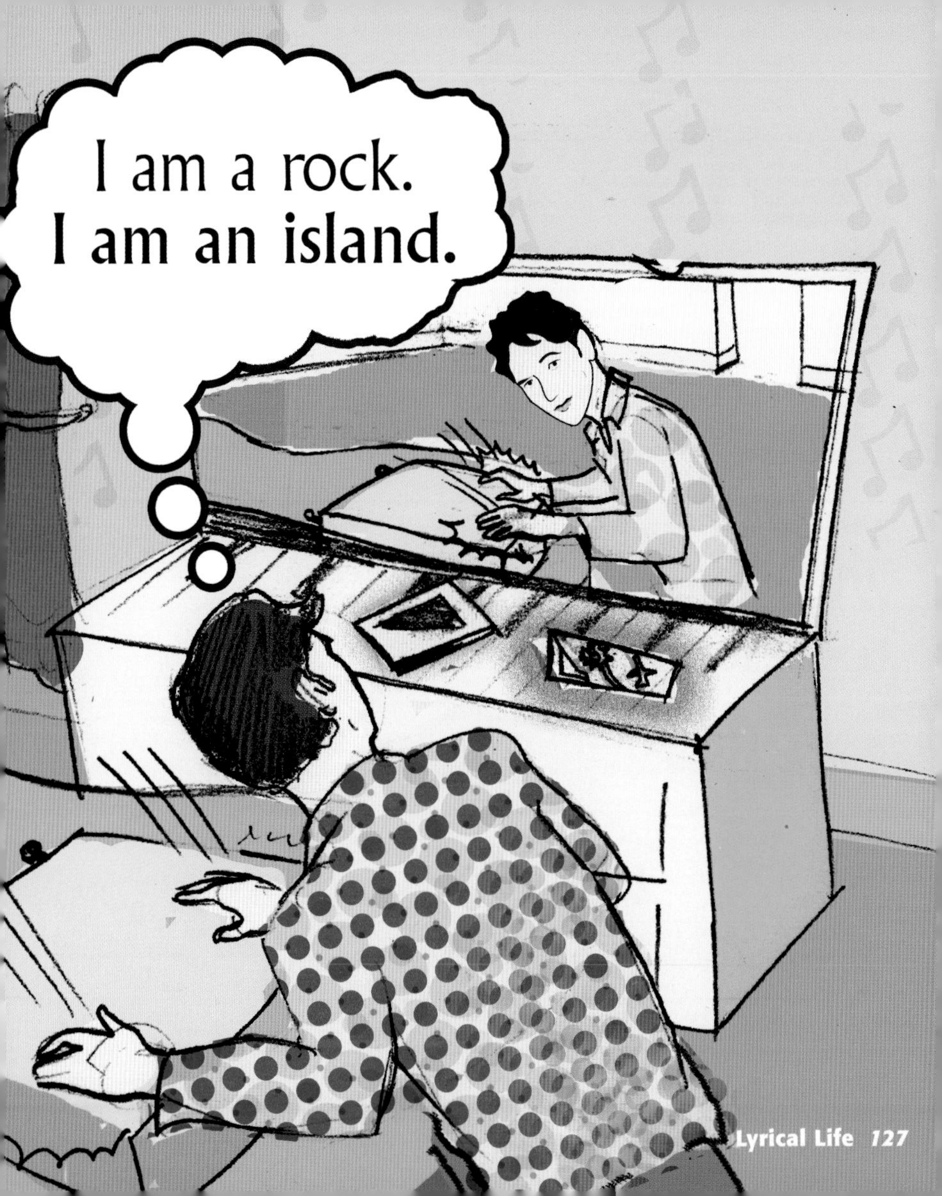
I am a rock.
I am an island.

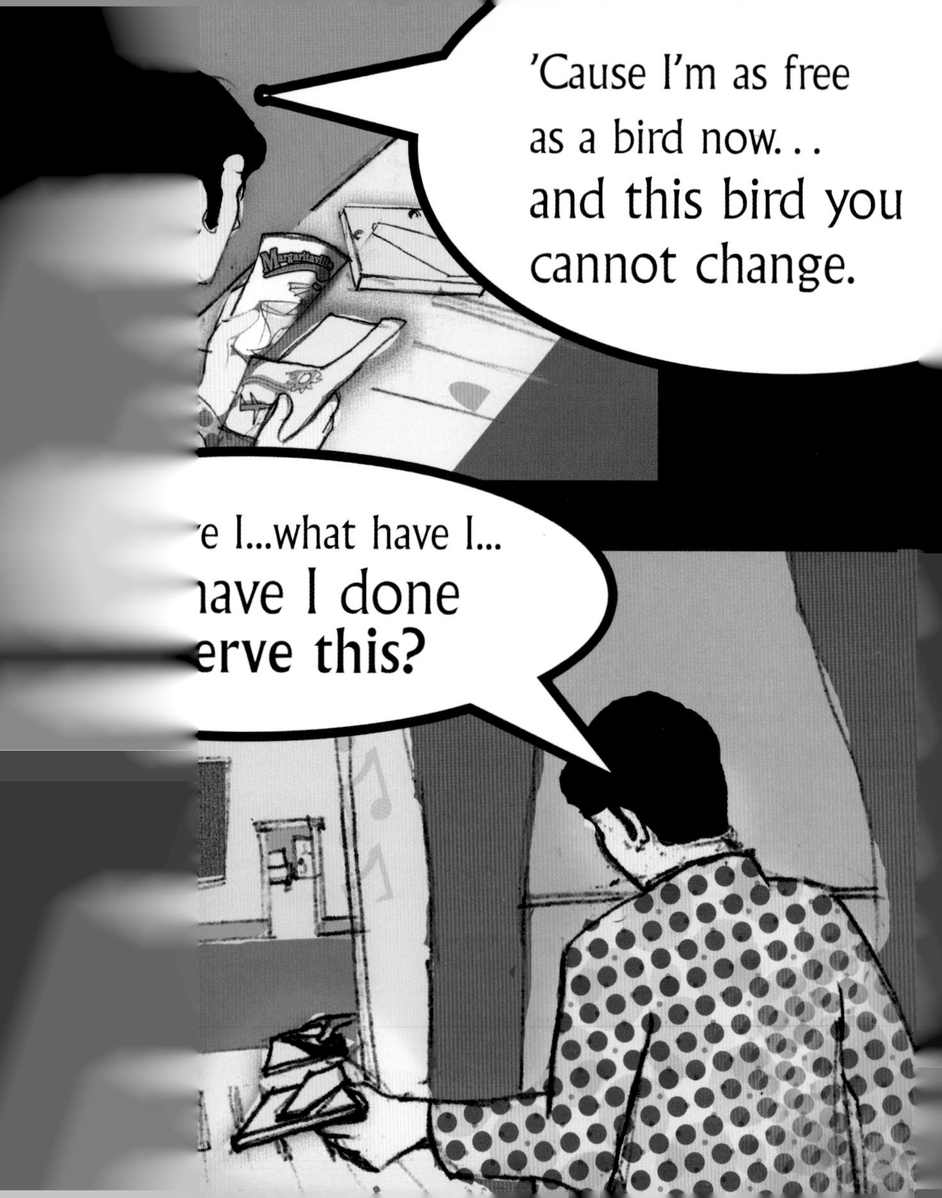
'Cause I'm as free as a bird now... and this bird you cannot change.
e I...what have I... ave I done erve this?

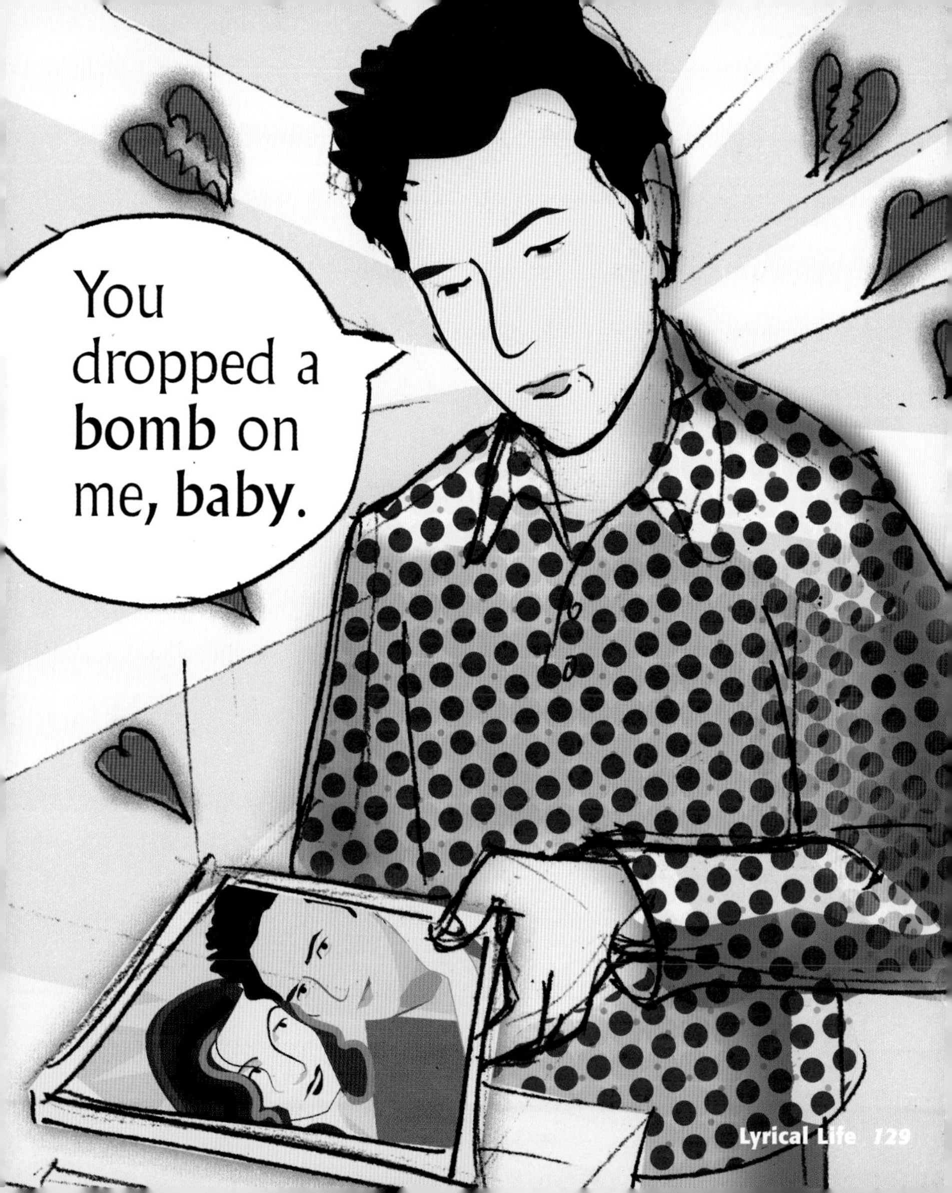
You dropped a bomb on me, baby.

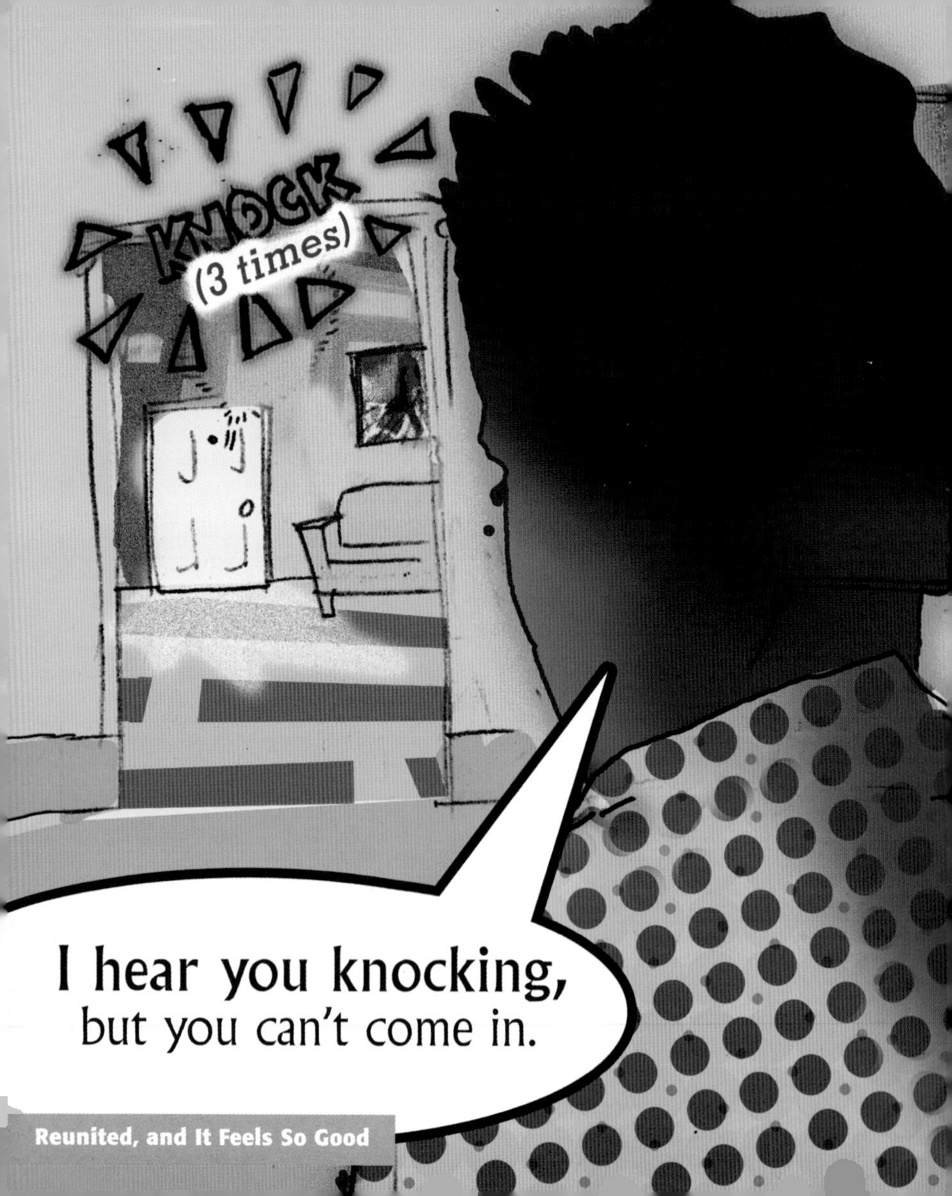
KNOCK
(3 times)
I hear you knocking,
but you can't come in.

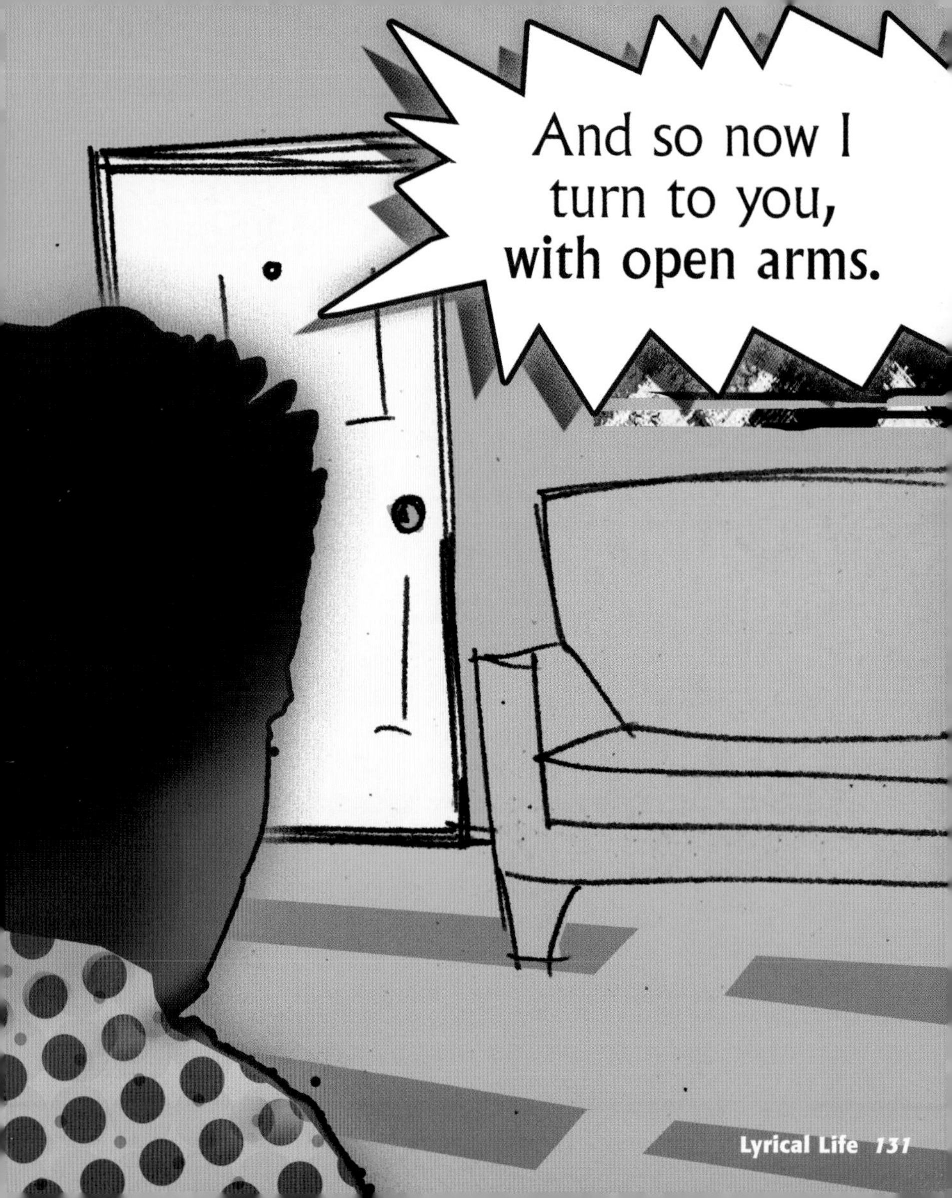
And so now I turn to you, with open arms.

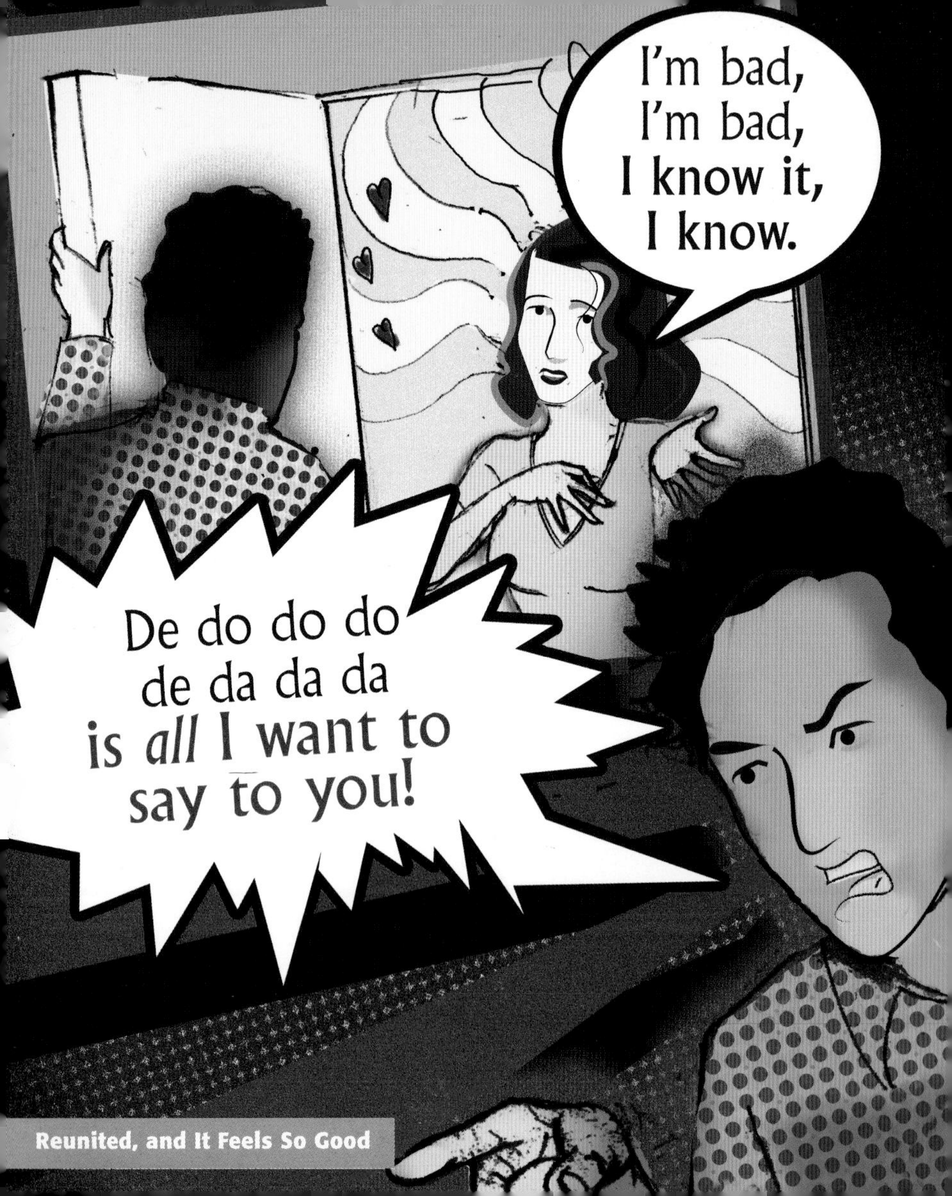
I'm bad, I'm bad, I know it, I know.
De do do do de da da da is *all* I want to say to you!

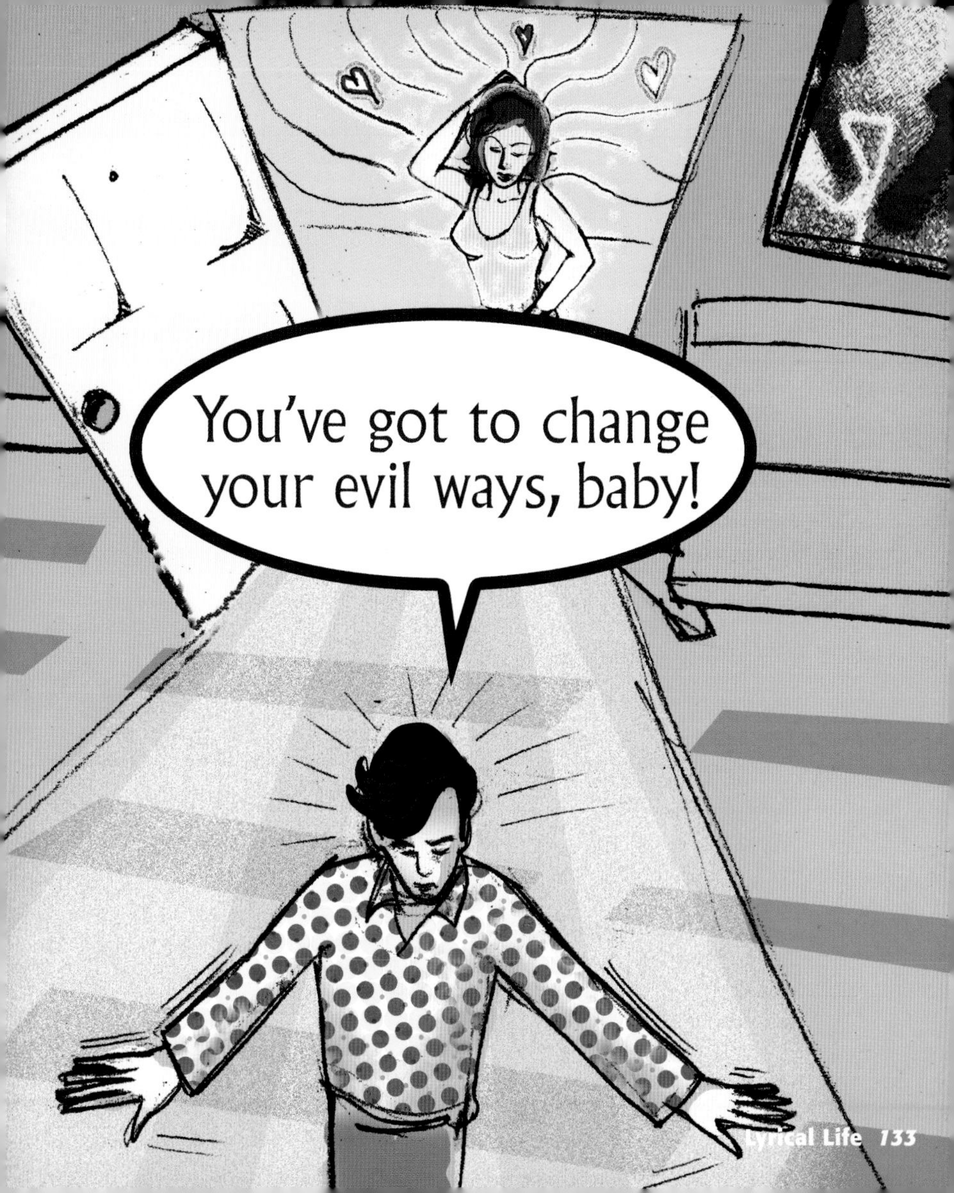
You've got to change your evil ways, baby!

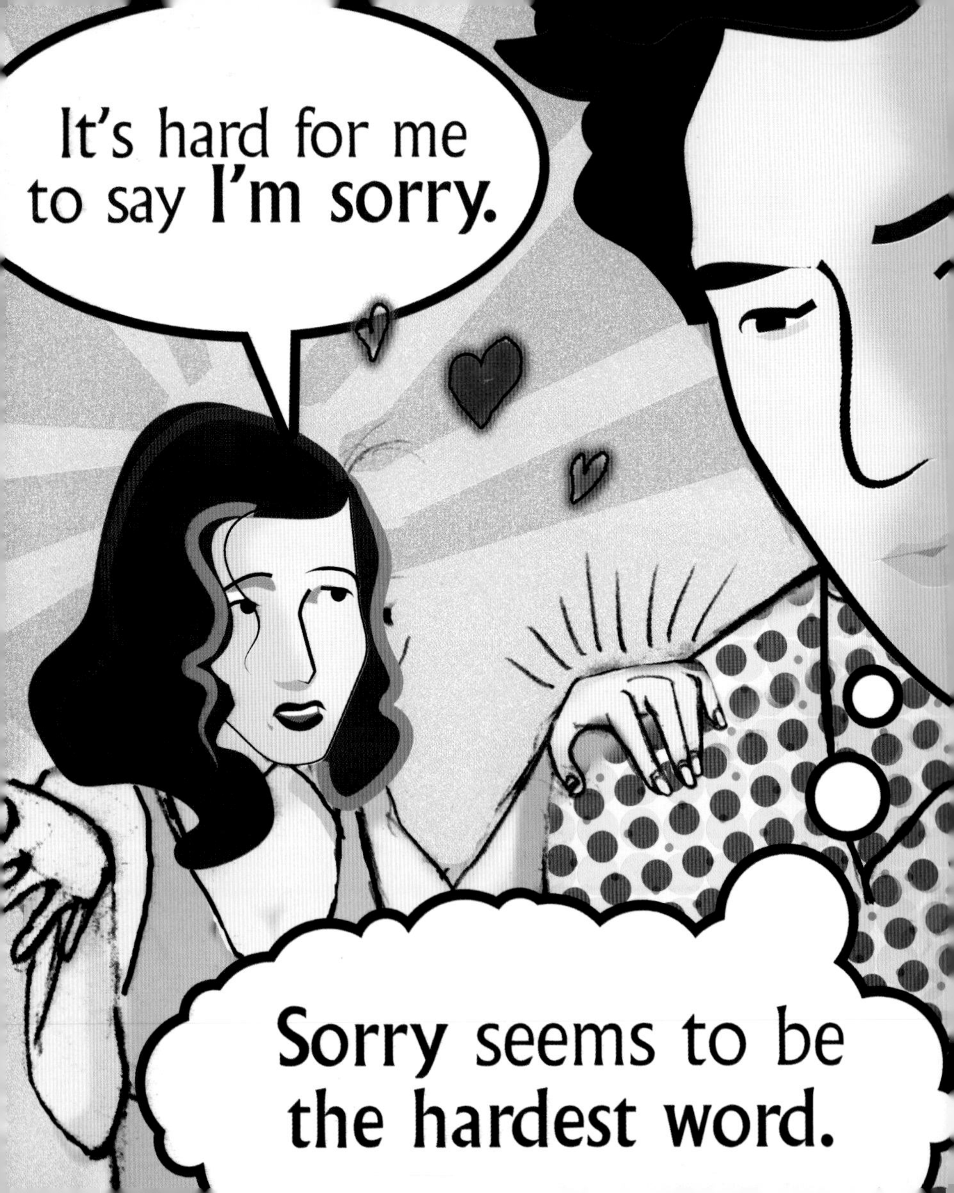
It's hard for me to say I'm sorry.
Sorry seems to be the hardest word.

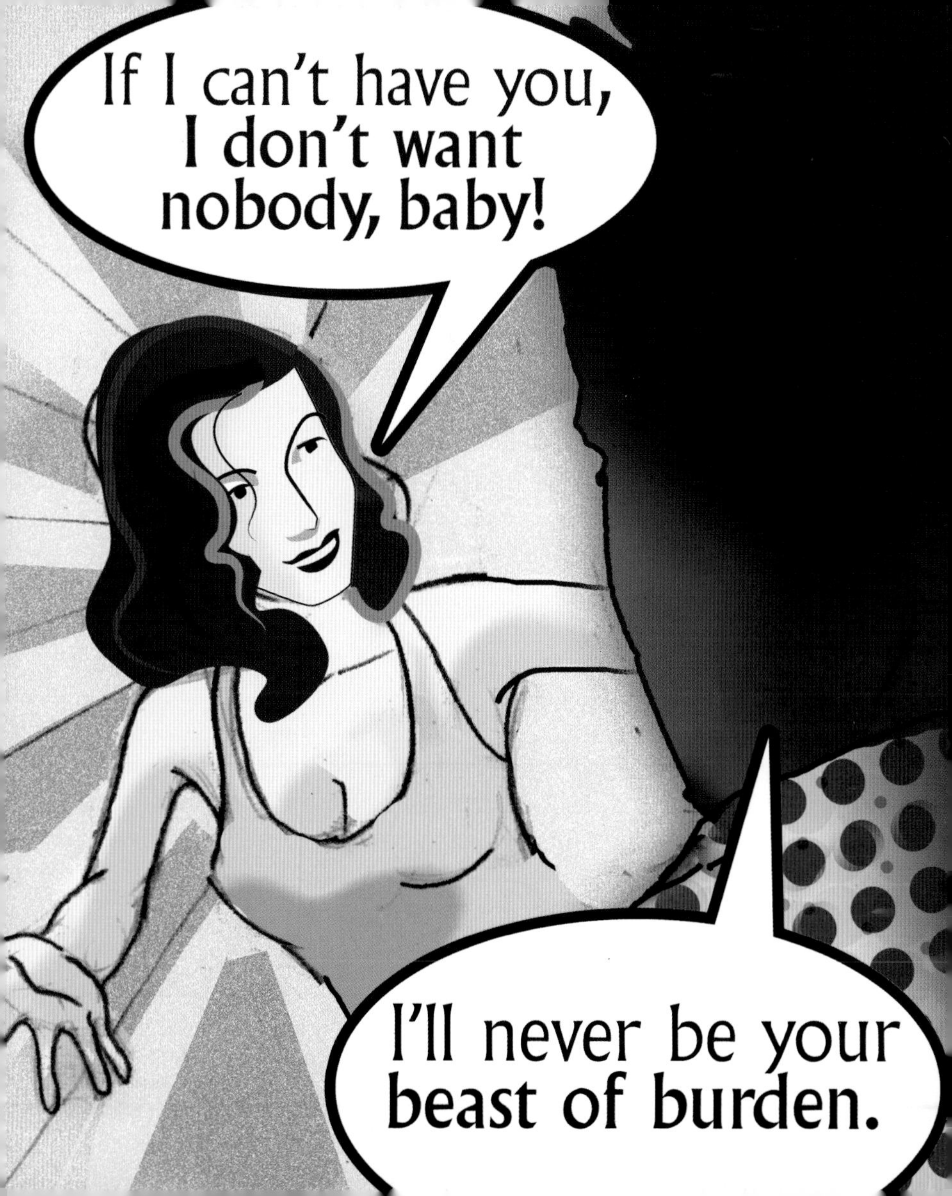
If I can't have you, I don't want nobody, baby!
I'll never be your beast of burden.

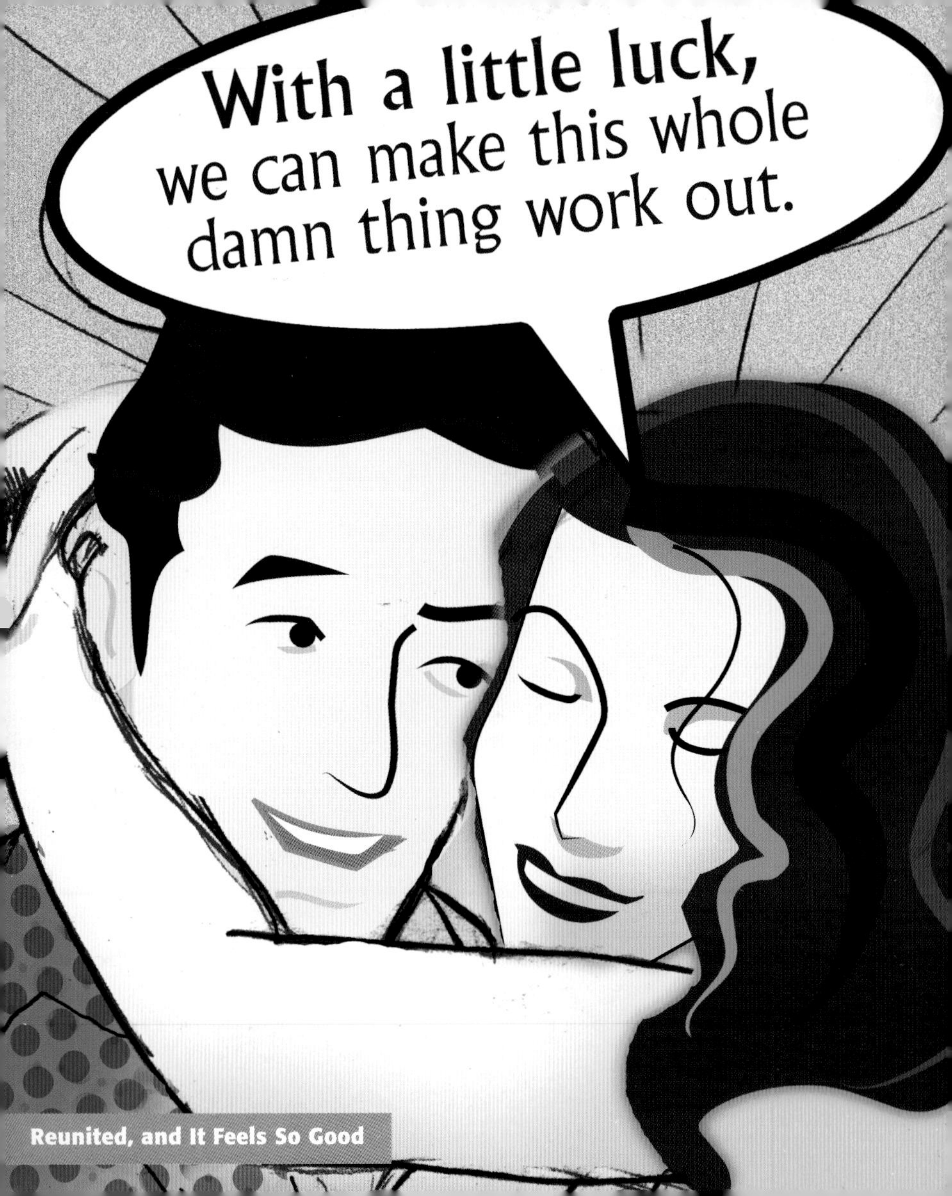
With a little luck, we can make this whole damn thing work out.

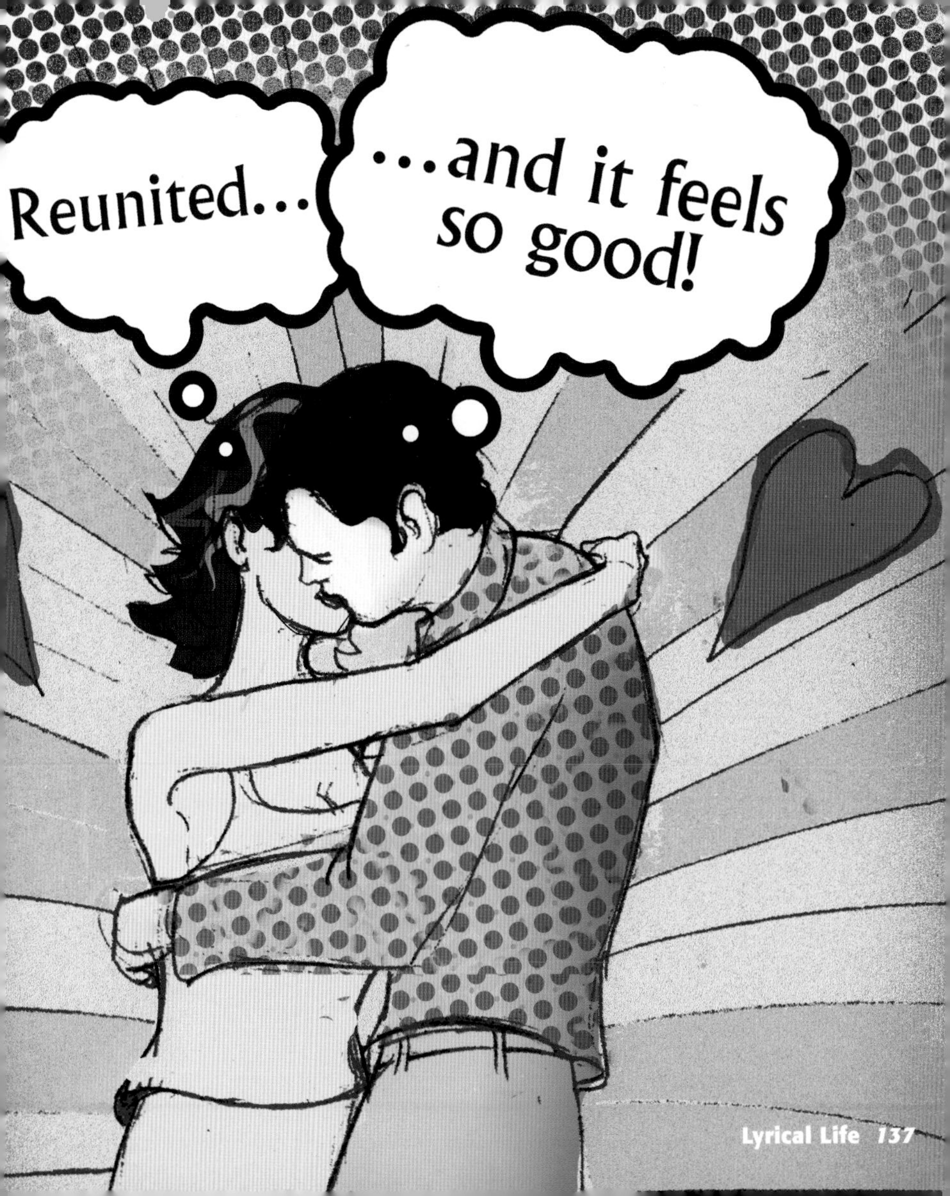
Reunited…
…and it feels so good!

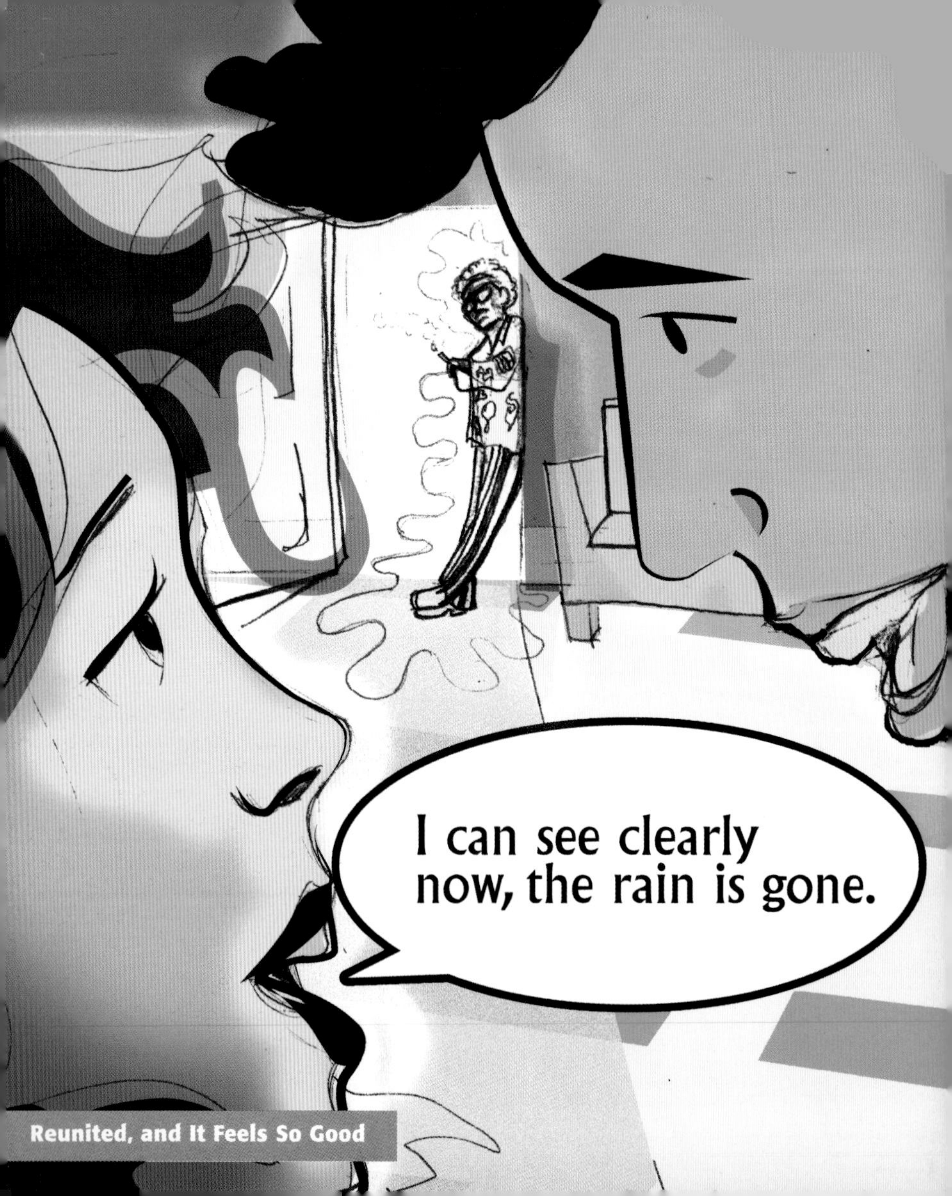
I can see clearly now, the rain is gone.

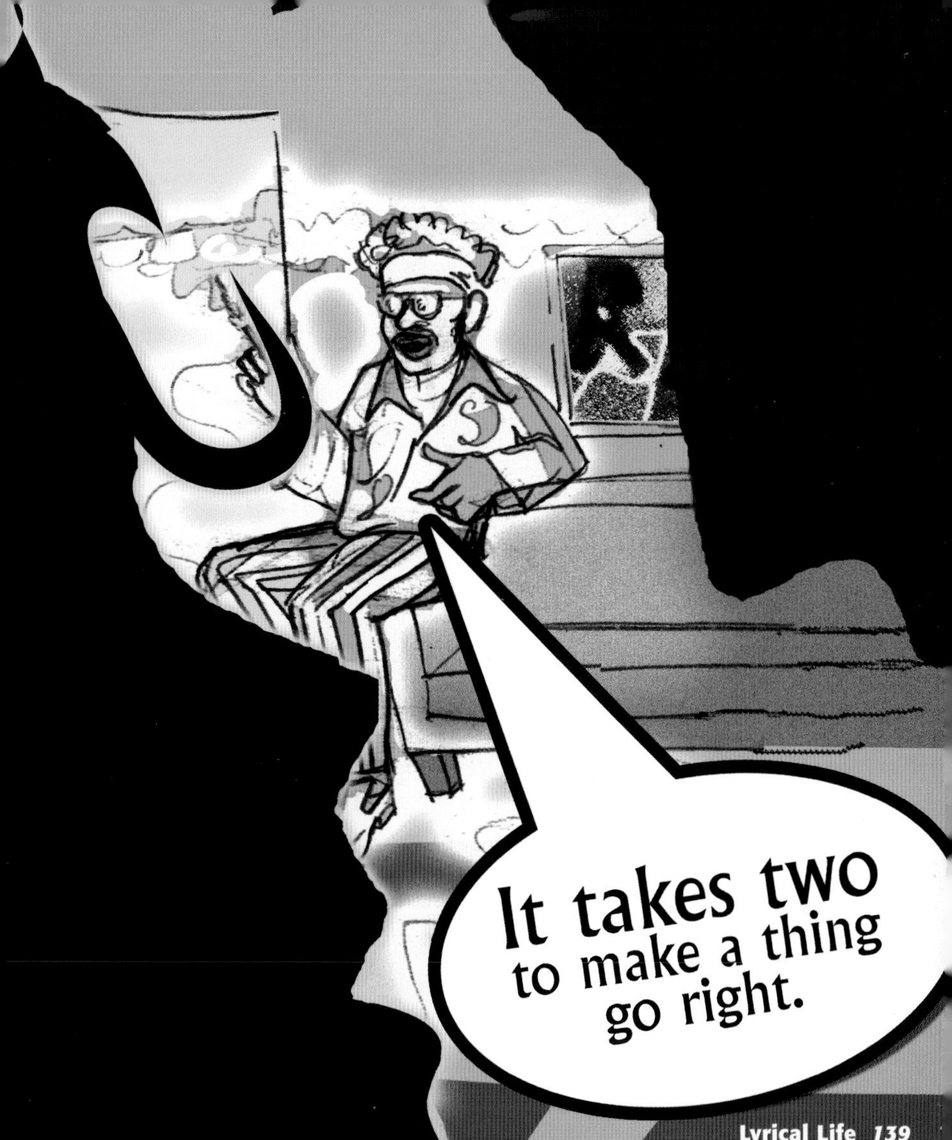
It takes two to make a thing go right.

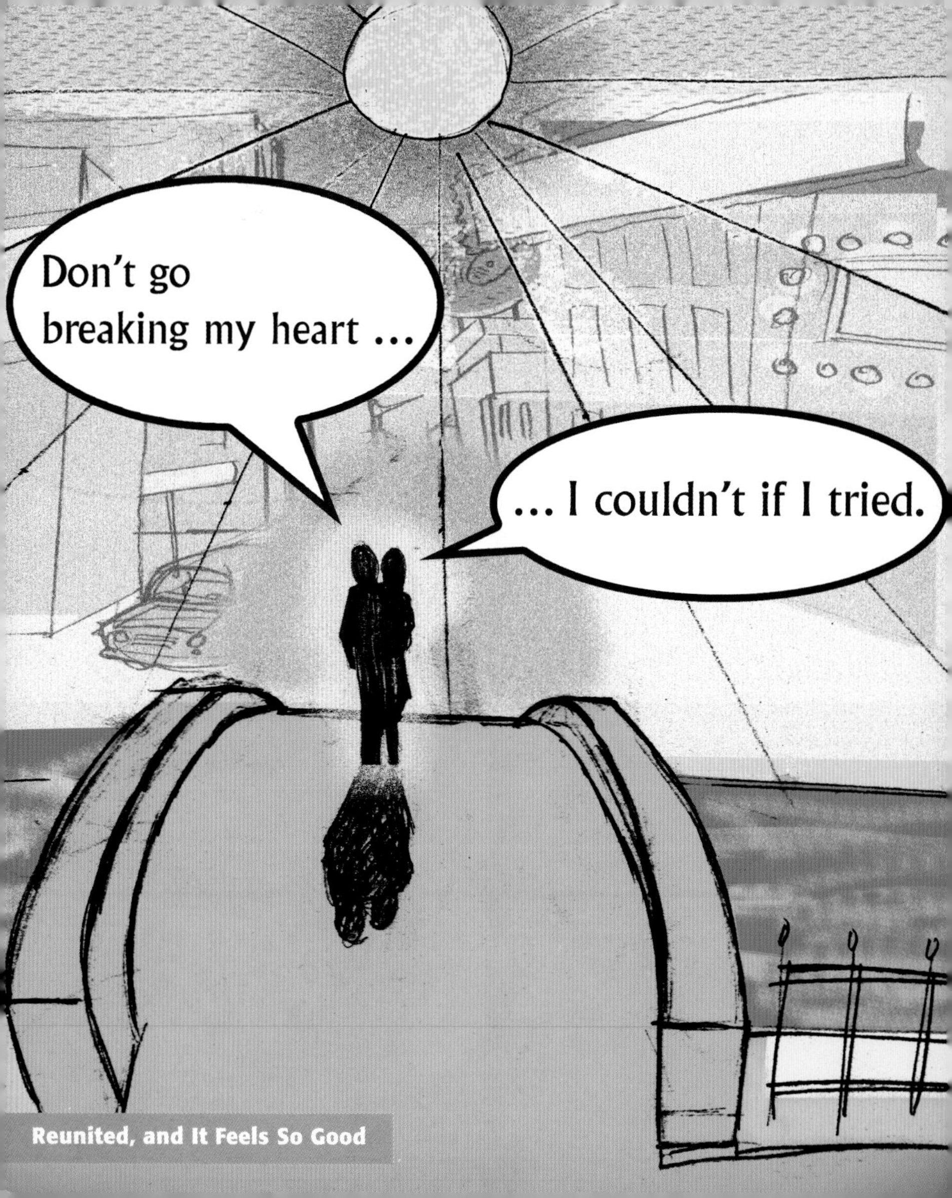
Don't go breaking my heart ...
... I couldn't if I tried.
Reunited, and It Feels So Good

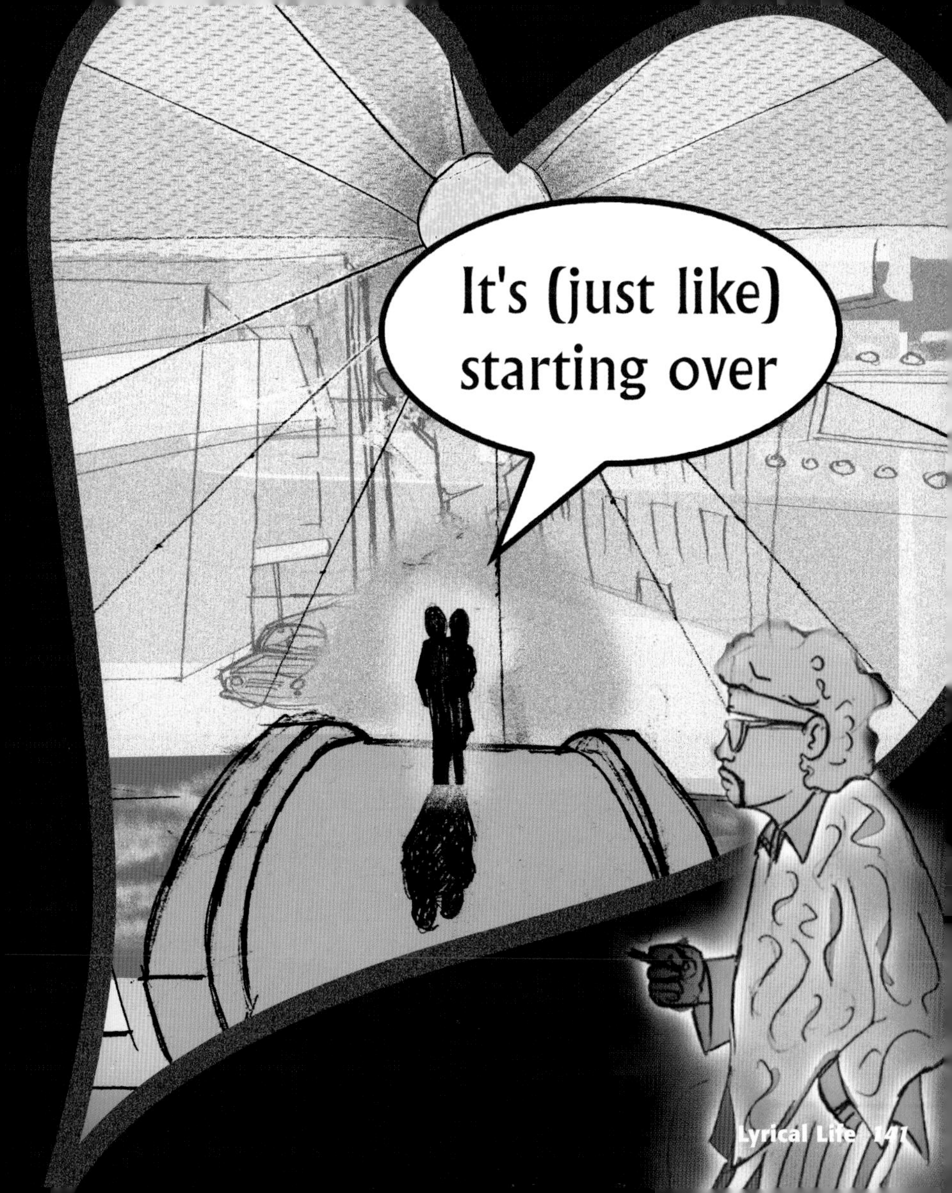
It's (just like)
starting over

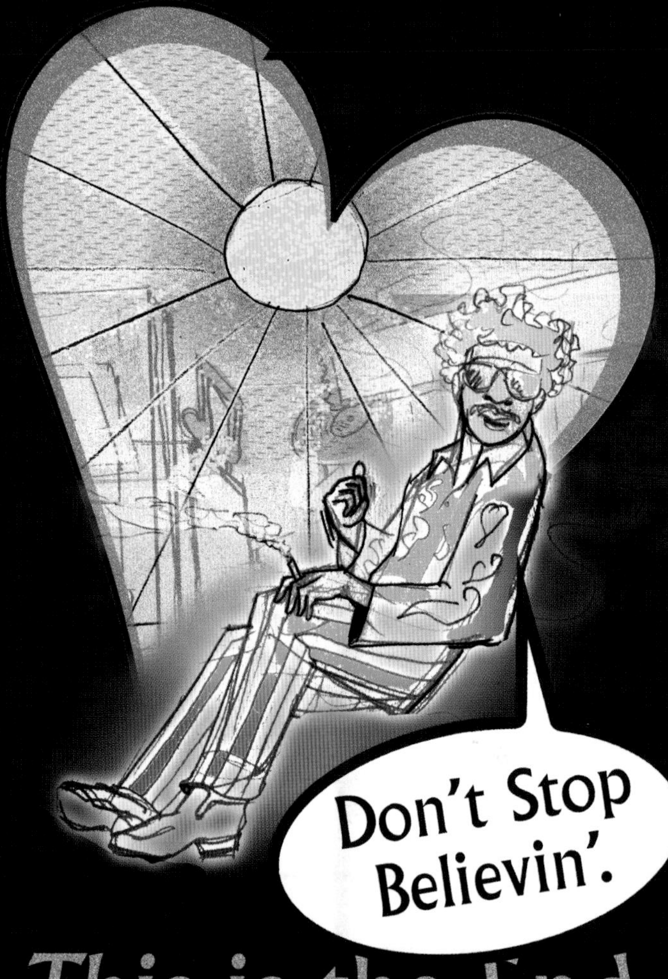
Don't Stop
Believin'.

This is the End
Beautiful Friend

CREDITS

CHAPTER 1 : Dialogue

Piano Man Billy Joel (Joel) **9 to 5** Dolly Parton (Parton) **Hey, Joe** Jimi Hendrix (Roberts) **Whipping Post** Allman Brothers (Allman) **Two Tickets to Paradise** Eddie Money (Money) **Should I Stay or Should I Go?** The Clash (The Clash) **I Love Rock 'n' Roll** Joan Jett & The Blackhearts (Merrill, Hooker) **Addicted to Love** Robert Palmer (Palmer) **To All the Girls I've Loved Before** Julio Iglesias & Willie Nelson (David, Hammond) **Jessie's Girl** Rick Springfield (Springfield) **Dancing Queen** Abba (Anderson, Anderson, Ulvaeus) **I'm a Believer** The Monkees (Diamond) **Copacabana (At the Copa)** Barry Manilow (Manilow, Sussman, Feldman) **Don't You Want Me** Human League (Oakey, Wright, Callis) **One Bourbon, One Scotch, One Beer** George Thorogood (Hooker) **Owner of a Lonely Heart** Yes (Rabin, Anderson, Squire, Horn) **Hello, I Love You** The Doors (The Doors) **Lola** The Kinks (Davies) **Luka** Suzanne Vega (Vega) **Never Say Never** Romeo Void (Romeo Void) **Show Me the Way** Peter Frampton (Frampton) **Baby, I Love Your Way** Peter Frampton (Frampton) **Who Let The Dogs Out?** Baha Men (Douglas) **ABC** Jackson 5 (Perren, Mizell, Richards, Gordy Jr.) **Is She Really Going Out with Him?** Joe Jackson (Jackson) **The Way It Is** Bruce Hornsby & The Range (Hornsby) **The Look of Love** ABC (Fry, White, Singleton, Palmer) **Waiting for a Girl Like You** Foreigner (Jones, Gramm) **Call Me** Blondie (Moroder, Harry) **Isn't She Lovely** Stevie Wonder (Wonder) **Bette Davis Eyes** Kim Carnes (Weiss, DeShannon) **Just What I Needed** The Cars (Ocasek) **Love Stinks** J. Geils Band (Justman, Wolf)

Chapter 1: Scenery

FunkyTown Lipps, Inc. (Greenberg) **We Built This City** Starship (Taupin, Page, Wolf, Lambert) **The Sad Café** The Eagles (Henley, Frey, Walsh, Souther) **In Dreams** Roy Orbison (Orbison) **Back to Life** Soul II Soul (Romeo, Law, Hooper) **Crosstown Traffic** Jimi Hendrix (Hendrix)

Chapter 2: Dialogue

Faith George Michael (Michael) **867-5309/Jenny** Tommy Tutone (Call, Keller) **Hello** Lionel Richie (Richie) **Moondance** Van Morrison (Morrison) **Saturday Night** Bay City Rollers (Martin, Coulter) **All I Wanna Do** Sheryl Crow (Cooper, Crow, Bottrell, Baerwald, Gilbert) **I'll Be There** Jackson 5 (Gordy, Davis, Hutch, West) **Pretty in Pink** Psychedelic Furs (Butler) **I'm Too Sexy** Right Said Fred (Fairbrass, Fairbrass, Manzoli) **Wanna Be Startin' Somethin'** Michael Jackson (Jackson) **Sharp Dressed Man** ZZ Top (ZZ Top) **Tonight's the Night** Rod Stewart (Stewart) **Yummy Yummy Yummy** Ohio Express (Resnick, Levine) **Small Town** John Mellencamp (Mellencamp) **A Horse with No Name** America (Bunnell) ? & The Mysterians **Spooky** Classics IV (Cobb, Buie) **Electric Avenue** Eddy Grant (Grant) **Everybody Have Fun Tonight** Wang Chung (Wang Chung, Wolf) **1999** Prince (Prince) **Dude (Looks Like a Lady)** Aerosmith (Tyler, Perry, Child) **Every Little Thing She Does Is Magic** The Police (Sting) **Abracadabra** Steve Miller Band (Miller) **I'll Melt with You** Modern English (Modern English) **Sexual Healing** Marvin Gaye (Gaye, Ritz, Brown) **Barracuda** Heart (Fischer, Wilson, Wilson, Derosier) **That's the Way (I Like It)** KC & The Sunshine Band (Casey, Finch) **Maneater** Hall & Oates (Allen, Hall, Oates) **Why Do Fools Fall In Love?** Frankie Lymon & The Teenagers (Levy, Lymon)

Chapter 2: Scenery

Dock of the Bay Otis Redding (Cropper, Redding) **Alice's Restaurant** Arlo Guthrie (Guthrie) **MacArthur Park** Richard Harris (Webb)

Chapter 3: Dialogue

I Will Survive Gloria Gaynor (Fekaris, Perren) **Somebody to Love** Jefferson Airplane (Slick) **Who Can It Be Now?** Men at Work (Hay) **Let My Love Open the Door** Pete Townshend (Townshend) **We've Got Tonight** Bob Seger (Seger) **You Better You Bet** The Who (Townshend) **Goody Two Shoes** Adam Ant (Adam Ant, Pirroni) **The Stroke** Billy Squier (Squier) **Sex Machine** James Brown (Brown, Byrd, Lenhoff) **Let's Get It On** Marvin Gaye (Gaye, Townsend) **People Are Strange** The Doors (The Doors) **More, More, More** Andrea True Connection (Diamond) **Macho Man** Village People (Morall, Belolo, Willis, Whitehead) **You Spin Me Round (Like a Record)** Dead or Alive (Dead or Alive) **I Got You (I Feel Good)** James Brown (Brown) **When Will I See You Again?** The Three Degrees (Gamble, Huff) **Tomorrow** *Annie soundtrack* (Charnin, Strouse) **Do That to Me One More Time** The Captain & Tennille (Tennille) **Vacation** The Go-Gos (Caffey, Valentine, Weidlin) **I Can't Drive 55** Sammy Hagar (Hagar) **Hotel California** The Eagles (Henley, Frey, Felder) **Diamonds Are a Girl's Best Friend** Marilyn Monroe (Robin, Styne) **Material Girl** Madonna (Brown, Rans) **Whole Lotta Love** Led Zeppelin (Page, Plant, Jones, Bonham) **Little Red Corvette** Prince (Prince) **Take Me Home, Country Roads** John Denver (Denver, Danoff, Nivert) **Mrs. Brown, You've Got a Lovely Daughter** Herman's Hermits (Peacock) **We Are Family** Sister Sledge (Rodgers, Edwards) **Our House** Crosby, Stills & Nash (Nash)

Chapter 3: Scenery

Knock Three Times Tony Orlando & Dawn (Levine, Brown) **It's the End of the World As We Know It (And I Feel Fine)** R.E.M. (R.E.M.)

Chapter 4: Dialogue

Some Guys Have All the Luck Rod Stewart (Fortgang) **Heaven on the 7th Floor** Paul Nicholas (Bugatti, Musker) **Love Machine** The Miracles (Moore, Griffin) **Heartache Tonight** The Eagles (Souther, Henley, Frey, Seger) **Can't You Hear Me Knocking?** The Rolling Stones (Jagger, Richards) **Mickey** Toni Basil (Chapman, Chinn)

Witchy Woman The Eagles (Leadon, Henley)   **Tempted** Squeeze (Difford, Tilbrook)   **Magic Number** De La Soul (De La Soul)   **Girls Just Wanna Have Fun** Cyndi Lauper (Hazard)   **Jeopardy** Greg Kihn (Kihn)   **I Didn't Mean to Turn You On** Robert Palmer (Harris, Lewis)   **You're No Good** Linda Ronstadt (Ballard)   **Heartbreaker** Pat Benatar (Gill, Wade)   **Don't Stand So Close to Me** The Police (Sting)   **Build Me Up, Buttercup** The Foundations (McCauley, D'Abo)   **Don't Come Around Here No More** Tom Petty & The Heartbreakers (Petty, Stewart)   **Do You Really Want to Hurt Me?** Culture Club (O'Dowd, Moss, Craig, Hay)   **Mysterious Ways** U2 (U2)   **Oops! . . . I Did It Again** Britney Spears (Martin, Rami)   **Poison Arrow** ABC (Fry, White, Singleton, Lickley)   **Another One Bites the Dust** Queen (Deacon)

Chapter 4: Scenery

Wham

Chapter 5: Dialogue

I Ran (So Far Away) A Flock of Seagulls (Score, Score, Maudsley, Reynolds)   **Feelin' Groovy** Simon & Garfunkel (Simon)   **Centerfold** J. Geils Band (Justman)   **Take It Easy** The Eagles (Browne, Frey)   **Running on Empty** Jackson Browne (Browne)   **Goin' Out of My Head** Little Anthony & The Imperials (Randazzo, Weinstein)   **Desperado** The Eagles (Henley, Frey)   **Time in a Bottle** Jim Croce (Croce)   **Does Anybody Really Know What Time It Is?** Chicago (Lamm)   **Damn! I Wish I Was Your Lover** Sophie B. Hawkins (Hawkins)   **Hit The Road Jack** Ray Charles (Mayfield)   **Alone Again (Naturally)** Gilbert O'Sullivan (O'Sullivan)   **Fly Away** Lenny Kravitz (Kravitz)   **Destroyer** The Kinks (Davies)   **Homeward Bound** Simon & Garfunkel (Simon)   **Mr. Pitiful** Otis Redding (Redding, Cropper)   **Always Something There to Remind Me** Naked Eyes (Bacharach, David)   **Little Red Corvette** Prince (Prince)   **Jump!** Van Halen (Van Halen, Roth, Anthony, Van Halen)   **Help!** The Beatles (Lennon, McCartney)   **Bad Case of Loving You (Doctor, Doctor)** Robert Palmer (Martin)   **All Shook Up** Elvis Presley (Blackwell, Presley)   **19th Nervous Breakdown** Rolling Stones (Jagger, Richards)   **Nineteen** Paul Hardcastle (Hardcastle)   **Love Is the Drug** Roxy Music (Ferry, Mackay)   **Breakdown** Tom Petty & The Heartbreakers (Petty, Stewart)   **Crazy Train** Ozzy Osbourne (Osbourne, Rhoads, Daisley)   **Crazy Little Thing Called Love** Queen (Mercury)   **Wild World** Cat Stevens (Stevens)   **Doctor My Eyes** Jackson Browne (Browne)   **I Am the Walrus** The Beatles (Lennon, McCartney)   **I Wanna Be Sedated** The Ramones (Hyman, Cummings, Colvin)   **Whip It** Devo (Mothersbaugh, Casale)   **Don't Cry Out Loud** Melissa Manchester (Sager, Allen)   **Parents Just Don't Understand** DJ Jazzy Jeff & The Fresh Prince (Harris, Smith, Townes)   **Get Off My Cloud** Rolling Stones (Jagger, Richards)   **Jive Talkin'** The Bee Gees (Gibb, Gibb, Gibb)   **Shout** Tears for Fears (Orzabal, Stanley)   **You May Be Right** Billy Joel (Joel)   **Stayin' Alive** The Bee Gees (The Bee Gees)   **White Rabbit** Jefferson Airplane (Slick)   **Go Your Own Way** Fleetwood Mac (Buckingham)   **Thank You** Sly & The Family Stone (Stewart)   **Money (That's What I Want)** The Beatles (Bradford,

Gordy)   **Manic Monday** The Bangles (Prince)   **I Will Survive** Gloria Gaynor (Fekaris, Perren)

Chapter 5: Scenery

News of the World (album) Queen   **Red Red Wine** UB40 (Diamond)   **Crash into Me** Dave Matthews Band (Matthews)   **Heartbreak Hotel** Elvis Presley (Axton, Durden, Presley)   **Bridge over Troubled Water** Simon & Garfunkel (Paul Simon)   **Dr. Love** Kiss (Simmons)   Kajagoogoo   Soft Cell   The Cure   The Fixx   **Love Potion #9** The Searchers (Leiber, Stoller)   **Still Crazy After All These Years** Paul Simon (Simon)   **Super Freak** Rick James (James, Miller)   **Maybe Baby** Buddy Holly (Petty, Hardin)   **Ready to Take a Chance Again** Barry Manilow (Gimbel, Fox)

Chapter 6: Dialogue

On the Road Again Willie Nelson (Nelson)   **I Am a Rock** Simon & Garfunkel (Simon)   **Free Bird** Lynyrd Skynyrd (Collins, Van Zant)   **What Have I Done to Deserve This?** Pet Shop Boys (Lowe, Tennant, Willis)   **You Dropped a Bomb on Me** The Gap Band (Wilson)   **I Hear You Knocking** Dave Edmunds (Edmunds)   **Open Arms** Journey (Perry, Cain)   **Bad** Michael Jackson (Jackson)   **De Do Do Do De Da Da Da** The Police (Sting)   **Evil Ways** Santana (Henry)   **Hard to Say I'm Sorry** Chicago (Cetera, Foster)   **Sorry Seems to Be the Hardest Word** Elton John (John, Taupin)   **If I Can't Have You** Yvonne Elliman (The Bee Gees)   **Beast of Burden** The Rolling Stones (Jagger, Richards)   **With a Little Luck** Paul McCartney & Wings (McCartney)   **Reunited** Peaches & Herb (Fekaris, Perren)   **I Can See Clearly Now** Johnny Nash (Nash)   **It Takes Two** Rob Base & DJ EZ Rock (Base, Rock)   **Don't Go Breaking My Heart** Elton John & Kiki Dee (Blanche, Orson)   **Don't Stop Believin'** Journey (Perry, Schon, Cain)   **The End** The Doors (Doors)

Chapter 6: Scenery

Jet Airliner Steve Miller Band (Pena)   **Margaritaville** Jimmy Buffett (Buffett)

Front Cover

Should I Stay or Should I Go? The Clash (The Clash)   **Don't You Want Me** Human League (Oakey, Wright, Callis)

Back Cover

It's De-Lovely Ella Fitzgerald (Porter)   **I'm a Believer** The Monkees (The Monkees)   **Lose Yourself** Eminem (Eminem)   **Don't Think Twice, It's All Right** Bob Dylan (Dylan)   **Everyday I Write the Book** Elvis Costello & The Attractions (Costello)